HODDER
English

Sue Hackman · Alan Howe · Patrick Scott

Hodder & Stoughton
A MEMBER OF THE HODDER HEADLINE GROUP

ACKNOWLEDGEMENTS

The publishers would like to thank the following contributors:

John Rowley and David Watkinson	–	Unit One, *Viral Reality* and Unit Four, *Serial Thriller*
Kevin Eames	–	Unit Two, *Experience into Words*
Perdita Davidson and Kevin Eames	–	Unit Three, *Talking Heads*
Jean Moore and John Catron	–	Unit Five, *Heroes and Heroines*, Unit Seven, *The Reading Odyssey* Unit Eight, *Witch Hunt*
Jan Malt	–	Unit Six, *Dead Man Walking*

and also Anne Barnes, GCSE Principal Examiner for the Northern Examination and Assessments Board (NEAB), for her comments in Unit Nine, *Preparing for your exam.*

Copyright photographs:

p14 photographs Tanya Piejus, by courtesy of Sylvonne Bailey and Phil Caisley, © Hodder & Stoughton; pp16, 17 © Zefa; p22 photographs Tanya Piejus, by courtesy of Hooi-Leng Dunnett, Philip Walters, Mel Thompson and Catherine Boulton, © Hodder & Stoughton; pp42, 44, 45 © Hulton Deutsch Collection; p46 © Richard Alton; p58 © BFI Stills, Posters and Designs; p62 © Associated Press/Topham; pp67, 72 © APL; p69 © Hodder & Stoughton; p73 © Topham Picture Library; p76 © Kobal Collection; p81 [left] © Sky One, [right] © Sky One; p90 © Mary Evans Picture Library; p91 © Topham Picturepoint; p92 © Ronald Grant Archive; p94 © Mary Evans Picture Library; p100 © Emma Lee/Life File; p101 © Disney/Aquarius; p102 [top right and left] Heath, The Independent, 6 September 1996, [below left] © Press Assoc./Topham, [below right] London News Service; p103 © BBC; p104 in *Janet and John book 1* by Mabel O'Donnell, Rona Munro and Muriel Warwick, James Nisbet and Co. 1949; p105 [left] © Disney/Ronald Grant Archive, [right] in *Household Tales by the Brothers Grimm*, illustrated by Mervyn Peake, Eyre & Spottiswoode, 1946; p108 © The Kobal Collection; p110 © Walt Disney Pictures/ Kobal Collection; pp112, 115 © The Kobal Collection; p116 © MGM/ Kobal Collection; p122 © Hulton Deutsch Collection; pp124, 128 © Topham; p125 © BBC/Aquarius; p131 Aquarius; p137 [left] © Aquarius, [right] BFI Stills, Posters and Design; p138 photographs Tanya Piejus, by courtesy of Scott Elton, © Hodder & Stoughton; p139 photographs [top three] Tanya Piejus, © Hodder & Stoughton, [below] © Katheryn Walden/Hodder & Stoughton; p146 © Seychelles Tourist Office, London; p148 by courtesy of Daniel Mayhew, © Hodder & Stoughton; p152 © Nicole Swengley/*Independent on Sunday*; p155 [above] Photographer Nick Nicholson/Hawkley Studios, © Hodder & Stoughton, [below] © Castle Rock Entertainment/Aquarius Library; pp156, 157 greetings cards © Hambledon Studios; p158 © Venice Simplon Orient Express; p160 © Ronald Grant Library; p162 © 1995 Sony Pictures Entertainment Co./The Kobal Collection; p163 © Guild Films; pp166, 167, 168, 173 in *A History of Witchcraft* by Jeffrey B Russell, Thames and Hudson 1982; p172 © 20th Century Fox/Aquarius Library; p175 © Donald Cooper/Photostage; p180 © Associated Press/Topham; p185 © Ronald Grant Archive; p191 © J. Allan Cash Ltd.

Copyright text:

p26 'Flesh-eating bug killed my mother in 20minutes' by Sydney Young, in *The Daily Mirror*, 23 May, 1994; p28 'The bug that ate into our imagination and sent us mad' by Sean Ryan, Lois Rogers and Margaret Driscoll, *The Sunday Times*, 29 May, 1994; p31 'No longer in the eye of the beholder' *The Education Guardian*, 4 Sept 1990; p34 Extract from 'Rebel with a Cause' by Alison Fell, in *Truth, Dare or Promise: Girls Growing Up in The Fifties*, (ed) Liz Heron, Virago Press, 1985; p37 Extract from *Cider with Rosie* by Laurie Lee, Penguin, 1962; p40 Extract from *A Welsh Childhood* by Alice Thomas Ellis, Collins Educational, 1995; pp41, 51-52 Extracts from *Owning Up* by George Melly, Penguin, 1970; p43 Extract from *In a Wiltshire Village: Scenes from Rural Victorian Life* by Alfred Williams, Alan Sutton Publishing, 1981; p44 Extract from 'From Deepest Kilburn' by Gail Lewis, in *Truth, Dare or Promise: Girls Growing Up in The Fifties*, (ed) Liz Heron, Virago Press, 1985; p45 Extract from *The Lost Continent* by Bill Bryson, Abacus, 1990; p46 'Brats' from *What's What* by Julie O'Callaghan, Bloodaxe Books, 1991; p47 'Very Simply Topping up the Brake Fluid' from *Zoom* by Simon Armitage, Bloodaxe Books, 1990; p67 Extract from 'Through the Farm Gate' © The Women's Farming Union; p69 Extract from 'Hidden Suffering' © The Farm Animal Welfare Network; p82 Extract from *Brighton Rock* by Graham Greene, Heinemann, 1938; p82 Extract from *Jaws* by Peter Benchley, Andre Deutsch; pp84-85 Extract from *Talking in Whispers* by James Watson, Lions Tracks; p95 Extract from *The Ghost Road* by Pat Barker, Penguin, 1995; p106 *The Paper Bag Princess* by Robert H Munsch, Scholastic, 1982; p126 'Breslau Prison, December 1917' from *Letters from Prison* by Rosa Luxemburg; pp127, 130 Extracts form *The Chamber* by John Grisham, Arrow, 1994; p131 Extract from *Dead Man Walking; An Experience of Death Row* by Helen Prejean, HarperCollins, 1993; p133 Extract from 'The very last Scripps heard...' by Paul Harris, in *Daily Mail*, 20 April 1996; p134 © *Empire*, April 1996; p135 [top] © *The Guardian*, March 1996, [below] © *Timeout*, March 1996; p136 © *Daily Mail*, March 1996; p141 Extract from *A Sense of Freedom* by Jimmy Boyle; p149 Extract from 'Brave New World' by © Emma Cook, Independent on Sunday, 17 December 1995; p152 Extract from 'A Passage to the South Pacific' by Nicole Swengley, *Independent on Sunday*, 23 June 1996; p157 'True Romance' © *Sugar* Magazine (Feb 1996); p159 Extract from 'The Challenge of Love', © *My Weekly*; pp166-167 Extract from *A History of Witchcraft* by Jeffrey B Russell, Thames and Hudson, 1982; pp173-174 Extract from *Salem Possessed: the social origins of witchcraft* by Paul Boyer and Stephen Nissenbaum, Harvard University Press, 1974; p185 Extract from *The Witches* by Roald Dahl, Puffin 1983; p186 Extract from *Bessie Dunlop: Witch of Dalry* by John Hodgart and Martin Clarke, Hodder & Stoughton 1995.

Every effort has been made to trace copyright holders of material reproduced in this book. Any rights not acknowledged here will be acknowledged in subsequent printings if notice is given to the publisher.

British Library Cataloguing in Publication Data

Hackman, Sue
   Hodder English 4
   1.English Language - Usage - Juvenile literature 2.English literature - Juvenile literature
   I.Title II.Howe, Alan III.Scott, Patrick, 1949-
   428

ISBN 0 340 67952 2

First published 1997
Impression number 10 9 8 7 6 5 4 3 2
Year   2001

Copyright © 1997 Sue Hackman, Alan Howe and Patrick Scott

Designed and typeset by Mind's Eye Design, Lewes.

Printed in Dubai for Hodder & Stoughton Educational, a division of Hodder Headline plc, 338 Euston Road, London NW1 3BH

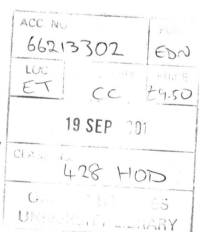

INTRODUCTION

Welcome to *Hodder English 4*. This course book and its companion Literature Study Books represent a quality English curriculum for Key Stage 4 and valuable resource material for Standard Grade. *Hodder English 4* has been planned and written to maintain a challenging, vigorous and progressive ethos in the classroom. The course book builds directly on *Hodder English 1, 2, and 3*, although its use is not dependent on having followed the Key Stage 3 series. Teachers may use *Hodder English 4* to supplement their own schemes of work, or link the materials and activities in the book with other materials. It offers pupils at Key Stage 4 a stimulating, varied and challenging experience of English that is designed to prepare them fully for GCSE English and, in conjunction with the Literature Study Books, for GCSE Literature.

RAISING STANDARDS, COVERING NATIONAL CURRICULUM REQUIREMENTS, AND PREPARING FOR EXAMINATIONS

We have taken as our prime directive the advancement of pupil learning. All the materials in *Hodder English* have been trialled in the classroom by English teachers to offer the very best of current practice. Units have been developed to cover the National Curriculum in England, Wales and Northern Ireland, and to provide a wealth of material appropriate to the 14–16 Guidelines in Scotland. The course book addresses literary and non-literary texts, poetry and drama, and offers opportunities for reading, writing, speaking and listening. Pupils are also offered many different purposes and audiences for their own writing. There is strong and relevant emphasis on studying and producing a range of media texts in a number of the units.

The course book is specifically designed to ensure that pupils fully cover the requirements for GCSE English and Literature, linked with the Literature Study Books for set texts. Pre-twentieth century literature is amply represented in both fiction and non-fiction. You will find a catholic range of genres, tones and forms, with a particular emphasis on helping pupils to broaden and extend the range and depth of their experience of language. We have made particular efforts to ensure that speaking and listening is fully represented as a purposeful activity in its own right as well as an essential approach to working through the activities and tasks. Several units lead to an oral course work component.

STRUCTURE

Hodder English 4 consists of an integrated course book containing eight units of work and a short section to help pupils prepare thoroughly for the examination. Each unit represents approximately a half term's work. The units have been arranged to cover years 10 and 11, and offer opportunities to establish, revisit and consolidate key skills. Although units have been placed in an order which offers pupils a varied and progressive experience of English, you can use the book in a flexible way, linking units with others, with texts you plan to teach, and with the Hodder English Literature Study Books.

Each unit has been written to strict specification, guaranteeing a rich mix of oral, written and reading activities. Language study and key skills are integrated in the context of the work. We have assumed that teachers will continue to support individual pupils by giving them feedback on their oral and written performance, and that spelling, punctuation and grammar will be part of this continuing work. This work is supported in the books by basic skills teaching in the context of the unit, all tackled at points where pupils will have the models and the motivation to learn from them. Explicit guidance is provided in accompanying Help boxes.

PROGRESSION

Hodder English 4 forms an incremental programme of work with clear goals written with the expressed intention of raising standards in English. The course offers far more than a sequence of self-contained lessons or starting points because progression is built into each unit, and across the course as a whole. *Hodder English 4* builds directly on the approach in the Key Stage 3 scheme in *Hodder English 1, 2* and *3*, but can also be used successfully whatever the experience and content of the Key Stage 3 course followed by pupils.

DIFFERENTIATION

Each unit offers accessible ways into all the programmes of study, including pre-twentieth literature, the literary heritage and a range of high quality modern writers. There is support for the less able, as well as challenging extension tasks for more able pupils.

ASSESSMENT

Assessment is an integral part of each unit. However, checklists, recording sheets and assessment grids are not included, as the different GCSE boards generally provide these, and you will most likely have already developed a workable system. Teaching by units enables you to collect evidence of pupils' achievements periodically, and systematically, at the end of each unit. The book provides pupils with focused tasks and explicit criteria for evaluating how well they are doing, and what they need to improve on. Each unit begins with a clear set of teaching aims and objectives, which will need to be talked through with pupils and revisited as the unit progresses. You will be able to plan the precise nature of your assessments against these aims and objectives. Pupils' own self-assessment is also vital: the units encourage pupils to think carefully about how to plan their work and how to succeed in carrying out these activities. At the end of a unit, pupils are invited to reflect on what they have done and to review their progress. Every unit offers clearly signposted opportunities for planning and submitting course work assignments and for examination preparation and practice.

USING *HODDER ENGLISH*

Many of the units can be used in association with Hodder English Literature Study Books. There are some direct links that can be made – for example, pupils studying *The Crucible* will find that the unit 'Witch Hunt' in *Hodder English 4* offers a range of background reading on attitudes to witchcraft and scapegoats in society that will enhance their understanding and appreciation of the play. Other units focus on themes that are reflected in the Literature Study Books – for example, the unit 'Heroes and Heroines' can be used in conjunction with a wide range of literature, and pupils studying *Lord of the Flies* will find much that is useful in the unit 'The Reading Odyssey'. Other units introduce pupils to elements of writers' techniques that can be applied to literature texts – for example, the unit 'Experience into Words' helps pupils to analyse similarities and differences in style and technique.

ACTIVITIES

The initial material and activities of each unit are designed to introduce pupils to the focus for the sequence of work, and to engage their interest. There is a series of tasks designed to help pupils to develop specific areas of knowledge, understanding and skill. Each activity includes guidance for working alone, in pairs or in groups and concentrates on reading, writing, speaking and listening. Each unit finishes with either a series of extension tasks or a choice of activities designed to consolidate learning and contribute to a course work folder.

CONTENTS

continued over

DEAD MAN WALKING

Emphasis on how the issue of capital punishment is reported in the media and treated in poetry, fiction, and film.
Includes:

- reading closely a wide range of texts and discussing information in order to build up a personal dossier of facts and ideas;
- analysing different texts in order to build up a picture of the writers' differing points of view;
- writing an extended piece of media course work;
- presenting ideas and views orally, considering the needs of an audience.

THE READING ODYSSEY

Emphasis on the way that different writers explore and develop the theme of 'islands' or 'romance', and the various meanings conveyed through the theme.
Includes:

- reading a range of twentieth and pre-twentieth century texts, investigating and discussing similarities and differences;
- researching ideas and developing different ways of recording information;
- developing understanding of the way some writers use a theme to reinforce commonly held ideas, whilst others use the same theme to challenge or extend the reader.

WITCH HUNT

Emphasis on close reading of a range of information texts, writing in a range of formal styles, and media work.
Includes:

- developing skills in reading for information, sifting evidence and selecting relevant details;
- using the information as the basis for a range of formal styles of writing;
- considering similarities and differences between modern and historical prejudices about 'outsiders';
- planning a television documentary based around the information.

PREPARING FOR YOUR EXAM

Emphasis on planning for the written examination and course work assignments. Helps students to identify what counts as success in English.
Includes:

- detailed commentary on what an examiner is looking for in speaking and listening, writing and study of literature;
- planning a revision timetable including time to revisit set texts;
- examination techniques.

GUIDELINES FOR TEACHERS

UNIT ONE – VIRAL REALITY

This unit is a strong mix of oral, written and reading work based on the mass media. It is organised as a semi-simulation in which pupils work through the dilemmas and demands of reporting a developing situation. The story is based on a virus and obvious links suggest themselves to the BSE scare, the Ebola virus, AIDs, and other public panics.

Teaching points

The unit would be well-served by reference to current media stories. Watch out for parallel stories in rival newspapers and news bulletins. Pace and pressure are important factors in managing this unit: issue tight deadlines, working in real time to give pupils the experience as well as the knowledge of working practices in the media.

UNIT TWO – EXPERIENCE INTO WORDS

Although the main aim in this unit is to help pupils with the personal/imaginative writing component of their course work, there is considerable scope for work on understanding and evaluating the linguistic and structural devices used by writers. There is scope, too, for cross-referencing and for exploring relations and comparisons within and between texts. A methodical framework has been offered for writing about and comparing texts, intended to help pupils with the perennial problem of finding things to say about literature.

Teaching points

The overall organisation is intended to move from textual analysis to the writing of pupils' own texts which incorporate what has been learnt in the earlier stages of the unit. The methodical framework offered in Part One, for analysing and comparing texts, will provide valuable support for lower- and middle-attaining pupils, whereas higher attainers will cover the ground suggested and beyond, developing their own individual approaches.

Part Two can be visited at different times during the course, and some of the comparisons can be made in discussion rather than in writing, as the teacher feels to be appropriate.

Part Three suggests ideas for writing which focus on particular teaching points and which might best be put into practice as 'short burst', early-draft pieces of writing. They could form the basis of, or be integrated within, the full-length final course work assignment with which the unit ends.

UNIT THREE – TALKING HEADS

This unit deals with the ways in which speech-writers use rhetorical techniques to persuade their audiences. Students learn to recognise these techniques in fiction, in televised 'soundbites', and in television programmes which argue a point of view. There are group discussions of two speeches offering opposing views of modern farming and from here, students are led into organising their own debate.

Teaching points

Although the unit focuses mainly on speaking and listening, much of the subject matter offers opportunities for reading and writing. For example, teachers could encourage pupils to compare the speeches by Old Major (*Animal Farm*) and Neil Kinnock. Looking at persuasive speeches from some set texts might also be appropriate, such as Ralph's addressing the assembly in *Lord of the Flies*. It could be useful, too, if pupils had access to videos featuring great orators such as Martin Luther King, Nelson Mandela, or Winston Churchill.

UNIT FOUR – SERIAL THRILLER

This unit identifies and teaches some of the key features of the thriller genre. The first half of the unit considers the structural design of the genre, from 'hooks' and thrills to engage the reader's interest at the beginning of a story, to the cliffhangers and suspense that develop the intrigue. The latter half of the unit suggests the dangers of the genre, moving into discussion of censorship and just endings.

Teaching points

The unit can draw successfully on students' own experiences of the genre. Immediate source material for lessons can be gleaned from the week's soap operas, popular films, or current reading. Most of the techniques studied (such as the cliffhanger ending) can be related to set texts, and lead to personal writing. It would be useful, in the preceding days, to collect relevant snippets from the media.

UNIT FIVE – HEROES AND HEROINES

This unit is about developing more critical and discriminating readers. The metaphor of the writer as 'puppet-master' that runs through this unit is important. It draws attention to the fact that the creation of a character is not about holding a mirror up to nature, but about making a series of authorial choices, many of which are about literary techniques such as how to construct a narrative. Almost all of the extracts that have been used to illustrate this will be familiar to pupils and this should help to reinforce the point when they meet them elsewhere in the course.

Teaching points

The structure of this unit encourages pupils gradually to build up their own theory about how characters are created and presented in fiction. For this reason, it is particularly important that the unit is treated as a sequence of lessons rather than as a series of self-contained slots. Pupils are asked to return to their previous ideas and will need to be well organised if they are to retrieve notes made in earlier lessons or records of group discussions. If pupils are not studying any of the texts referred to in this unit, extracts from other set texts could be selected to complement the unit, so that pupils see the direct relevance of character study to the texts they are studying.

UNIT SIX – DEAD MAN WALKING

This unit takes a contemporary issue – the use of judicial execution in various parts of the world – in order to introduce students to differences in the way that an issue is reported and treated in both fiction and in various media. There is a particular emphasis on what constitutes 'good quality' eye-witness reporting.

Teaching Points

Ideally, preparation for teaching this unit should involve gathering together a book box of additional articles, novels, autobiographies and media accounts surrounding the topic. The short reading list provided at the end of the unit should be helpful here. In addition, the

media element of the unit, although it can be taught without any supplementary material, will be enhanced by making available the video of the film *Dead Man Walking*, especially the section related to the extract in the unit. The focus of the unit is on how different writers treat the raw material they encounter – not on exploring the full extent of the issue itself. So, whilst it will be important to get the students interested and engaged with the 'rights and wrongs' of the issue, their attention should always be directed towards the literary and journalistic qualities of the various writings they are encountering.

UNIT SEVEN – THE READING ODYSSEY

This unit aims to help pupils explore the way in which their previous experiences of books influence the way in which they read, and also draw their attention to the fact that writers of different genres exploit this knowledge. By the end of the unit, pupils should be aware that books don't exist in a cultural vacuum. In terms of the syllabus, it provides a key opportunity for media work of all kinds.

Teaching points
As with other units, there are clear connections with many of the prescribed examination texts. 'Islands' can be used to prepare pupils for work on *Lord of the Flies*, and 'Romance' is relevant to any number of texts; extracts from *Jane Eyre*, *Hobson's Choice* and *Sense and Sensibility* are all included in the unit itself. However, the important point about the approach adopted in the unit is that it seeks to make the connection between popular culture and literary texts. For this reason, it would be useful to encourage pupils to collect other examples of material on islands and romance and to build on the suggestions for display work.

UNIT EIGHT – WITCH HUNT

This unit provides an opportunity to combine work on documentary material with study of an issue that is central to two of the most popular examination texts at this level, *Macbeth* and *The Crucible*. The use of original source material from the trials of the Salem witches offers a way of encouraging pupils to read and write non-fiction, now a required element in every syllabus. Although the material has a good deal of intrinsic interest, the activities are demanding and will challenge even the most able. The issues for discussion are not easily resolved, and the range of written styles that pupils are asked to tackle is wider than usual and includes some unfamiliar forms.

Teaching points
Although this unit stands by itself, many teachers will want to use it precisely because of the connection with *Macbeth* and *The Crucible*. The teacher should choose whether the material should be taught before or after the prescribed text. If it comes before, it will help to acclimatise pupils to the cultural differences between their world and that of the play. If the unit is used to follow up work on the plays, then it will help to shed new light on the text and encourage pupils to develop more considered judgements. The final activity in the unit, the production of a documentary programme about witchcraft, can be as ambitious as time will allow. To make the most of it, pupils could be encouraged to gather more original source material as part of a research exercise.

UNIT NINE – PREPARING FOR YOUR EXAM

This short unit offers guidelines on planning course work, on effective use of revision periods and on the best examination techniques. There is first hand advice from an examiner, giving students a fresh view of their aims. By using this reference guide in conjunction with the study skills practised within the context of the other units of the course, students will be able to develop their own strategies for successful study.

Teaching points
Although this unit is situated at the back of the book, teachers will need to draw students' attention to it at an early stage of the course, and encourage students to refer to the guidance at key moments – for example, before planning and preparing a course work assignment.

Viral Reality

In this unit you will assume several roles in an unfolding story. You will be at different times, journalists, editors, micro-biological research scientists and other people in the drama. You will develop your skills as:

SPEAKERS AND LISTENERS

by engaging in role play to express a point of view
by collaborating as a team to arrive at informed decisions
by delivering a news bulletin

READERS

by sifting and selecting relevant information
by analysing the features of different forms of report
by looking critically at media articles

WRITERS

by writing contrasting newspaper articles
by preparing a range of informative texts
by writing narrative in documentary form

The police have a dilemma: do they inform the public and risk a public panic? Or do they hope the thieves will be found and the virus recovered intact?

- In pairs, choose which course of action you support. Then consider:

What are the strong arguments in your favour? List them.

What will be the main objections (counter-arguments) to this point of view? List them.

Think of good answers to these counter-arguments. List them.

What will happen next if you get your way?

What will be the long-term consequences if you get your way?

- Team up with another pair who take the opposite point of view. Take turns to present your case and then talk through the issues. You could use the following prompts:

We believe that the best course of action is to…

Our main reason for thinking this is…

And there are other good reasons, such as…

Some people will object because… but this is not a sound argument because…

If we do not follow this course of action…

While we recognise the difficulties, we think it would be best to…

The decision is taken to hold a press conference, with Dr Williams and Chief Inspector Goode of Garton Police force.

When news of the press conference reaches the The Sentinel and The Planet, the Editors of both newspapers decide to send their best reporters to cover the story.

Anita Gold, reporter for The Planet, and Brian Doughty, who works for The Sentinel, have just been covering a story on an escaped puma in the town of Stockdale on Trent. The Planet is a **popular tabloid** newspaper, and covers stories in a very different way to The Sentinel, a more serious **quality broadsheet.** Both are national newspapers.

First look carefully at the two 'Puma' articles on the next two pages. What differences can you see in:

- the headlines
- the way the articles are set out
- the descriptions of the puma

- the descriptions of panic in Stockdale
- the descriptions of Fred Higgins
- the choice of quotations
- the use of humour
- the aspects of the issue in which the 2 papers are interested (their news values)

The differences in style are typical of tabloid and broadsheet newspapers. The terms refer to the size of paper: tabloid newspapers are smaller in size and they take a more sensational approach. Broadsheet newspapers are larger in size and take a more sober approach.

- List all the tabloid newspapers you can think of.
- List the broadsheet newspapers you can think of.

- Find a story that has been covered by a tabloid and a broadsheet in different ways. List all the differences and display your findings to the class.

LOADING VOCABULARY

Tabloid headline writers like words of one syllable – words that are short and punchy. Look at the table below – what else do you notice about the words editors choose?

BROADSHEET	TABLOID	BROADSHEET	TABLOID
anger	fury	infected	struck down
avoid	shun	patient	victim
criticise	slam, blast	proposal	plan
dangerous	deadly	quickly	with terrifying speed
disagreement	clash	replace	oust
dismissed	dumped, axed	reprove	rap
fatal fall	death plunge	unpleasant	horrific
happening	drama	virus	death bug, killer bug

- What words might you find in a tabloid newspaper for:
      annoyance
      cancel or withdraw
      resign
      possibility
      question
      setback

- Loading vocabulary to influence your readers is a technique used by all writers in all kinds of writing – advertisements, letters, drama, comedy, poetry, campaigns, and so on. What alternative terms are there for these words?

  fat   thin   small   child   old person

  How easy is it to group your answers as **positive, negative** or **neutral**?

Circulation of *The Planet* is 5 million copies daily with an estimated readership of 11.7 million.

PUBLICAN FRED'S PUMA PINT IS A KNOCKOUT!
Anita Gold Reporting

Super-cool publican Fred Higgins saved petrified regulars from the hungry jaws of an escaped puma – by serving him a pint of bitter! 'Make mine a double' the killer cat seemed to be saying, as he leapt up on the bar at The Wheatsheaf – and cool-as-a-cucumber Fred, father of two, was only too keen to oblige!

"I've had a few dodgy customers in the past," declared heroic pint-pulling Fred, "but this was something else!"

The killer cat brought sleepy Stockdale on Trent to a knee-knocking standstill after nipping out behind zoo keeper Chris Connolly's legs at feeding time. Two hours of 'puma panic' followed as:
• terror-struck travellers fled from the bus station!
• desperate drivers jumped red lights!
• fear-crazed fishermen jumped in the river!
But the one thing Pat the puma had not bargained for was the knock-out punch packed by a pint of real Stockdale beer.

Circulation of *The Sentinel* is 450,000 copies daily with an estimated readership of 1.5 million.

PUMA ESCAPE RAISES ZOO LICENCE DOUBTS
by Brian Doughty

The October renewal of the licence of Stockdale on Trent's local zoo was jeopardised today when an escaped puma – not known for its aggression towards humans – caused panic in the quiet, country town. The puma, an eight year old male named Patrick, escaped from the local zoo at feeding time. Two hours later the animal was recaptured in The Wheatsheaf, a pub three miles from the zoo on the other side of the town.

There were reports of fleeing motorists and shoppers, as news of the escape became known. Many appear to have panicked without reason, as all confirmed sightings of the puma were in quiet back streets.

Eventually, the puma was captured in the lounge bar of The Wheatsheaf, whose publican Mr Fred Higgins was praised by police for his calm handling of the situation.

Later Mr John Banks, owner of the zoo, defended his zoo's record of four escapes by large cats in the last five years. "It's extremely unfortunate, but I can assure the public that all possible steps are being taken to make sure nothing of this nature can happen again."

The police are apparently far from convinced. "This escape caused a great deal of distress to the public, and wasted a great deal of police time," said Inspector Rowley of Stockdale Police. He refused to confirm, however, that the police would oppose the renewal of the zoo's licence.

PRESS CONFERENCE

After the press conference, both Anita and Brian have the same tape recordings of the questions and answers given:

Inspector Goode: First of all, ladies and gentlemen, I would like to give you the basic facts of what has happened. Dr Williams worked at Broughton Microbiology Research Centre until his retirement two months ago. Earlier today Dr Williams visited Broughton and hid a quantity of Blue Squirrel virus in his briefcase. That briefcase was stolen at approximately 4pm from Eastgate Motorway Services on the M43. It is extremely important that the virus is recovered and we are keen that anyone who was at the service station at that time and saw anything suspicious, gets into contact as soon as possible. The number is Garton 346678.

Q: Anita Gold, The Planet. Why on earth did you want the virus in the first place, Dr Williams?

Dr Williams: It's simple. I had been working on the Kolona virus (that's the Blue Squirrel virus) at the time of my retirement, and I was on the point of discovering the antidote. I have a laboratory at my farmhouse and I was hoping to go on with my work. But I needed a sample of the virus first.

Q: How dangerous is the virus?

Dr Williams: It might be extremely dangerous. Those who have suffered from the virus fall into a coma, become paralysed and die.

Q: How is the virus passed on?

Dr Williams: There is very little evidence of how the virus is passed on, because it has only been discovered on an island, Herella, in the Pacific Ocean. But on Herella whole villages have been found dead. We have to assume that the virus is airborne.

Q: So anyone who is breathed on could get it?

Dr Williams: That's possible.

Q: Is there a possibility that the inhabitants of Herella have a special susceptibility to the virus?

Dr Williams: Yes, that is perfectly possible. My work involved finding an antidote, in case the virus could have the same effect in the United Kingdom. It's possible that in this country the virus could lead to serious symptoms, such as coma, but not lead to death. At the moment we just don't know.

Q: What other symptoms are there?

Dr Williams: Blue spots appear on the body.

Q: Didn't it occur to you, Dr Williams, that carrying a test tube of such a deadly virus down a motorway on a motorbike was not a very intelligent thing to do?

Dr Williams: I've always travelled on a motorbike. I didn't want to arouse the suspicions of my colleagues by changing my routine. But, yes, I do realise it was stupid thing to do. I had become obsessed with my work, and wanted to successfully conclude my research, that's all.

Q: Brian Doughty, The Sentinel. Will Dr Williams be charged with theft, Inspector?

Inspector Goode: No decision has yet been taken. The priority seems to be that Dr Williams returns to Broughton to complete his work on an antidote.

Q: So that if the thieves do open the briefcase and come into contact with the virus, there will be a hope they can be saved?

Inspector Goode: Well, as Dr Williams has said, it is not certain that the virus will have the same effect in the United Kingdom as it does on the island…

Dr Williams: Herella.

Inspector Goode: Right. Now, ladies and gentlemen, if there are no more questions, I have the important task of tracking down the thieves before they are exposed to possible harm. Dr Williams has the task of completing his research so that, in the unlikely circumstances that the virus has the same effects in our country, an antidote is readily available. Thank you all for coming.

- Write the two articles that Anita and Brian submit to their editors. Base your articles on the information given in the press conference.

As these are reporters' drafts submitted to the editor, you do not need to worry about headlines or layout. Focus on getting the styles and tones right.

To help you, look at how Anita Gold and Brian Doughty reported the puma incident and what you have learned about tabloids and broadsheets.

SAINT OR SINNER?

Brian and Anita visit neighbours, and speak to friends of the Doctor at the centre of this major news story. Although Anita and Brian have gone to the farm together, that does not mean they will write the same story – or that they will take the same view of Dr Williams.

Tabloid newspapers tend to present people in strong emotive terms, dividing the world into saints or sinners. A sinner, such as a convicted murderer, for instance, might be described as a 'fiend' or 'beast'. The publican in Anita's puma story, on the other hand, is described as 'super-cool' and 'heroic'. The purpose of language like this is to make readers take sides and become more strongly involved – in much the same way as readers 'take sides' with characters in a novel.

Broadsheet newspapers do not present people in this way, tending to keep their distance. Brian Doughty's article on the puma is not mainly concerned with personalities, but the issues raised by the escape. There is no mention of heroics, although a quotation is given, praising the publican's calm behaviour.

"QUOTE ... UNQUOTE"

- Again Anita and Brian have articles to write. But, taking into account the fact that Dr Williams has disappeared, and there is no sign of the missing virus, what angle will Anita and her editor now adopt?

- Bearing this in mind, and all that the two journalists have seen at the farmhouse, look at the following quotations that Anita and Brian manage to gather from people who know Dr Williams. What view of Dr Williams do you think a tabloid journalist like Anita Gold might now give her readers? In what way might Brian Doughty offer a different view to his readers?

John Carlton, farmer and nearest neighbour:
He was just a bit forgetful and went everywhere on his motorbike. I think he was wrapped up in his experiments.

Jessie Williams, Dr Williams's sister and only surviving relative, who lives in Wales:
He was a lovely man, a lovely man. Do anything for you. He just wanted to make this country a safer place to live in. Nothing wrong in that, is there?

Broughton Research Centre:
Dr Williams no longer works at this establishment.

A police spokesperson:
Dr Williams cannot be found.

Mike Durrant, pensioner, who saw Dr Williams occasionally in the pub:
He was a funny bloke. You could never be sure what he was thinking. Liked to be on his own, couldn't be bothered with the likes of me!

Dr Susan Sherwood, Broughton microbiologist who entered Pacific Village 5 years ago with Williams:
The Herella business really got to him. He never forgot what he saw in that village. It changed him ...

Former colleague Dr Henry Hall:
John Williams was a man of brilliance, and held his views strongly. That is all I have to say.

Dr Sheila Williamson, another former colleague:
No, I wouldn't say he was someone you could trust. He wanted fame and recognition for his work and everything else came a poor second.

- One way in which journalists offer a particular view (or slant) on a story, is by choosing quotations that back up their point of view.

Very different pictures of Dr Williams can be given depending on which quotes are chosen. He could be shown as:

an eccentric, but harmless, forgetful old man

a dangerous, untrustworthy maniac on the loose

an ambitious, selfish scientist more concerned with winning a Nobel prize than saving lives

a maverick, disturbed and dangerous loner

a missing, talented scientist with the ability to help solve this crisis

Which of the quotations would Anita Gold use in her article to support her view of Williams? Which quotations would Brian Doughty use to support his point of view?

Give reasons for your choices.

- Anita and Brian have access to several pictures of Dr Williams: some show him at the press conference looking angry, looking confident, looking anxious; some are from science journals showing him at work, and showing him accepting an award for achievement; and some have been supplied by Dr Williams's sister, showing him laughing, and showing him sitting on his motorbike. There is also an artist's impression of Dr Williams's face. Consider which pictures Anita and Brian might select to back up their articles. What captions might they write?

- Write the headline for each article.

A **caption** is the writing underneath a photograph or picture in a book or newspaper. Captions help to interpret the points of what is shown.

PRESSURE

As Anita is choosing pictures to complement her article on Dr Williams's disappearance, the Editor of The Planet calls her into his office…

Harry: Anita, that was Downing Street on the 'phone – I've been summoned, along with Ben Kowalski from The Sentinel.

Anita: About the Williams business?

Harry: They wouldn't say – I'm guessing that's it. I'll have to leave everything in your hands till I get back.

Later, at 10 Downing Street …

Prime Minister: We need your help in the delicate matter of the Kolona virus. The Home Secretary will brief you on developments since your journalists illegally entered Dr Williams's property.

Home Secretary: The unconscious female has been identified as Sophie Gannon, a known petty thief. It is believed that when she heard how deadly the virus is, she tried to return it. She was disturbed – perhaps by Dr Williams. It is suspected that a struggle followed, during which drops of the substance containing the virus were spilt on Miss Gannon. Her boyfriend was probably with her at the time – he was found unconscious in a hamburger bar in Garton some hours later.

Health Minister: Mr Sampson was taken to Garton Hospital. It was when police searched the flat he shared with Miss Gannon that Dr Williams's briefcase was recovered. Mr Sampson and Miss Gannon are both in isolation – they have both developed blue spots.

Prime Minister: We have had our differences in the past, but its essential that we all co-operate at this time – what happened at the farmhouse must not be divulged to the general public. We are in the process of tracking down all who may have come into contact with Miss Gannon and Mr Sampson, and the last thing we need is widespread panic and hysteria. I am sure you agree that it is in national interest to have a news blackout.

Ben Kowalski: And where's Williams? Is he infected?

Home Secretary: MI5 are investigating his disappearance. It is unlikely that he has been infected – if that was the case, we would have found him before now. However, we cannot be sure.

At *The Sentinel* a meeting is held to decide whether or not to follow the Government's request, or go ahead and publish. The Editor passes on the Prime Minister's request, and acknowledges that the Police and health authorities fear a public panic if news leaks out.

There are good reasons for not alerting the public to the danger:

▶ there is no known antidote to the virus, so if anyone at risk was told, nothing could be done for them

▶ both Sophie Gannon and Michael Sampson are now in isolation, so no further harm is being done

▶ if a public panic did close Garton Hospital many patients would suffer, and some might die

▶ it is not known for certain that the disease will follow the same course as it did on the island of Herella; the coma may be temporary and both Sophie and Michael may recover

The Editor (Ben Kowalski): very aware of the serious and responsible stance taken by the paper on all issues. At the same time dedicated to freedom of the press, and the public's 'right to know'.

The Circulation Manager: aware of falling sales, and very keen on a 'scoop' that would undoubtedly boost circulation.

The Deputy Editor: aware of the responsible and serious stance taken by the newspaper and keen to avoid a scare story later shown to be false. At the same time deeply suspicious that the Government is probably only giving them the information it suits them to give. Is *The Sentinel* being fooled?

The Health Correspondent: very keen to publish the story, on the grounds that people have the basic right to be kept informed if their life is at risk. At the same time concerned that if the hospital is closed, unnecessary suffering could be caused to patients.

● In groups of four, take a role each. The Editor should start by recounting his visit to Downing Street and the points raised. Then, throw open the discussion and consider the rights and wrongs of publishing the article. The Editor must close the discussion by reviewing what he sees as the key issues, and arrive at a decision.

LATE NEWS

Half way through your discussion there is fresh news. Tony Bevan, the ambulance driver who picked up Michael Sampson at the hamburger bar, has been found dead. Police are at the house and no further details have been given. How does this news change the situation, if at all?

The Planet has ignored the Prime Minister's request and published its story.

Panic follows and frightened Garton residents set up road blocks, denying access to routes in or out of the hospital. As police attempt to clear the barricades, fights break out. An army helicopter lands inside the hospital grounds issuing a warning over a loud-speaker – they carry supplies for the hospital and anyone interfering will be fired at.

A patient, desperate to escape the hospital grounds, tells the crowd that three other patients have died. A porter, catching up with the patient, says that the ones who have died were critically ill and would have been expected to die.

• YOU ARE GOING OUT **LIVE** IN FIVE MINUTES ON NATIONAL TELEVISION! YOUR REPORT SHOULD LAST FROM 90–120 SECONDS. GIVE YOUR NEWS REPORT. (Video if you have the facility.) Your teacher will count you down to transmission time.

Follow the advice in the help box.

HELP

ORGANISING A NEWS BULLETIN

Prepare your report in sections

1 Attention-grabbing opening

2 Filling in the background to the crisis
   'Here at Garton hospital the crisis deepens…'

3 Update on latest developments/new deaths: 'So far we have been told of…'

4 Important quotations

5 Next developments

6 Own comment/analysis

7 Signing off
   'This is ____ for ____ at Garton General Hospital.'

FACING THE FACTS

The world now awaits the latest news from Garton Hospital. Naturally the hospital would like the road blocks removed and the panic to die down. At the same time, it would be wrong to publish information that was misleading, and lives must be protected.

A meeting of the Hospital Management Committee is held to review the situation. The plan is to put out a **press release**, that puts the problem into perspective.

THE FACTS

Michael Sampson and Sophie Gannon are still unconscious, but after three days are still alive. They still have blue spots. Their breathing is regular and their lives do not appear to be in immediate danger.

The ambulanceman who picked up Michael Sampson died in his sleep. There was no trace of blue spots. Tests are being carried out to try to establish the cause of death. His family has a history of heart disease.

Four deaths have taken place at the hospital since the admission of Michael Sampson and Sophie Gannon. All four patients had been seriously ill. In two of the four cases, blue spots had appeared, but Kolona virus has not been established as the cause of death. Paralysis had not taken place.

Six other patients have contracted blue spots and have fallen unconscious. But, as with Gannon and Sampson, their heartbeats are regular.

All six patients had been in the ward to which Michael Sampson had been admitted.

HELP

WHAT IS A PRESS RELEASE?

A press release is a written statement you give to the press. Instead of them hounding you for information, you supply it to them. You don't get caught out this way: you can consider your words and you can control the information. You can present the information in the way that suits you.

What are the ground rules?

Do keep it brief
Do keep it factual
Do write in formal language
Don't lie
Don't sensationalise
Don't discredit yourself

What goes in a press release?

First paragraph: strictly factual information about the current situation

Second paragraph: more detailed information about the practical steps taken to resolve the situation

Third paragraph: hard evidence such as statistics or scientific findings to reassure the public

Fourth paragraph: what steps are intended next (if anything)

Fifth paragraph: summary of viewpoint – 'We believe that …'

Sixth paragraph: Details of the person to contact for further information or about future plans

- Write this press release. Your aim, in this case, is to:

   defuse the panic,

   put the record straight by releasing accurate information,

   give the hospital a good image.

A LULL

For three days, there are no developments in the story of the virus.

If any of the following events were to occur, which would you make the lead story instead of the virus?

A plane crash in Mongolia

A successful England football performance in the semi-final of the World Cup

A political scandal involving a minister

A sex scandal involving a minister

A famous member of a pop group quits

A small terrorist bomb goes off in London (no-one is injured)

An ex-prime minister dies

Freak floods – 5 die

National Lottery roll-over biggest ever

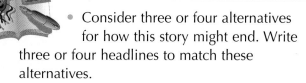

• Make a list of the factors which make stories important and number the stories in order of priority.

Would this order be different for tabloid and broadsheet newspapers?

RESOLUTION

What fresh developments would push the virus back into the headlines?
If the victims recovered, would it be headline news?

• Consider three or four alternatives for how this story might end. Write three or four headlines to match these alternatives.

• In a group, prepare a handful of contrasting documents to bring the story to your favoured conclusion. The documents displayed together should be enough to show how the story worked out.

You might include, for example:

A press release, e.g. '5 patients are recovering from …'

A TV news bulletin, e.g. 'French eruption of Blue Squirrel virus'

A statement by the Prime Minister in the House of Commons, e.g. 'It is my sad duty to inform you …'

An interview, e.g. 'The families of victims speak out …'

An article, e.g. 'Should biological research be ended?'

A diary of someone involved, e.g. 'This may be my last entry …'

A letter, e.g. 'I think I have the answer…'

A radio broadcast, e.g. 'If anyone out there can here me …'

A page from a history textbook published in 2015: 'The Great Virus'

CASE STUDY: FLESH-EATING BUGS

In 1994 reports of a frightening flesh-eating bacteria appeared in the newspapers. Read the following extracts and tackle the tasks at the end.

AGONY OF 7 VICTIMS IN MUTANT MICROBE MYSTERY

FLESH-EATING BUG KILLED MY MOTHER IN 20 MINUTES

A deadly flesh-eating bug killed one victim in just TWENTY MINUTES, it was revealed last night.

The mystery bug, which devours inches of body fat an hour, has struck seven people from the same area in the last four months.

Three have died. Three have been left scarred for life and the seventh is fighting for her life in hospital. One victim, a 69-year-old woman from Cheltenham, died on a train as she returned home from Scotland.

Her daughter, who doesn't want to be named, said last night: "She boarded a train in Dundee feeling very unwell and by the time it pulled into Kirkcaldy 20 minutes later she was dead. At first they thought she had died of a heart attack. But they found these blisters on her leg."

The bug feeds on dead tissue and eats away at humans with terrifying speed, leaving gangrene in its wake.

The bacteria is a common, and usually harmless, sore-throat bug found in about 10 per cent of the population.

Experts believe a virus, preying on the germ, may have turned it into a killer.

Nearly all the victims have suffered from a skin infection or some other previous underlying illness.

SPREADS

But why has it struck in such a small, 25 mile wide area of Gloucestershire?

Survivor Les Christie, who became ill 24 hours after a hernia operation, said yesterday: "It is like something from a science fiction film the way it spreads. I have been told that if they had not operated on me to remove the affected skin within eight hours I would have been wheeled out in a coffin."

Mr Christie, 58, from Chalford Hill in Stroud, was one of two patients who fell ill after having minor operations at

Stroud General Hospital in February.

A neighbour from Chalford Hill, 64-year-old Mrs Helen Sackett, was in hospital for a varicose vein operation at the same time and was also hit by the bug – called *streptococcal necrotising fasciitis*.

The pair had emergency surgery and skin grafting at Frenchay Hospital, Bristol.

The Stroud Operating theatre was closed for a week for a clean-up.

But suspicions of a link with the hospital faded when a retired local GP, Dr David Somervell, was struck down by the infection.

Dr Somervell, 64, from France Lynch, near Stroud, had not visited the Stroud hospital recently.

He was taken to the Gloucestershire Royal Hospital with the bacteria spreading rapidly through his right leg.

His kidneys failed as the infection ravaged his body – and surgeons had to amputate his leg to save him.

Dr Somervell spent two months in hospital.

He is now recovering but it is likely to be a year before he is fully back to normal. Dr Somervell's wife Margaret said, "How he got it is a mystery, because he had not had any wound which could have been infected."

The next three victims all died. One was a Gloucester man in his fifties, the second a woman in her sixties from Forest of Dean and the third, the Cheltenham woman who died on the train.

RARE

Irwin Wilson, general manager of Gloucestershire Royal Hospital, said there was no known connection between the victims. He added, "It is a very rare condition." Previously, the infection has turned up only once or twice a year in different parts of the country.

Dr Keith Cartwright, head of Gloucestershire's public health laboratories, said four of the latest victims were suffering from different sub-types of streptococcal bacteria. He added, "The germ itself is widespread in the community. What is unusual here is that it is causing this serious invasive illness. The same organism can also cause arthritis, blood poisoning, and all sorts of other things."

HOW HORROR GERM STRIKES

Victims of the killer bug break out in blisters, have diarrhoea and feel generally unwell.

They are treated with high doses of antibiotics. But in the worst cases, surgery is the only hope.

A special committee of consultants, hospital managers and senior nurses has been set up to combat the outbreak.

Doctors have been unable to discover any previous similar cluster of cases anywhere in the world. They believe it is caused by lowered resistance, changes in the bug itself – or

simply by chance.

Experts stress that most people with sore throats should not worry about falling victim to the bug. The odds against this happening are several thousands to one.

One scientist, Thomas Pennington, said, "This sounds like the gangrene outbreaks in hospitals 150 years ago. The big question is: What has happened to make it come back again?"

The Professor from Aberdeen University, added, "This bug seems to have extra special properties and once it starts attacking there is a chain reaction as it obviously feeds on dead tissue and eats away at humans.

"This is a cunning organism and we need to be on our guard against it."

THE BUG THAT ATE INTO OUR IMAGINATION AND SENT US MAD

Last week death followed its usual pattern, 32 people perished from septicaemia in the hospitals of England and Wales. Meningitis killed another nine and food poisoning at least one more. Whether the victims of these bacterial infections were children or adults, their families will have experienced shock and grief. The vast majority of such cases are private affairs, unnoticed by the press.

Instead the tabloids focussed on a bacterium, far rarer and more than 50 times less likely to kill us than the organism responsible for blood poisoning: the 'mutant flesh-eating bug', group A beta haemolytic streptococcus.

Editors fought for the most lurid headline. 'KILLER BUG ATE MY FACE' (Daily Star) was followed by 'FLESH BUG ATE MY BROTHER IN 18 HOURS' (The Sun) and 'FLESH-EATING BUG KILLED MY MOTHER IN 20 MINUTES' (Daily Mirror). The Star then came up with a headline guaranteed to jam surgery switchboards: "It started with a sore throat but you can die within 24 hours." One Scottish GP arrived to find five croaky patients waiting anxiously on his doorstep.

Streptococcus A, as we all now have embedded in our minds, can cause necrotising fasciitis ('Flesh-eating disease') or NF. It does not eat people's bodies, but produces toxins which destroy flesh. Nor is this new: NF has been familiar to doctors since it struck the British Home fleet in the 1790s, astonishing naval surgeons with the speed at which is stripped away skin and muscle, killing scores of sailors.

Streptococcus, first identified in human blood by Louis Pasteur, is known to appear in more than 80 different forms which cause anything from skin rashes to bubonic plague.

Up to one in five of us carry it. Most forms are harmless; a few are capable of making toxins which destroy the body's cells to devastating effect.

At its peak in the 19th Century, scarlet fever caused by Streptococcus A caused 35,000 deaths a year in Britain. Alexander Fleming's discovery of penicillin in 1929 heralded its downfall, and it has been close to the bottom of the league table of lethal organisms ever since.

However the genetic make-up of bacterial cells sometimes changes spontaneously, and several strains of streptococci A are thought to have recently mutated into a more dangerous form after invasion by viruses which have boosted their resistance to antibiotics.

In common with other bacteria, these streptococci have tentatively renewed their assault on mankind. Scientists have alerted health authorities to this mysterious setback in their war against microbes. They have revealed that diseases in long-term decline such as dysentery and tuberculosis are returning with a vigour some doctors put down to the misuse of antibiotics. Patients who fail to finish their course of pills only kill weaker organisms, allowing more powerful strains to multiply.

The FOUR isolated NF cases confirmed in Gloucester might have remained a medical curiosity had it not been for their timing. To national news editors, numbed by acres of worthy but dull coverage of Labour's leadership, the bug was a gift from God.

The killer bacteria could have been created by Steven Spielberg, and it was poised to eat into the hearts and minds of the public as surely and as fast as it had eaten its way through its victims.

Coinciding with an epidemic of sore throats, it caused a frisson of fear as people took (only half-jokingly) the first sign of any illness as the precursor to their bodies being eaten away.

Television was as guilty as the newspapers. "The killer bacteria claims more victims: government says don't panic" intoned ITN. Solemn bulletins were illustrated by high-tech graphics that showed viruses clamping themselves onto bacteria and squirting poison from their legs like malevolent insects. Here was a modern plague, turning its victim black and eating through it at a rate of an inch an hour. Every day, it seemed, new survivors and new victims were found. The coverage grew with the death toll; first seven, then 10, 12 and, by Friday, 17 in the Daily Mirror, 15 in the Daily Star and 14 in Today.

It is now clear that some families made baseless claims that a relative died from Necrotising Fasciitis.

No less bemused by the storm than the doctors who vainly tried to point out that the chances of being attacked by the bug were similar to being struck by lightning were the two journalists who had found the story in the first place. Three months ago, Andy Read, a reporter on the weekly Stroud News and Journal, and Jeremy Griffin, the paper's news editor, were both told on the same day about a local councillor, Les Christie, who was ill in hospital and fighting for his life. Christie had become infected after a routine hernia operation, as had a local woman, Helen Sackett, who had been operated on for varicose veins.

The same day the Stroud General's operating theatre was closed. It was Wednesday, the day the paper appeared, so the two had to sit on their scoop for a week, hoping that nobody else would find out. To head the story off, the hospital issued a press release two days later, explaining that two patients had fallen ill with tissue infection and that, as a precaution, the theatre was to undergo a programme of 'deep cleaning'.

By the time the story appeared the following week, it had been relegated to page two. Unknown to the journal, a third case had been diagnosed. A fourth followed publication. Official; it was a cluster, and the story moved off onto the national agenda.

"The whole thing really went on a roll because of the cluster," said Griffin. "We hadn't a clue that it would escalate this way. It's been grabbed because it's such a ready-made story, perfect for writing gruesome stories and headlines."

The same ordeal has been endured more phlegmatically in other countries whose health authorities profess themselves bewildered by the response in Britain. Many have detected increases in bacterial infection which can be caused by mutations of the organisms, complacent use of antibiotics, lifestyles or even the weather, but all insist that the number of cases is relatively small. None has found public reassurance as difficult as the authorities in this country.

The first report appeared in a tabloid newspaper – *The Daily Mirror*. The second appeared in a broadsheet newspaper – *The Times*.

- Compare the two accounts of the flesh-eating bug story.

- In the second article what is the writer's attitude to the way the tabloid press reported the story?

- What turned the story from a page 2 item in a regional newspaper to a national story both on TV and in the press?

- Compare the number of facts given in both articles about Streptococcus A.

- Tabloids often accompany an article with a bullet-pointed box, in this case probably TEN ESSENTIAL THINGS YOU NEED TO KNOW ABOUT THE FLESH-EATING BUG. Write that list making your language as lurid and sensational as possible.

- Could you defend the way the tabloids reported this story?

- Take a current news story and compare how it is treated in a tabloid and a broadsheet.

'IT MUST BE TRUE – I READ IT IN THE PAPER'

To what extent are newspapers obliged to give the whole truth and nothing but the truth? If the information offered as 'news' is misleading, we may not know what to believe.

- Read the article 'The Camera Never Lies' on the opposite page. Split a page of A4 into two columns. Call the left hand column 'Changes made to photographs'. Call the right hand column 'Reasons for changes'. Find as many examples as you can and set out as below (one is done already, to give you a start):

Changes made to photographs	Reasons for changes
Model's skin – blemishes removed	Improve advertisement

- Using the information you have collected, write a letter to an editor of a newspaper, in which you make clear your views of the practice of tampering with photographs. You may wish to make clear the kinds of changes to photographs you feel are reasonable, and the kinds of changes you feel are wrong and should be stopped.

- Look at the following list of things of which newspapers are sometimes accused. Newspapers are accused of many more 'crimes' than just altering photographs! Accusations include:

Invasion of privacy (when a telephoto lens is used, for instance, to take a photograph of which the subject knows nothing)

Misquotation (changing the words someone has used in talking to the journalist)

Quoting 'out of context' (taking one sentence from a lengthy interview to give a false idea of what was said)

Apologies tucked away where no-one can read them

Sensationalism (for instance, many people objected to the photographs of the Hillsborough Stadium disaster, that showed football fans being crushed to death against the fencing)

Indecency (topless 'page 3' girls)

Racism (some newspapers do not print the colour of a suspect when reporting a crime. Other papers might refer to 'black muggers')

Sexism (if an article concerns a man, the article gives his name and perhaps his profession. If the same article is written about a woman it might start 'attractive mother of two, Joan Smith …')

- Write a set of rules, headed **Code of Practice,** that you think newspapers should keep to. List your rules in order of importance. Cover at least six points from the above list, more if you wish. Note: a rule should state something a newspaper should not do. But it is also important to say how a mistake should be avoided, or, if a mistake has been made, how it should be put right. For example, a rule to cover the changing of a photograph to fit a space (as the baby Alexandra Griffiths example) might read as follows:

Newspapers should always try to print a photograph in its original form. If a change is made to fit the space, the caption underneath should always include the words 'altered photograph'.

- Imagine you are the editor of the *Daily Mirror* on the day after *The Sun* had published the picture of the lorry driver that you believe has been altered. Write the editorial that would be in the *Mirror* Comment section. You are allowed 300 words maximum.

Background detail – the driver Paul Ashwell had been imprisoned in Greece for transporting, unknowingly, parts for the Iraqi supergun. The *Daily Mirror* mounted a successful campaign for his release.

THE CAMERA NEVER LIES

Can a bald man be given hair? Can you be thinner at the touch of a button? Today's technology means that any photograph can be put onto a scanner and the image converted to electronic signals which are transmitted to a computer. The computer can then form a representation of the image on the screen in the form of thousands of tiny dots, like on a television screen. Groups of dots can then be moved or copied using the mouse and placed elsewhere in the picture. For example, a photograph of a man with a bald patch could be scanned, and the computer operator could use the mouse to select part of the picture which shows some of the man's hair, copy this part and repeat it over the bald patch. The photograph would now show the man with a full head of hair! Or, by combining a photograph of a small group of people in an office with a photograph of a small group of people in a park, you could make up a picture of a large crowd in the park.

Some newspaper editors were asked their opinion on the subject of cropping and changing photographs:

The Sun's picture desk: "We don't do it. The Press Council would be down on us, as we've found out in the past. People think we do it all the time - but it certainly doesn't go on here. We have an electronic picture desk but all we do is change the colour balance."

Picture editor of *Hello!* magazine: "We don't do it at all because we never have time and don't really believe in it. We wouldn't touch out wrinkles, or if someone had unattractive legs we wouldn't crop them out. We only crop if there's someone in a photograph we can't identify, if there's too much of a boring area or if it's artistically ugly."

Picture editor of the *Guardian*: "We would never retouch a photograph; if something did not happen in a certain way, then it would be unethical to say that it did. However, we do use a technique called 'photo-montage' which is the sticking together of different pictures. In this case, we would always write 'photo-montage' on the bottom. We would also highlight certain aspects of a photo - for instance, if there was a telegraph pole behind someone, we would not hesitate to make it lighter so that the person stands out more. We're not perfect though; we may have been guilty of moving the odd football in the past . . ."

GOOD OR BAD?

- A company advertising moisturiser removes blemishes from the face of the model in the picture.
- The pictures in a travel agent's brochure are changed to show partially-built hotels as finished, and holiday-makers with deeper suntans.
- A couple's wedding photographs are made lighter so that the weather appears to have been better than it was.
- A photograph in a magazine of a man who has lost a lot of weight is changed to make him look even thinner.
- A mysterious ghostly image is introduced into a picture for a book about the supernatural.

Baby Alexandra Griffiths was kidnapped from a hospital in January 1990. When she was found and reunited with her mother, *The Sunday Times* couldn't fit the photograph into the space available in their news report, so they moved the baby closer to her mother.

Lorry driver Paul Ashwell appeared in *The Sun* newspaper wearing a Sun T-shirt. *The Daily Mirror* took *The Sun* to court for allegedly faking the picture because, claimed the *Mirror*, Paul was wearing a *Daily Mirror* T-shirt when released from a Greek jail.

WHAT NEXT?

When you have completed this unit, look back over the work you have done. Use what you have learned to tackle one or more of the following written assignments:

- You are the Editor of a national newspaper alone in your office at night. Your paper is set to print a front page story the next day concerning the private life of a young star of a popular 'soap' on television. Such a story will boost sales, which will please your publisher. You have just received a phone call from the mother of the young star, pleading with you not to run the story, as her son recently attempted suicide after a similar article appeared in the press. You know this to be the truth.

    Either

    Write a story describing your thoughts and feelings as you struggle to reach a decision on whether to go ahead with the story.

    Tell the story from the mother's point of view, as she waits by the telephone for the Editor to ring back with his/her decision.

    Or

    Write a story of your own **either** about a journalist involved in inaccurate reporting **or** about a victim of the press.

- A journalist has been granted an interview with a member of the royal family, with whom he/she has been on friendly terms for several years. The Editor of the newspaper for which the journalist works has insisted he/she plant a 'bug', a small microphone, in the house during the interview.

    Describe the interview and the efforts the journalist makes to reach a decision whether or not to obey the Editor's instructions.

- Do you believe newspapers should be subjected to far more restraints on their ability to invade the privacy of the rich and famous, or would such restrictions deny ordinary people the right to know what is really going on? Give your views.

RECOMMENDED FURTHER STUDY

Fiction

   The Andromeda Strain by Michael Crichton

   Plague 99 by Jean Ure

   The Hot Zone by Richard Preston

On Media

   'Shot Actress – Full Story' by H. E. Bates, in *Short Stories of our Time* published by Hassap

Film

   Outbreak, Warner Brothers

UNIT TWO

Experience Into Words

Most of us like listening to well-told stories, and most of us like telling stories about the things that have happened to us. In the first part of this unit, you will see how two writers introduce you to their earliest memories. You will also learn how to compare two descriptions – a skill which will prove useful in examinations. The second part of the unit provides extracts in which writers have used a variety of techniques to recreate their experiences in the mind of the reader. Finally, you will consider ways in which you might write your own course work piece based on your own experiences, trying out the techniques you have been studying.

As you work through the unit, you will develop your skills as:

SPEAKERS AND LISTENERS

by discussing and comparing texts which draw on writers' own experiences
by working in response groups to discuss your own writing as it develops, and to help your partners with their drafts

READERS

by reading a range of original writing based on the writers' experiences
by investigating the techniques writers use to bring their experiences to life
by looking at similarities and differences between texts

WRITERS

by using what you learn about comparing and contrasting texts to produce organised written work
by exploring your own ideas and developing them into original writing for your course work folder

PART ONE – EARLIEST MEMORIES

In the first extract, Alison Fell describes her experiences of growing up in Scotland just after the Second World War.

  When you have read the following extract, capture your first reactions in a five or ten minute burst of silent writing. What were your feelings about what you read? What could you see in your mind? What could you hear? Did it make you think of anything, or did it remind you of anything?

In 1944 mothers' milk leaves a lot to be desired: a sense of grievance starts early. I can see my mother, pretty, acned, skinny with fretting, on a packed train from Scotland to South Wales. That bawling six-week-old the troops dandle is me: always hungry, never knowing whether to spit out this thin stuff or yell for more, nearly starving before the doctor twigs.

  We're off to Barry to meet my father, who has bombed Hamburg and Dresden and D-Day France, and has survived. …On the station platform my father, seeing his new daughter for the first time, will blurt out: 'Och, Doris, what a penny-faced wee article', and my mother, exhausted, will burst into tears. It was a boy they'd wanted, anyway, not this peely-wally thing, not another girl when they've got Sheila already.

  By 1945 they will be feeling more optimistic. Well, they won the war, didn't they, and they're alive, more than can be said for some, and now Nye Bevan's going to see the working man all right at last: we'll have the National Health, and school milk will be free, and even daughters will have the education they deserve.

  Times are still tough, though, in 1949 in grey Lanarkshire, with sweetie rationing as well. We've moved, the four of us, to a two-room basement in Hamilton, a cramped, sooty, outside-lavvy type of tenement opposite the Public Baths and the steamie. I start school at Beckford Street Primary in red lacing clogs (cheaper than shoes) and spend my first day in the headmistress's office clutching a rag doll and howling for my mammy to come back. Later I behave myself and write ABCs with hard grey chalk on screaming slates and stand still once a month for the Public Health nit inspectors.

  At nights there are forbidden pit byngs to slide down, allotments to raid and rival gangs of kids to stone. 'Dirty Papes' we yell from behind dustbin lids and the dark mouths of concrete closes: ignorant, tattered and ragamuffin, the lot of us. 'Proddy Dogs', they howl back and we have no idea what that means either; we only know the aggro is obligatory.

  If religious differences are way above this five-year-old's head, so too is the notion of gender. She has no real idea what she is – except dirt poor, and frightened. For her these are dangerous times. Dangerous if you tear your hand-me-down coat. Dangerous if you just cannae get bread and butter pudding (so slimy and white) down your throat at the tea table. Dangerous if you accidentally break a rationed egg. So full of beatings and beltings. Twenty or more years later those chickens will all come home to roost, and in a therapy group I'll hear an awful young scream sirening up from that black basement place: 'It isn't fair, it isn't fair.' I've done nothing wrong: why, then, the punishment? Even now, all traps and enclosures in my life bring me back to this angry question, this banging around in a box. No wonder, then, that I put up such a fight for justice, equality, socialism and what have you: it's no mere matter of ideology or principle, but an obsession in the very flesh.

From *Rebel with a Cause* by Alison Fell

peely-wally – sickly
Nye Bevan – ministerof health 1945
Papes – Papists/Catholics
Proddy – Protestant

DEVELOPING YOUR RESPONSE

When you've written down your first reactions, share them with one or two partners. Did your partners react in the same way as you? Did they notice anything that you didn't?

• With a partner, work through the extract methodically, so that you can explain in detail why you responded as you did. Use the following methods to examine and make notes on the extract. (It's useful to have a method to help you in an exam, as well as in course work.)

Stage 1 – The Title:
Does the title help you understand what the writer is trying to say?

Stage 2 – 'Chains':
Look for chains of words, phrases, and ideas that run through the extract. Start with the first word or phrase in the chain, and write down the words/phrases/ideas connected with that first link. Then write down what you think the writer is trying to show. Here's a short chain that starts with Alison Fell's mother:

My mother – skinny with fretting – exhausted – burst into tears: **shows Alison Fell's pity for her mother. Gets across the difficulty of coping with a new-born baby that cries all the time, especially when her husband doesn't seem to appreciate what she's been through.**

Chains can be short or long, and can re-use links from other chains. Here's another one starting with Alison Fell's mother. See how far you can take it, then explain what it shows:

Mother – milk – sense of grievance – always hungry – nearly starving – school milk – sweetie rationing

Possible words in other chains have been marked purple in the extract. What chains can you put together from them? What do these chains show? Are there any chains which you can make from words that haven't been marked?

Stage 3 – Paragraphs:
Now that you've picked out some of the threads running through the extract, you can look at how the writer organises her ideas overall. In your notes, give each paragraph a letter (A to F in this case), and write beside each letter a short phrase or two to sum up the topic of the paragraph. Note down also any ideas, words or phrases that make links between the paragraphs. For example:

Paragraph A: On the train to meet father.

Paragraph B: Meeting father. First reactions.
(Link phrase: 'On the station platform'.)

Stage 4 – Techniques:
Finally, look closely at each paragraph in detail to pick up the techniques used by the writer. Features to watch for:

Viewpoint. Who's telling the story? Look at the way Alison Fell varies the **pronouns** referring to herself. She uses 'I', as you might expect, but she also uses 'she' and 'you'. What effect does this have? In the first two paragraphs, she also includes details that she couldn't possibly remember, but which she must have been told about by her parents. What effect does this have? Also, look at the way she uses the pronoun 'they' (referring to her parents) in paragraphs B and C. What effect does this viewpoint have?

Use of Detail. What kinds of words are used, and why? Look at how Alison Fell builds up an impression of what her early life was like by giving us details about it. To focus more clearly on the impression she gives us, look in particular at the **adjectives** and the **verbs.**

For example, look at some of the **adjectives** in

[continued over]

paragraph D: *grey* Lanarkshire'; *'two-room* basement', 'a *cramped, sooty, outside-lavvy* type of tenement'; 'a *rag* doll'; *'hard, grey* chalk'; *'screaming* slates'. What impression do these adjectives give you? Pick out some of the adjectives in the next two paragraphs. Again, what effect do they have?

Look now at the **verbs** in paragraph E: *to slide* down; *to raid; to stone; yell; howl.* Again, what impression do they give of how Alison Fell spends the evenings after school has finished?

The **tenses** of the verbs throughout the extract are interesting. They are mainly **present tense** ('I *start* school'), with some examples of **future tense** (*'will have* the education'). Normally, you would expect writing about memories to be in the **past tense** (such as 'I *started* school'), so why has Alison Fell chosen to write it like this? What effect does her choice of tense have?

Sentence structure. Another technique that writers often use is creating **patterns** of sentences, and of words within sentences. For example, in paragraph F, Alison Fell writes a series of **short** or **incomplete sentences** (from 'She has no real idea of what she is' to 'beatings and beltings'). What impression does she want to give by doing this? She also uses **repetition** in this paragraph

('Dangerous if you …') How do we react to this repetition? (Think as well about the pronoun that's being used.)

In paragraph E, too, she gives us **lists**, in which she repeats particular types of words: 'pit byngs *to slide* down, allotments *to raid* and rival gangs of kids *to stone'* (verbs) and *'ignorant, tattered* and *ragamuffin'* (adjectives). Listing is a common technique used by writers. What effect does it have here?

Speech. Writers make use of what people say and how they say it, because the sound of speech can bring writing vividly alive. Alison Fell makes use of her regional **dialect** in the **direct speech** she writes down – for example in what her father says when he first sees her (paragraph B), or in the insults the children shout at each other (paragraph E). In addition, she scatters dialect vocabulary ('peely-wally', 'byngs', 'cannae') and slang ('before the doctor twigs', 'sweeties', 'outside-lavvy', 'aggro') throughout this extract. More usually, you might expect writers to use standard English, and only to use dialect in direct speech. So, why does Alison Fell choose to use dialect throughout the text? And what does she do in paragraph C?

Now that you have looked in detail at the first extract, compare the way Alison Fell writes about her earliest experiences with the approach taken in the following extract 'First Light' by Laurie Lee. He tells us about his earliest memory, dating to a time before the First World War, when his family moved to a new house.

FIRST LIGHT

I was set down from the carrier's cart at the age of three; and there with a sense of bewilderment and terror my life in the village began.

The June grass, amongst which I stood, was taller than I was and I wept. I had never been so close to grass before. It towered above me and all around me, each blade tattooed with tiger-skins of sunlight. It was knife-edged, dark and a wicked green, thick as forest and alive with grasshoppers that chirped and chattered and leapt through the air like monkeys.

I was lost and didn't know where to move. A tropic heat oozed up from the ground, rank with sharp odours of roots and nettles. Snow-clouds of elder-blossom banked in the sky, showering upon me the fumes and flakes of their sweet and giddy suffocation. High overhead ran frenzied larks, screaming, as though the sky were tearing apart.

For the first time in my life I was out of the sight of humans. For the first time in my life I was alone in a world whose behaviour I could neither predict nor fathom: a world of birds that squealed, of plants that stank, of insects that sprang about without warning. I was lost and I did not expect to be found again. I put back my head and howled, and the sun hit me smartly on the face, like a bully.

From *Cider with Rosie* by Laurie Lee

• *First reactions.* As you did with the previous extract, jot down your initial reactions without discussing them. How did you feel about it? What could you see or hear? Did it remind you of anything? Did it make you think of anything? Did it give you a fresh way of looking at anything?

• *Developing your response.* When you've written about your first reactions, compare your response with your partner's. Then, with your partner, work methodically through the four stages of developing your response (see pages 3–4), in the same way as you did with *Rebel with a Cause.* The first three stages (**title; chains; paragraph** lettering/topics/links) will help you to understand the extract more thoroughly. The fourth stage (**techniques:** viewpoint; use of detail; sentence structure; dialect) will help you explain the techniques the writer uses.

Although you will be able to look for similar things in both passages, there is one extra technique used in this extract. Laurie Lee uses **metaphors** to help bring his description alive for the reader. For example, he tells us that the blades of grass are 'knife-edged'. Here, he is comparing the edges of the grass blades with the edges of knife blades. Why does he do that? What impression does he want to give us about his feelings as a three-year-old in this situation?

Simile – using 'like' or 'as', compares one thing with something completely different to show a common aspect, e.g. 'the sun *is like* an orange'.	**Metaphor** – one thing described *in terms of* another to show common aspects, e.g. '*snow-clouds* of elder-blossom'.

• Now look again at paragraphs B, C and D. In each paragraph, pick out at least one metaphor or simile. In each case, you need to explain what is being compared with what, and why. What effect on the reader does each metaphor or simile have, and why? Can you find a metaphor in *Rebel with a Cause?*

(You can find ideas about using the extracts from *Rebel with a Cause* and *Cider with Rosie* for your own original writing on page 49).

COMPARING TEXTS

Now that you know how to analyse a text, you can go on to
compare one with another. It will be useful to follow a framework
so that you can write about two extracts in a structured way.

• Compare the extracts from *Rebel
with a Cause* and *Cider with Rosie*.
Explain which of the two extracts involves you
more as a reader, or whether you liked them
equally. You should comment on:

How you responded to each extract.

The techniques used by the writers to
influence your response.

When you write your comparison, try to organise
your ideas using the framework in the following
help box.

HELP

To extend and develop your writing, try using
this framework: it will help you to explain the
things you need to.

Remember to paragraph your writing. You
should aim to write about 600 to 800 words
altogether. (Remember, too, that you don't
have to prefer one extract to the other. You
can like or appreciate them both equally.)

COMPARING TEXTS – A FRAMEWORK

ALWAYS REMEMBER TO: MAKE A POINT
                       GIVE EVIDENCE (short quotation or reference)
                       EXPLAIN WHAT THE EVIDENCE SHOWS

step 1 *The extract I preferred was …*
Write about the extract that appealed to you most and **why.** (Perhaps you liked the tone
or style of writing? Perhaps you felt the writer succeeded in making you sympathise
with the character?)

step 2 *When I read [the other extract], I …*
Write about your response to the other extract and why you reacted as you did.
(Perhaps, for example, you felt there should be more information, or perhaps you found
the tenses or viewpoint offputting?)

step 3 *These two extracts are similar in a number of ways …*
Write about the similarities of the three extracts. (Do the writers use any similar
techniques? Do they encourage the reader to imagine events from a similar viewpoint?)

step 4 *The extracts are different in that …*
Write about the contrasts of the two extracts – how they are different from each other?
(Perhaps one uses adjectives to describe something while the other uses speech?
Perhaps they make use of different tenses for different purposes?)

HELP

You do not have to begin your sentences as shown in the framework. Try a selection of these phrases to help you explain and develop your ideas.

It made me think about ..., because ...

I could sympathise with ..., because ...

I could understand ...

It made me see ... by ...

I would have preferred ..., because ...

I would like to have found out ...

It made me feel ...

Alison Fell/Laurie Lee shows us what ... is like through her/his descriptions of ...

For example, s/he shows us ...

It tells us that ..., because ...

For example, when ... This word/phrase tells me that ..., because ...

Another way in which s/he shows ...

The phrase/words which give that impression is/are ..., because ...

The viewpoint s/he gives us ...

The pronoun gives us the impression that ...

The adjectives/verbs/details tell us that ... The tenses ...

The effect of the sentence structure is to make us feel ...

This use of dialect gives us the impression that ...

In this metaphor, s/he compares ... with ... They are similar because ...

This suggests that ...

Another similarity is ... In contrast,

This is different from ... because ...

However ... But ... Although ... Another difference is ...

This contrasts with ...

PART TWO – EXPERIENCES OF SCHOOL

Drawing on common experience is a useful way for writers to involve the reader in the text. School experiences are often highly formative and provide a rich source of material for vivid autobiographical writing.

Here are two views of schooldays – Alice Thomas Ellis's from her days in a small, local school in North Wales, and George Melly's from the independent, fee-paying school to which he was sent by his parents. The reader knows what it is like to be at school and so can sympathise with the feelings described by the writers. However, the reader can also easily recognise important differences between the writer's account and what school is like today. This helps to give a sense of time and place to the events described.

I went to the National School on the coast road and, since Penmaenmawr slopes as it does, my first classroom was half underground. In the winter it was warmed by an open stove and we did our sums on wood-framed slates using slate pencils which, licked and held in a certain way, made the sort of noise that drives some people mad – like a long fingernail scratching a nylon stocking. Certain of my friends, having discovered the power of this noise, would slide the last part of the road to school down the slate-lined gutters with a granite chipping under foot. I had enemies too. There was a boy called Robert who lived in Penmaenan (all our enemies lived in Penmaenan, which was out of bounds except for raiding parties) who had thick glasses and a chronic dribble, and used to chase me round the playground. He caught me and kissed me one day, and I was reprimanded by the headmaster, who said he would never have expected such a thing of me. I have never recovered from the injustice of this and I hope Robert has had a rotten life. Then there was a little English boy whose name I never knew, who didn't even attempt to fraternize with the natives but played trains all by himself, going choo choo and working his elbows like pistons. The badder boys jeered at him in the playground and he

once made a response so dignified and so touching that I wept. I can't remember what it was, but the memory still brings tears to my eyes. I dare say today I should want to smack him.

As time went by our teacher, G.O. Jones, taught us, among other things, to write properly, with a pen. This involved penholders and nibs and wipers and ink monitors whose duty it was to refill the inkwells on each desk, which must have been quite tricky since most of us used them as receptacles for the cod-liver oil capsules and iron pills which a caring authority deemed necessary for our health. G.O. had been gassed in the First World War and as a result he spat a bit as he spoke, and our exercise books came up in moisture bubbles when he stood beside us. He, too, had trouble with Robert whose mother used to burst in roaring when her boy had been quite correctly caned. G.O. said she was a blackguard and I admired this sophisticated choice of words, although I wouldn't have cared to cross her myself. There were several women like this around, gypsy-like and intimidating, and quite unlike the majority who wore black straw hats and gloves to Chapel and high-necked, black garments and never swore.

From A Welsh Childhood by Alice Thomas Ellis

---

fraternize – make friends with
blackguard – pronounced 'blaggard' – foul-mouthed person, scoundrel

---

• As usual, approach the extract on the opposite page methodically. Jot down your first reactions, then develop your understanding more thoroughly (title; chains; paragraph lettering/topics/links), before looking at the techniques the writer uses (viewpoint; use of detail; sentence-structure; dialect/sound of voice; metaphorical language). Look out for the little touches of sly humour. Pay particular attention to the paragraphing – the way Alice Thomas Ellis has a clear topic for each paragraph, but towards the end she prepares the reader for the paragraph that is to come. How does she do this for each paragraph in this extract?

FILTHY JAZZ

My prep-school headmaster was a fat bald brute, who aimed, in the decade before the war, to turn little Liverpudlians, whose parents could afford the fees, into tiny Tom Browns.

Looking back I believe he must have been mad, or perhaps he drank. In fairness to my mother and father they had no idea what went on. He was constantly stressing that a term's notice was required, and we had seen too much of what happened to boys living through that term to complain.

'Proditor – masculine – a traitor,' he would mutter as he set about them, for he believed Latin prose to be the foundation of everything.

During the summer term, if a Test Match was taking place, we were expected to eat our bright pink mince and leaden jam roll in attentive silence, and listen, with real or simulated interest to the B.B.C. commentary. Any whispering, if detected, led to either a slippering or being hauled to our feet by the skin of the cheek and shaken to and fro.

'It's the pestilential day-school system,' he would shout as he hammered the side of our skulls with the knuckles of his free hand.

In me he sensed a contrary spirit, and almost every day would fire questions as to who bowled the last over or was fielding at silly mid-off. As I never knew ('give me your slipper, Melly Major'), I was very relieved when rain stopped play, and even now the sentence 'and we return you to the studio' holds an irrational beauty.

Very often the announcer, in a suitably apologetic voice, would introduce a record by Ambrose and his Orchestra or Roy Fox and his Band. At this the headmaster, with the hysterical violence which characterized all his movements, would push back his chair and attempt to silence the ancient set before the first note.

If, as usually happened, the switch came off in his hand, he would drown the music, as he fumbled to replace it on its axle, by shouting 'filthy jazz!' at the top of his voice.

Sitting po-faced under a sepia photograph of giraffes in the East African bush, I would mentally add jazz to Bolshevism and the lower classes ('Spurni profanum vulgus'), as things I was in favour of.

From Owning Up by George Melly

Tom Brown – a fictional public school boy	po-faced – looking serious
pestilential – diseased or dangerous to morals	Bolshevism – revolutionary socialism
irrational – cannot be explained logically	

• Again, approach this passage methodically, jotting down your first reactions, before developing your understanding of what the extract is saying, and the techniques the writer uses. Look at the paragraphs – they are much shorter than those used by Alice Thomas Ellis. What effect does this have? How does George Melly capture the voice of his prep-school headmaster? What use, in particular, does he make of brackets?

• Both of these extracts have touches of humour. Compare the two passages, using the framework and a selection of the phrases on pages 38 to 39.

You will find ideas on using these passages for your own original writing on page 49.)

WINTER MEMORIES

William Wordsworth lived in and wrote about the Lake District. The countryside in this part of the north west of England is very beautiful, and each season held special memories for the poet. Here is an extract from 'The Prelude', a poem Wordsworth published in 1805. In the extract, he describes what it was like to skate on one of the frozen lakes on a cold winter evening.

And in the frosty season, when the sun
Was set, and visible for many a mile
The cottage windows blazed through twilight gloom,
I heeded not their summons – happy time
It was indeed for all of us, for me
It was a time of rapture! Clear and loud
The village clock tolled six – I wheeled about,
Proud and exulting like an untired horse
That cares not for his home. All shod with steel
We hissed along the polished ice in games
Confederate, imitative of the chase
And woodland pleasures, – the resounding horn,
The pack loud chiming, and the hunted hare.
So through the darkness and the cold we flew,
And not a voice was idle; with the din
Smitten, the precipices rang aloud;
The leafless trees and every icy crag
Tinkled like iron; while far distant hills
Into the tumult sent an alien sound
Of melancholy, not unnoticed, while the stars
Eastward were sparkling clear, and in the west
The orange sky of evening died away.
Not seldom from the uproar I retired
Into a silent bay, or sportively
Glanced sideway, leaving the tumultuous throng
To cut across the reflex of a star
That fled and flying still before me gleamed
Upon the glassy plain.

heeded not – paid no attention to
rapture – bliss, delight
exulting – delighting in his ability
confederate – joining together with others
smitten – struck
tumult – uproar, noise
reflex – reflection

- Although this is a poem, you can still use the methodical approach that you've worked with before. Jot down your first reactions, then develop your understanding more thoroughly (title; chains; paragraph lettering/topics/links), before looking at the techniques the writer uses (viewpoint; use of detail; sentence structure; dialect/sound of voice; metaphorical language).

- However, because it is a poem, you will need to consider the effects of the verse form and rhythm, and of the sound patterns. Consider the following points and note down any examples you find of each one:

The verse form and rhythm. Each line has ten syllables, but there is no rhyme. Wordsworth uses run-on lines (where the meaning runs from one line to the next, without a punctuation mark) to give the impression of a speaking voice. What examples can you find? He also uses run-on lines, and regular patterns of stresses to imitate or suggest physical action. Again, can you find examples?

The sound patterns. He uses repeated patterns of consonants (alliteration) to give an impression of the sound or actions he is describing. What examples can you find?

Alfred Williams, who was writing at the end of the nineteenth century, was a steam-hammer operator in the Great Western Railway works in Swindon. In his best-known book, called *In a Wiltshire Village,* he describes the everyday life of people at that time; the winter, with its opportunities for skating, was as memorable to him as to William Wordsworth:

In the winter, provided there is frost enough, there will be abundant skating and sliding on the pools, and often in the water-meadows as well, though the ice there will not be as stable.

The country boys do not often possess skates, but content themselves with sliding instead. Their heavy nailed boots are very well adapted for this; they glide along over the smooth surface for a long distance. If one of the nails in their boots should happen to be sharp and cleave a long white line in the ice, they call this a 'steak of fat bacon.' He who can effect the longest streak is counted above the average among the juveniles. The farm youngsters often meet with accidents in sliding and skating on the ice, and frequently get severe wettings at it. Sometimes they attempt the ice before it bears properly, or slide into a spot sheltered by trees or bushes, or, if it is in the water-meadows, they may be deceived with a current which has retarded the frost, and come to grief that way, but they do not care very much about it, and continue with the sport. Once, in my boyhood, when I was in the habit of coming home from the farm by way of the ice on the canal several successive nights in the starlight, I suddenly found myself struggling in the middle of the water nearly to my shoulders. While I was in this predicament the testy old farmer at the house near by, being warned of the accident by his man-servant, who was in waiting for me, hearing that I had slid into the hole, thrust his head outside and cried: 'An sard un devilish well right, too; a no business an ther.' The ill-natured old man had had the holes broken on purpose to entrap the skaters.

retarded – slowed down

• Discuss this extract to develop your understanding of it, and then write about the techniques the writer uses. Pay attention to viewpoint by thinking about the pronouns Alfred Williams uses in the first two thirds of this extract. What impression do these pronouns give you of his focus, here? How does this focus contrast with what Wordsworth is interested in, when he writes?

William Wordsworth and Alfred Williams write in a literary dialect which would have been the equivalent of our standard English. There aren't many differences between the language they use and modern standard written English, but there are some.

• Find examples of differences under the following headings, and rewrite them in modern standard English:

Vocabulary – some of the words and phrases used would be uncommon nowadays, for example, 'imitative of the chase', where we would say 'imitating the chase'.

Syntax – the order of words in the sentence differs from what we would expect, for example 'happy time / It was indeed for all of us'. What would the word order be nowadays, in standard written English?

Alfred Williams goes beyond the literary written dialect, and gives examples of the spoken Wiltshire dialect of that time. There's the metaphor the country boys use for the line in the ice (a 'steak of fat bacon'). There's also the dialect spoken by the 'ill-natured' old farmer.

• What are the Wiltshire words for 'he'/'him'/'on'? What is significant about the dialect syntax of 'A no business an ther'? What effect does this use of dialect have?

• Compare these two extracts using the framework you have practised. Make sure you bring out the differences between prose and poetry.

(You will find ideas for original writing on page 50.)

GRANDPARENTS

The next two extracts portray the writers' memories of their grandparents. In *From Deepest Kilburn*, Gail Lewis writes about the food at her grandmother's house, and how it contrasted with the food she ate at home. Look out, in the second paragraph, for the way she moves from memories of food to other memories. Is the transition she makes a completely new direction, or does she link it in any way with the topic she's been focusing on?

The difference between the Jamaican and English aspects of my life at that time often revolved around food. Saturdays really exemplified it. Saturday-morning breakfast would usually be fried dumpling and egg or saltfish fritters, sometimes sardine. If it was at my Nan's it would be cornflakes or porridge, the Scottish way, with salt – my Grandad was from Edinburgh. Then for Saturday dinnertime (lunch) my Mum would let me go and have pie, mash and liquor at the pie and mash shop. She would give me a shilling and I would go off and eat this very English working-class food sitting on a wooden bench at a marble table. I was the only black person in the shop. Now when I pass one of the few pie and mash shops still left in London and see that green, slimy-looking liquor I really wonder how I ever came to eat it, but it still serves to remind me of my roots. Dinner in the evening would be either saltfish and ackee (still one of my favourite meals); home-made oxtail or pea soup, or maybe pigs' trotters and rice.

This stark difference would be replayed throughout the week with English dinner at nursery or school and something more Jamaican in the evening. At my Nan's, of course, it was English all the time (although there may have been Scottish variations of which I was unaware). In particular I remember the high tea on Sundays – bread, celery, tomatoes, ham, prawns, perhaps some mussels or cockles, eggs, and of course salad cream. Occasionally Nan would cut up an avocado pear that my Dad might have given her if he'd managed to get some down at the Shepherd's Bush market. Another thing that reminds me of the 'old days' is horse-drawn carts. That's because the milkman would do his round with a horse-drawn carriage; he and his weekend helper would sit at the front. The milkman's horse was called Ginger and it was a huge great orange-coloured horse that would take lumps of sugar from you if you were brave enough to offer them. I was always too frightened to do that but I did eventually pluck up enough courage to stroke him, taking great care not to go too close to his back legs – I'd been told that if you do, horses have a tendency to kick you. Being very much a city girl, I had no idea whether this was true or not, but I sure as hell wasn't going to risk finding out the hard way. But it was really nice on weekend days to lie in bed and hear the clip-clop of Ginger's hooves on the cobbled street.

- Make notes about this extract as you have for others in the unit. Consider the style of language and the techniques the writer uses.

- Discuss your views of the extract. What do you learn about the writer's character as a young girl and what can you tell about her character now?

In *The Lost Continent*, Bill Bryson writes about returning to the USA, where he grew up. In the following extract, he remembers family visits to his grandparents.

Arriving in Winfield was always thrilling. Dad would turn off Highway 78 and bounce us down a rough gravel road at far too high a speed, throwing up clouds of white dust, and then to my mother's unfailing alarm would drive with evident insanity towards some railroad tracks on a blind bend in the road, remarking gravely, 'I hope there's not a train coming.' My mother didn't discover until years later that there were only two trains a day along those tracks, both in the dead of night. Beyond the tracks, standing alone in a neglected field, was a Victorian mansion . . . Beyond the mansion was a wide field, full of black and white cows, and beyond that was my grandparents' house, pretty and white beneath a canopy of trees, with a big red barn and acres of lawn. My grandparents were always waiting at the gate. I don't know whether they could see us coming and raced to their positions or whether they just waited there hour after hour. Quite possibly the latter because, let's face it, they didn't have a whole lot else to do. And then it would be four or five days of fun. My grandfather had a Model T Ford, which he let us kids drive around the yard, to the distress of his chickens and the older women. In the winter he would attach a sleigh to the back and take us for long cold rides down snowy roads. In the evenings we would all play cards around the kitchen table and stay up late. It was always Christmas at my grandparents' house, or Thanksgiving, or the Fourth of July, or somebody's birthday. There was always happiness there.

When we arrived, my grandmother would scuttle off to pull something fresh-baked out of the oven. This was always something unusual. My grandmother was the only person I ever knew – possibly the only person who ever lived – who actually made things from the recipes on the backs of food packets. These dishes always had names like 'Rice Krispies 'n' Banana Chunks Upside-Down Cake' or 'Del Monte Lima Bean 'n' Pretzels Party Snacks'. Generally they consisted of suspiciously large amounts of the manufacturer's own products, usually in combinations you wouldn't think of except perhaps in an especially severe famine. The one thing to be said for these dishes was that they were novel. When my

grandmother offered you a steaming slab of cake or wedge of pie it might contain almost anything – Niblets, sweet corn, chocolate chips, Spam, diced carrots, peanut butter. Generally it would have some Rice Krispies in it somewhere. My grandmother was particularly partial to Rice Krispies and would add a couple of shovelfuls to whatever she made, even if the recipe didn't call for it. She was about as bad a cook as you can be without actually being hazardous.

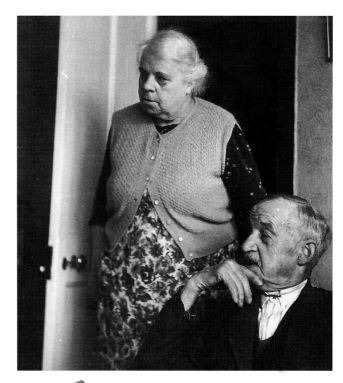

• When you've finished writing about and discussing this extract, compare it with *From Deepest Kilburn*. Note in particular the humour in the extract from *The Lost Continent*. Pick out the humorous words and phrases, and explain why they have the effect they do. Look also at the way Bill Bryson covers a wide range of details – not just food – about what visits to his grandparents were like.

(You will find suggestions for original writing on page 50.)

LISTEN TO THEM TALK!

To use your own experiences in original writing, you don't always have to write autobiographically, from an 'I' viewpoint. Writers use things that have happened to them, or things they have seen or been told about, and they write about them from an outside, second- or third-person viewpoint ('you' or 'she'/'he'/'they'). Here are two poems which could have been written about the writers' own experiences, or about events they have observed. The first is by a young American poet, Julie O'Callaghan, who now lives and works in Ireland. It shows how you can create original writing from even the most ordinary-seeming incidents and experiences.

BRATS

Tell Wanda ta shut her trap, Mom.
– What's wrong with humming, knucklebrain?
Mom, will ya tell her?
– I can hum when I want – right, Mom?
Not while I'm watching something, sap.
– Reruns of the Beverly Hillbillies?
Mom, tell her or I'll bash her one.
– Your son is threatening me, Mother.
Wait till Dad gets home, smarty pants.
– Oh, I'm so scared!
Why won't ya tell her to shut her big dumb mouth?
– Quit bossing Mom around.
No stupid, put a cork in it.
– He called me stupid, Mom.
I'm watching something you goddamn moose.
– Now, Mom, he's swearing.

• Write and talk about this poem in the usual way. Your first jottings will probably include thoughts and feelings about incidents like this that you've seen or experienced yourself. When you develop your understanding further, and look at the poet's techniques, you won't be able to find things to say under all headings. For example, there's not a lot of metaphorical language, unless you can count 'you goddamn moose'. You can't say much about paragraphs or sections either, but you can comment on the layout, on the way you can tell who's speaking. You can also pick up quite a lot about the personalities of the two 'brats' (and perhaps about their mother) from the things they say to each other.

The second poem is by Simon Armitage, a young writer who works in Huddersfield. You will be able to work out the situation quite easily – who is talking to whom, where they are, and what is going on. Look out for the way Simon Armitage communicates the personality of the speaker.

VERY SIMPLY TOPPING UP THE BRAKE FLUID

Yes, love, that's why the warning light comes on. Don't
panic. Fetch some universal brake-fluid
and a five-eighths screwdriver from your toolkit
then prop the bonnet open. Go on, it won't

eat you. Now, without slicing through the fan-belt
try and slide the sharp end of the screwdriver
under the lid and push the spade connector
through its bed, go on, that's it. Now you're all right

to unscrew, no, clockwise, you see it's Russian
love, back to front, that's it. You see, it's empty.
Now, gently with your hand and I mean gently,
try and create a bit of space by pushing

the float-chamber sideways so there's room to pour,
gently does it, that's it. Try not to spill it, it's
corrosive, rusts, you know, and fill it till it's
level with the notch on the clutch reservoir.

Lovely. There's some Swarfega in the office
if you want to wash and some soft roll above
the cistern for, you know. Oh don't mind him, love,
he doesn't bite. Come here and sit down Prince. Prince!

Now, where's that bloody alternator? Managed?
Oh any time, love. I'll not charge you for that
because it's nothing of a job. If you want
us again we're in the book. Tell your husband.

• Write about your first reactions, then develop your response in the usual way and look at the techniques the writer uses. In particular, look at the way Simon Armitage captures the sound of the speaker's voice by using run-on lines, and by using dialect. What

does Simon Armitage think of this man, and of his attitude to the woman he's talking to? How does he communicate that attitude?

• Now compare the two poems.

(Suggestions for writing are on page 50.)

PART THREE

ORIGINAL WRITING FROM YOUR OWN EXPERIENCES

This section gives you ideas for writing, making use of what you have learnt from the extracts you have studied. Each suggestion is based on one of the pairs of texts you have been studying in Parts One and Two of this unit. Use the suggestions as ideas to try out, putting into practice the techniques you have been looking at in the earlier parts. It is probably best at this stage to keep your writing in early draft form, and then develop one of your drafts into a full-length course work piece of between 600 and 900 words. The final extract in this section will focus on structuring a piece of this length.

When you are gathering ideas in your draft, you might follow this procedure:

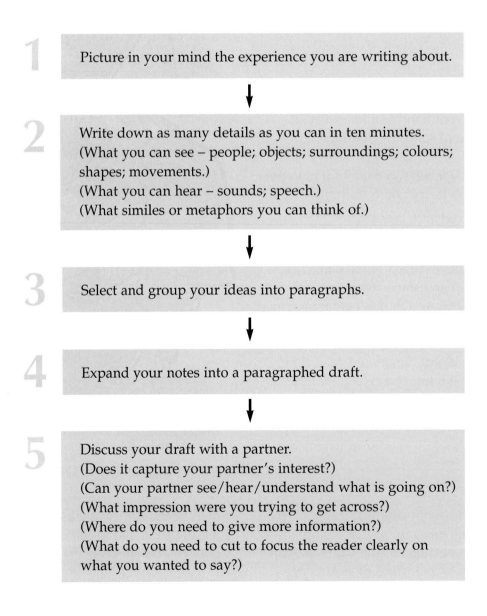

1   Picture in your mind the experience you are writing about.

2   Write down as many details as you can in ten minutes.
(What you can see – people; objects; surroundings; colours; shapes; movements.)
(What you can hear – sounds; speech.)
(What similes or metaphors you can think of.)

3   Select and group your ideas into paragraphs.

4   Expand your notes into a paragraphed draft.

5   Discuss your draft with a partner.
(Does it capture your partner's interest?)
(Can your partner see/hear/understand what is going on?)
(What impression were you trying to get across?)
(Where do you need to give more information?)
(What do you need to cut to focus the reader clearly on what you wanted to say?)

Here are some ideas you might use as starting points.

Earliest Memories

Always a good place to begin! Look back at the two extracts on pages 34 and 37, and refresh your memory about what they say, and the techniques the writers use. Bearing these in mind, make notes on your own earliest memories using the procedure suggested on the previous page. When you get to the fourth stage of working on the draft, think about:

- **The keynote of your writing** – what's the main idea, or the feeling that you want to communicate?

- **The viewpoint** – Alison Fell describes her experiences from the outside; Laurie Lee uses a first-person viewpoint. Which would be most effective for your own writing? Could your parents give you information that would be useful?

- **Your use of detail** – how might you build up a picture of people, places, events and reactions through detailed description? Look again at the way Alison Fell and Laurie Lee use adjectives to build up impressions of colour, sound and texture, or to give you other important details. Look, too, at the verbs they choose. Use a thesaurus to make sure you have chosen an effective range of verbs. Have you chosen exactly the right ones?

- **Sentence structure** – could you use sentence patterns such as lists, repetition, short or incomplete sentences? What effect would you be aiming for? Could you vary the order of phrases within sentences or clauses?

  For example, Laurie Lee wrote: '… and there with a sense of bewilderment and terror my life in the village began'. How would the effect have been different if he'd changed the order of phrases within this clause to read: '… and my life in the village began there with a sense of bewilderment and terror'?

  See if you can find any sentences, or

clauses, where you can alter the order of phrases. Does it produce a different effect, providing variety or giving a slightly different emphasis or meaning?

- **Dialect** – have you used any dialect or slang? What effect did you intend to give? Would it improve the effect if it was all standard English, or if you increased the amount of dialect or slang?

- **Metaphorical language** – did you use any metaphors or similes? Look again at the metaphorical language used by Laurie Lee. Are there any places where you could use metaphors to make the reader see the subject in a fresh way?

Finally, having discussed your draft with your partner, consider how your partner reacted – was his or her attention grabbed by the beginning? Did he or she feel that the ending was satisfying and fitted the rest of the story? Were there any things your partner couldn't follow or wanted more information about? Could your partner see and hear what you were describing?

Experiences of school

Again, there are many possibilities here. You could:

- Write a three-paragraph piece, like the extract by Alice Thomas Ellis on page 40. Focus on the details of the place, on the people (friends, enemies, teachers, parents) and on any striking incidents you can remember. Each paragraph should be on a particular topic, but should lead into the following paragraph in the same way as the paragraphs written by Alice Thomas Ellis. When you are writing, think about how the sentences link up with each other too. Try to make each paragraph about 150 to 200 words.

- Write a portrait of a former teacher, like in George Melly's writing on page 41, using short paragraphs, with snatches of speech, some included within brackets. Make sure that you punctuate accurately when writing speech –

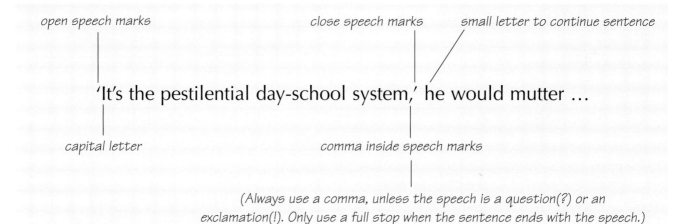

open speech marks   close speech marks   small letter to continue sentence

'It's the pestilential day-school system,' he would mutter ...

capital letter   comma inside speech marks

(Always use a comma, unless the speech is a question(?) or an exclamation(!). Only use a full stop when the sentence ends with the speech.)

Note also how the tense of many of the verbs ('would mutter', 'would shout', 'would introduce' etc) suggest something continuous, an action which is habitual, which the character does repeatedly. Try this effect at appropriate points in your portrait. You could use a similar structure to George Melly's, beginning paragraphs with:

My . . . was a . . ., who . . . S/her was constantly . . .

During the . . .

In me s/he sensed . . .

Very often . . .

If, as usually happened . . .

I would . . .

Make sure that the portrait is anonymous, and would amuse but not offend, unlike George Melly's!

To help with either of these pieces, look back at the notes on the previous page which draw your attention to the techniques writers use. Which techniques would be effective here? Use as many as possible.

Winter Memories

- Write a one-paragraph description (of about 200 to 250 words) of a particular place at a particular time of year (not necessarily winter). As William Wordsworth and Alfred Williams

do, (pages 42 and 43), build up details to give a wider view, at the start, of the place and what people do there. Then focus on yourself, your own experiences and your thoughts. This paragraph might form part of a longer piece of writing. Again, look back at the previous page to remind yourself of techniques to use.

Grandparents

- Look again at the extracts by Gail Lewis and Bill Bryson (pages 44 and 45), and write two or three paragraphs about your grandparents (or other relatives). Build up details about the place, the people, your feelings, and your memories. Remind yourself of the techniques on the previous page.

Listen to them talk!

Writing a poem like the ones on pages 46 and 47 would not make a course work piece on its own, but would be useful to help you practise dialogue or monologue.

- If you want to try a 16-line dialogue poem, remember to give the reader a clue with the title, then write alternate lines for the speakers. Look at how the beginnings of the lines are punctuated. Try to get a 'twist' or an appropriate line to finish the poem. If you choose to imitate the monologue, try to reveal the character of the speaker by the things they say. Run-on lines are essential to give the impression of a speaking voice.

STRUCTURING A STORY

Finally, let's return to George Melly's autobiography. As you read
this extract, think about the way the writer:

- introduces key ideas at the beginning,

- illustrates and develops those ideas,

- brings together the key ideas at the end.

On bass [there was] a newcomer called Alan
Duddington. We always seemed to be having new bass
players. Unlike other musicians connected with the
band, they had a high turnover.

Alan came from Lancaster. He was younger than
the rest of us, still in his early twenties, a neat precise
person ... with a very slight Lancashire accent. His
features were a little on the weak side, but redeemed
from mediocrity by a large and noble nose similar in
character to that of the first Duke of Wellington.

He was proud to be a musician, but not proud to be
in the Mulligan Band. Everything about it distressed
him – the music, our attitudes, the way we dressed –
and it was very surprising how long he stayed,
especially as he was teased unmercifully and without a
moment's respite.

Why did we tease him? There were in fact two
reasons. For one thing he reacted so splendidly,
concealing his mounting exasperation under a tight-
mouthed, straight-backed indifference with only an
occasional low sigh, or at most, a quiet if terse 'Very
amusing' to show we were getting through, but the real
reason was that he knew he was right about everything.
There was no question of doubt. There was no
possibility that any alternatives existed, or that some
things were a matter of personal taste. On every
subject, at every level, Alan Duddington was right. If
anyone disagreed with him, he didn't shout or even try
and argue. He just repeated his own opinion in a quiet
but firm voice until whoever was trying to contradict
him gave up.

Alan was a perfectionist. He had certain standards,
certain things he expected to happen. However far
short reality fell from his expectations, it never
affected his optimism. However often he didn't get
what he wanted, it never occurred to him to lower his
sights.

Opposite the Town Hall, Huddersfield, is a small
public house called 'The County'. It's a friendly little
pub, but as regards food anybody could tell at a glance
what you could expect: crisps, nuts possibly a pie or a
sandwich. One evening we arrived in Huddersfield
rather late and Mick told us we hadn't got time to go
and eat, but perhaps we could grab a sandwich in the
nearest boozer. Duddington looked at him coolly.

'I presume there's no objection if I have a crab salad
instead,' he asked.

'No, cock,' said Mick, 'but where?'

'In the public house,' explained Duddington as
though to an idiot child. We took it for granted that he
didn't know the pub, and that once he saw it, he would
realize there wasn't a chance, but that wasn't Alan. He
marched in, and ordered a small strong ale and a crab
salad. The old girl said they didn't do a crab salad.
Alan looked hurt and surprised.

He was very fussy about his small strong ales too. He
would first look along the bottles of beer until he had
spotted what he wanted – barley wine, Stingo,
whatever the local brewery supplied – and then order
it by name. Very few people drink these small and
potent ales, and quite often the barmaid would spend
a long time searching the shelves for it, and even
come back to Alan to tell him she didn't think they
had any. She would find him standing up as stiff as a
ramrod and pointing at the bottle he'd asked for.

It was his nose and personal fads which provided us
with most of our ammunition, and the van in which
we travelled was our usual theatre of cruelty.

His nose. How we went on about it! If he fell asleep,
somebody – usually Frank Parr, another group member
– would trace out a tiny head with a huge hooter on
the steamed-up window so that it was the first thing
he saw when he woke up. ('Very amusing.') Whatever
came up in conversation was, if it was in any way

possible, altered to include a reference to noses, e.g. 'Cat on a hot tin nose'. ('Very amusing.')

His habit of opening his suitcase at frequent intervals and producing a bar of chocolate which he unwrapped and ate with the formality which characterized all his movements was another moment in the day we never allowed to pass unremarked. There was a limerick we all knew about an old person from Silesia. Its last line was: 'if Jimmy the tapeworm don't seize yer!', and we pretended to believe that Alan's perpetual chocolate eating was because he had a tapeworm.

'Jimmy-time, Alan?' Frank would ask politely every time Alan opened his suitcase.

He tried to defeat us by forestalling this question.

'What time is it, Frank?' he'd ask as he reached for his suitcase.

'Jimmy-time,' said Frank in a matter-of-fact voice.

Even when he had left us, we didn't allow him to escape. We discovered that he was appearing at the Metropolitan Music Hall in the Edgware Road with a country and western group, and hatched a plan.

We all of us went to a joke shop one afternoon and bought enormous false noses. That evening we took a box at the Met as near as possible to the stage. We had previously got in touch with another member of the group whom we knew, and put him up to telling Duddington that he had met a beautiful girl who had

told him that she was mad about Alan, and would be sitting in a box that evening hoping that he would smile at her.

Just before Alan's turn was due, we hid below the level of the front of the box and put on our noses. As the curtains drew we slowly rose to our feet. Alan was staring at the box. Instead of a girl, there was the whole Mulligan band in their false noses.

What was nice about Alan was that he never bore any grudges. Despite our rotten teasing, despite even this final malevolent prank, he has always, on the occasions we have met since, greeted me in an open and warm way.

THINKING ABOUT STRUCTURE

- Develop your reactions and responses through the usual stages, with some adjustments:

  First, note that the extract is made up of paragraphs which are often quite short. Rather than lettering each paragraph and summing up in a short phrase what it says, look for longer sections (about four) to letter and sum up. Think about how each section is linked to the others.

  Second, when looking for chains of words, phrases and ideas that run through the extract, think about how George Melly structures the

  story he tells. Look at the adjectives used in the second paragraph ('neat, precise') to describe the kind of person that Alan Duddington is. How does George Melly develop these adjectives in the incidents he describes in the rest of the story? Look, too, at the way that the detail about Alan's 'large and noble nose' is developed, with references at the beginning, about halfway through, and at the end of the story. How do the chains relating to Alan's nose and his personality come together at the end?

STRUCTURING YOUR OWN WRITING

When you write your own piece for your course work folder, think about structure. Try to:

- Introduce two key ideas right at the beginning.

- Illustrate those ideas with incidents during your story.

- Bring the key ideas back at the end, with the story finishing as the two ideas are brought together.

   You could develop one of the drafts you have been working on, or you could write a completely new piece. In either case, remind yourself of the advice given earlier on drafting (page 48), and on the techniques writers use (pages 35 and 36). Try to use as many of the techniques as you can. Your final draft should be between 600 and 900 words long – don't worry if you go over the upper limit, as long as you have structured the story carefully, but make sure you haven't included details which don't add anything to the ideas you are trying to get across to the reader.

WHAT NEXT?

In this unit, you have studied a range of original writing based on personal experiences. You have looked at how to write about this kind of writing, and how to make comparisons between texts. You have also used what you have learnt in your own original writing. To practise the skills you have developed, you might try the following written assignment:

- Find and read the beginnings of some other autobiographies. Compare how the writers establish a scene and a point of view. Which do you prefer or consider most successful and why?

You might like to look for the following titles in a library. They are all based on the writer's personal experiences, or are rooted in the writer's life or community.

Some authors and titles:

Bill Bryson *The Lost Continent*
Roddy Doyle *Paddy Clarke Ha Ha Ha*
Alice Thomas Ellis *A Welsh Childhood*
Esther Hautzig *The Endless Steppe*
Liz Heron (ed) *Truth, Dare or Promise: Girls Growing Up In the Fifties*
Nick Hornby *Fever Pitch*
Clive James *Unreliable Memoirs*
Laurie Lee *Cider with Rosie*
George Melly *Owning Up*
Jean McCrindle and Sheila Rowbotham (eds) *Dutiful Daughters – Women Talk About Their Lives*
Blake Morrison *And When Did You Last See Your Father?*
Robert Roberts *A Ragged Schooling*
Flora Thompson *Lark Rise to Candleford*
Paul Theroux *The Kingdom by the Sea, The Great Railway Bazaar, Riding the Iron Rooster*
Keith Waterhouse *There Is A Happy Land*

SENTENCE SPOTTING: A SURVIVOR'S GUIDE

When you comment on what writers have said, you will find it useful to be able to identify sentences, and the phrases and clauses which make up sentences. If you can do this, you will be able to explain more easily your responses to extracts – this will be valuable to you in course work and exams.

Also, if you are confident about sentences, you will understand where full stops and commas go, and why.

Once you spot the basic pattern of sentences in written English, you will see that most are variations on a three-part structure:

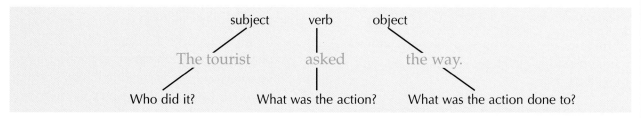

You can build on this basic sentence structure by adding single words or phrases to give more information. A phrase is, simply, a group of words which goes together, and forms part of a sentence:

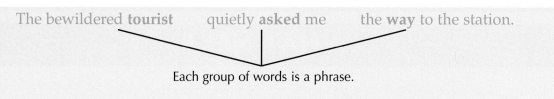

The main idea in each phrase (in bold) is called the headword.

The basic three-part pattern is called a **simple sentence.**

Write out this simple sentence and label the three-part structure:

> He got off the bus.

Simple sentences can be joined together using **conjunctions** to make a **complex sentence:**

After he got off the bus, the bewildered tourist quietly asked me the way to the station.
conjunction

Each part of the complex sentence is called a **clause** – in this sentence there are two – and they are separated by a comma. The **main clause** of the complex sentence could still stand as a sentence on its own, but the other clause could not stand alone because it is joined to the main clause by the conjunction. It is called a **dependent clause** – it *depends* on the main clause for its meaning.

Look at the following sentences. Pick out the conjunctions (the joining words):

Before the clock chimes, Uncle Tom goes to bed.

I will go in the car, then you can ride the motorbike.

When I write a letter, I use blue ink.

Sometimes the comma is unnecessary:

I use blue ink when I write a letter.

Now decide which are the main clauses and which are the dependent clauses in the same sentences.

Writers can also vary the arrangement, embedding the dependent clause into the main clause, rather than adding it at the end or at the beginning:

The bewildered tourist, after he got off the bus, quietly asked me the way to the station.

Most sentences have these basic patterns or variations of them. This summary is not the whole story, but it will help you to identify how sentences are put together. Look at your own writing, or any writing, for examples of phrases, clauses, the three-part pattern of simple sentences, and the dependent clause/main clause pattern of complex sentences. If you can identify the main clause in a complex sentence, you should be able to see how the sentence fits together.

UNIT THREE

Talking Heads

When speakers communicate with their audiences – whether they are presenting radio or television programmes, or whether they are in politics, industry, or education – what you see is only the final stage in a process of thinking and organisation. In this unit, you will look at the way speakers use different techniques to present their ideas in a range of contexts.

As you work through the unit you will develop your skills as:

SPEAKERS AND LISTENERS

by explaining your ideas clearly, in a well-structured way
by putting across your viewpoint convincingly
by adapting your style of presentation to interest your audience
by making contributions to discussions, and engaging with what others say

READERS

by discussing and analysing the style, organisation and language of speeches
by reading a speech aloud

WRITERS

by taking notes from speeches you listen to
by making notes and using them to present your views and arguments
by writing your own speeches, drawing on the techniques you have learnt in
    the course of the unit

Throughout our society, people will try to persuade you that their views are correct. This unit helps you understand how they do that, and shows you how to do it yourself. Begin by looking at the following speech which you may have come across before.

DOWN WITH THE OPPRESSORS!

Animal Farm, by George Orwell, is one of the most widely-known and widely-translated books in the world. In this book, Orwell attacks all those in positions of power (no matter what political approach they say they believe in) who run society to suit themselves, and who oppress ordinary people to do so. At the beginning of the novel, the animals on the farm have been badly treated and exploited by human beings for as long as can be remembered. In the extract you are going to look at, Old Major, a wise and elderly pig, is speaking to a gathering of all the animals on the farm. He is explaining to them how they are oppressed, and gives them a vision of a world in which they work for themselves, not for humans.

MAKING A START: GETTING THE AUDIENCE'S ATTENTION

Look at how Old Major begins his speech:

(a) He addresses them in a friendly way. What does the word 'comrades' tell you about how he sees the relationship between himself and his audience?

(b) The 'strange dream': he's drawing on something they have all heard about. He attracts their interest by promising to tell them about the dream – but later.

(c) He emphasises the importance of what he is going to say. The word 'duty', and the fact that he's got to pass his message on before he dies, tell them how important his speech will be to them.

(d) He also sets out his credentials for speaking on this subject. He speaks with authority, because of the length of time he has lived, and because of the amount of time he has spent thinking about things.

(e) He lets the audience know what he's going to talk about in the rest of his speech.

'Comrades, you have heard already about the strange dream that I had last night. But I will come to the dream later. I have something else to say first. I do not think, comrades, that I shall be with you for many months longer, and before I die I feel it my duty to pass on to you such wisdom as I have acquired. I have had a long life, I have had much time for thought as I lay alone in my stall, and I think I may say that I understand the nature of life on this earth as well any animal now living. It is about this that I wish to speak to you.

• Before you read the next section of Old Major's speech, work with a partner and consider what you now know about the audience he is speaking to, and his purpose in speaking to them. Decide what detailed examples he is going to give to illustrate what he means. Are there any questions in your mind at this stage about what he will say? (Predicting and asking questions like this will help you to read actively, with greater involvement.)

Now read the next section of Old Major's speech. As you read, see if he talks about what you predicted and whether your questions are answered.

'Now, comrades, what is the nature of this life of ours? Let us face it: our lives are miserable, laborious, and short. We are born, we are given just so much food as will keep the breath in our bodies, and those of us who are capable of it are forced to work to the last atom of our strength; and the very instant that our usefulness has come to an end we are slaughtered with hideous cruelty. No animal in England knows the meaning of happiness or leisure after he is a year old. No animal in England is free. The life of an animal is misery and slavery: that is the plain truth.

'But is this simply part of the order of nature? Is it because this land of ours is so poor that it cannot afford a decent life to those who dwell upon it? No, comrades, a thousand times no! The soil of England is fertile, its climate is good, it is capable of affording food in abundance to an enormously greater number of animals than now inhabit it. This single farm of ours would support a dozen horses, twenty cows, hundreds of sheep – and all of them living in a comfort and a dignity that are now almost beyond our imagining. Why then do we continue in this miserable condition? Because nearly the whole of the produce of our labour is stolen from us by human beings. There, comrades, is the answer to all our problems. It is summed up in a single word – Man. Man is the only real enemy we have. Remove Man from the scene, and the root cause of hunger and overwork is abolished for ever.

'Man is the only creature that consumes without producing. He does not give milk, he does not lay eggs, he is too weak to pull the plough, he cannot run fast enough to catch rabbits. Yet he is lord of all the animals. He sets them to work, he gives back to them the bare minimum that will prevent them from starving, and the rest he keeps for himself. Our labour tills the soil, our dung fertilizes it, and yet there is not one of us that owns more than his bare skin. You cows that I see before me, how many thousands of gallons of milk have you given during this last year? And what has happened to that milk which should have been breeding up sturdy calves? Every drop of it has gone down the throats of our enemies. And you hens, how many eggs have you laid this year, and how many of those eggs ever hatched into chickens? The rest have all gone to market to bring in money for Jones and his men. And you, Clover, where are those four foals you bore, who should have been the support and pleasure of your old age? Each was sold at a year old – you will never see one of them again. In return for your four confinements and all your labour in the field, what have you ever had except your bare rations and a stall?

'And even the miserable lives we lead are not allowed to reach their natural span. For myself I do not grumble, for I am one of the lucky ones. I am twelve years old and have had over four hundred children. Such is the natural life of a pig. But no animal escapes the cruel knife in the end. You young porkers who are sitting in front of me, every one of you will scream your lives out at the block within a year. To that horror, we all must come – cows, pigs, hens, sheep, everyone. Even the horses and the dogs have no better fate. You, Boxer, the very day that those great muscles of yours lose their power, Jones will sell you to the knacker, who will cut your throat and boil you down for the fox-hounds. As for the dogs, when they grow old and toothless, Jones ties a brick round their necks and drowns them in the nearest pond.

'Is it not crystal clear, then, comrades, that all the evils of this life of ours spring from the tyranny of human beings? Only get rid of Man, and the produce of our labour would be our own. Almost overnight we could become rich and free. What then must we do? Why, work night and day, body and soul, for the overthrow of the human race! That is my message to you, comrades: Rebellion! I do not know when that Rebellion will come, it might be in a week or in a hundred years, but I know, as surely as I see this straw beneath my feet, that sooner or later justice will be done. Fix your eyes on that, comrades, throughout the short remainder of your lives! And above all, pass on this message of mine to those who come after you, so that future generations shall carry on the struggle until it is victorious.

'And remember, comrades, your resolution must never falter. No argument must lead you astray. Never listen when they tell you that Man and the animals have a common interest, that the prosperity of the one is the prosperity of the others. It is all lies. Man serves the interests of no creature except himself. And among us animals let there be perfect unity, perfect comradeship in the struggle. All men are enemies. All animals are comrades.'

When you have finished this section of Old Major's speech, discuss whether any of your predictions were correct, or if any of your questions were answered. If they weren't, can you explain why? What did Old Major's speech mention which you didn't expect? What effect did that have?

- After you have discussed your predictions, questions, and what you have learnt, spend five or ten minutes writing to get further inside this section of Old Major's speech. Write as if you were a member of Old Major's audience, and describe your initial reactions. What effect did it have? What did it make you feel, visualise, hear and think of? (Take your pick of what animal you are.)

HOW THE SPEECH IS ORGANISED

Now look methodically at the speech, to see how it is organised and how it has its effect.

- Look first at the chains of words, phrases and ideas that run through the speech. These will give you a way into seeing how the speech is organised, and what it deals with. Start with an idea like 'the nature of life' for animals, which comes in the first paragraph. Write down the phrase, and list other words or phrases that are linked with it, in the rest of the speech. Then explain what that chain of ideas shows. For example:

the nature of life – our lives are miserable, laborious and short – the life of an animal is misery and slavery – this miserable condition – the miserable lives we lead are not allowed to reach their allotted span – all the evils of this life of ours – the short remainder of your lives.

Shows what the lives of animals are like under the existing set-up. Emphasises the misery and unhappiness of their situation. Shows they are killed by men; they don't die naturally.

Try finding a couple of other chains. There is one which starts with the idea of 'human beings'/'Man'. Track through the links in this chain, and explain what it shows. Are there any other chains that you can see?

- You also need to think about the way the ideas are grouped. Give each paragraph a number (with the introduction being number one). Write a brief summary of what the topic of each paragraph is, and how it links or contrasts with the previous paragraph.

Paragraph	Summary of topic
1	Introduction – gives his credentials – tells audience he's going to talk about nature of life.
2	Describes the 'plain truth' of what animals' lives are like. Link: explains the 'nature' of life mentioned in paragraph 1. (Link words – 'Now, Comrades')

HOW THE SPEECH HAS ITS EFFECT

Think again about how you would have reacted if you had been a member of Old Major's audience. *How* did he get those reactions from you? There are many techniques used by speech makers, and Old Major is obviously a master of them. Look at the techniques he uses:

Work either on your own or with a partner: build up a set of notes as you work through the following:

- Asking **rhetorical questions** (questions to which he does not expect an answer). There are two types – one type where Old Major asks a question so that he can give the audience the answer, and a second type where he asks a question which has a built-in, 'common-sense' answer. Can you find examples of both types? How would his audience react to the examples you have found? Sometimes, he also uses a question as the topic sentence of the paragraph. How many of these can you find? What would be his reason to do this?

- Using a particular **range of pronouns**. Old Major sticks mainly to the pronouns 'I', 'you', 'we', 'they'. Find examples of each of these pronouns and explain what effect each one would have on the audience. (Note that Old Major uses 'he' to refer to Farmer Jones, and to mankind in general. Try to explain the effect this has.)

- Using **lists of words**, such as adjectives ('our lives are miserable, laborious and short') or nouns ('To that horror we all must come - cows, pigs, hens, sheep, everyone'). Can you explain, in each of these cases, what effect these lists would have on the audience? Can you find any other examples, and explain the effects they have?

- Similar to the use of lists is **repetition**. Old Major repeats single words or phrases ('Man', 'you cows,' 'you hens,' 'you, Clover,' 'you, Boxer.') He repeats grammatical structures, too, such as 'We are born, we are given just so much food as will keep the breath in our bodies, and those of us who are capable of it are forced to work to the last atom of our strength.' Try to explain the effect of these examples, then find your own examples of repetition, and explain what effect they have.

- Old Major also makes use of **emotive language**, when he tries to provoke a strong emotion in his audience, such as anger, fear, disgust, or hatred. For example, he tells the assembled animals that 'every one of you will scream your lives out at the block within a year'. What emotions does he produce with this detail? What are the words that provoke those emotions, and why would the audience react to them in that way? Find and explain other examples of emotive language from the speech.

- **Building to a climax.** Look back at the notes you made on how the speech is organised. Discuss the way Old Major builds his argument towards the climax of the final paragraph. How does this last paragraph sum up what he has been saying?

'THE GREATEST BRITISH ORATOR OF HIS GENERATION'

Old Major was a great (if fictional) master of political rhetoric – the art of making persuasive speeches. The next speech was made by a real politician who, according to *The Penguin Book of Twentieth Century Speeches*, was known by supporters and opponents as 'the greatest British orator of his generation'. Unlike many politicians, Neil Kinnock (leader of the Labour Party 1983 – 1992) wrote his own speeches, and this one was made to an audience in Llandudno, North Wales. Extracts from it appeared on television at the time, and have been used occasionally since then. Look at the title, and try to predict two or three things the speech will deal with. Read the speech, and spend five or ten minutes jotting down your reactions as if you were a member of the audience. What did it make you feel, see, or think about?

Why am I the first Kinnock in a thousand generations to be able to get to university?'

We are democratic socialists. We care all the time. We don't think it's a soft sentiment, we don't think it's 'wet'.

We think that care is the essence of strength.

And we believe that because we know that strength without care is savage and brutal and selfish.

Strength with care is compassion – the practical action that is needed to help people lift themselves to their full stature.

That's real care – It is not soft or weak. It is tough and strong.

But where do we get that strength to provide that care?

Do we wait for some stroke of good fortune, some benign giant, some socially conscious Samson to come along and pick up the wretched of the earth?

Of course we don't.

We cooperate, we collect together, we coordinate so that everyone can contribute and everyone can benefit, everyone has responsibilities, everyone has rights. That is how we put care into action. That is how we make the weak strong, that is how we lift the needy, that is how we make the sick whole, that is how we give talent the chance to flourish, that is how we turn the unemployed claimant into the working contributor.

We do it together. It is called collective strength, collective care. And its whole purpose is individual freedom.

When we speak of collective strength and collective freedom, collectively achieved, we are not fulfilling that nightmare that Mrs Thatcher tries to paint, and all her predecessors have tried to saddle us with.

We're not talking about uniformity; we're not talking about regimentation; we're not talking about *conformity* – that's their creed. The uniformity of the dole queue; the regimentation of the unemployed young and their compulsory work schemes. The *conformity* of people who will work in conditions, and take orders, and accept pay *because of* mass unemployment that they would laugh at in a free society with full employment.

UK Prime Minister 1979–1992

That kind of freedom for the individual, that kind of liberty can't be secured by most of the people for most of the time if they're just left to themselves, isolated, stranded, with their whole life chances dependent upon luck!

Why am I the first Kinnock in a thousand generations to be able to get to university? Why is <u>Glenys</u> the first woman in her family in a thousand generations to be able to get to university?

his wife

Was it because *all* our predecessors were 'thick'? Did they lack talent – those people who could sing, and play, and recite and write poetry; those people who could make wonderful, beautiful things with their hands; those people who could dream dreams, see visions; those people who had such a sense of perception as to know in times so brutal, so oppressive, that they could win their way out of that by coming together?

Were those people not university material? Couldn't they have knocked off all their A-levels in an afternoon?

But why didn't they get it?

Was it because they were weak? – those people who could work eight hours underground and then come up and play football?

Weak? Those women who could survive eleven childbearings, were they weak? Those people who could stand with their backs and their legs straight and face the people who had control over their lives, the ones who owned their workplaces and tried to own them, and tell them, 'No, I won't take your orders.' Were they weak?

Does anybody really think that they didn't get what we had because they didn't have the talent, or the strength, or the endurance, or the commitment?

Of course not. It was because there was no platform upon which they could stand; no arrangement for their neighbours to subscribe to their welfare; no method by which the communities could translate their desires for those individuals into provision for those individuals.

And now, Mrs Thatcher, by dint of privatization, and means test, and deprivation, and division, wants to nudge us back into the situation where everybody can either stand on their own feet, or live on their knees.

That's what this election is about as she parades her visions and values, and we choose to contest them as people with roots in this country, with a future only in this country, with pride in this country. People who know that if we are to have and sustain real individual liberty in this country it requires the collective effort of the whole community.

Of course you hear the Tories talking about freedom. We'll be hearing a great deal of that over the next month from the same people who have spent the last eight years crushing individual freedoms under the weight of unemployment and poverty, squeezing individual rights with cuts and means tests and charges.

I think of the youngsters I meet. Three, four, five years out of school. Never had a job. And they say to me, 'Do you think we'll ever work?'

They live in a free country, but they do not feel free.

I think of the fifty-five-year-old woman I meet who is waiting to go into hospital, her whole existence clouded by pain.

She lives in a free country, but she does not feel free.

I think of the young couple, two years married, living in Mam and Dad's front room because they can't get a home. They ask, 'Will we *ever* get a home of own?'

They live in a free country, but they do not feel free.

And I think of the old couple who spend months of the winter afraid to turn up the heating, who stay at home because they are afraid to go out after dark, whose lives are turned into a crisis by the need to buy a new pair of shoes.

They live in a free country – indeed, they're of the generation that *fought* for a free country – but they do not feel free.

How can they – and millions like them – have their individual freedom if there is no collective provision?

How can they have strength if they do not have care?

Now they cannot have either because they are locked out of being able to discharge responsibilities just as surely as they are locked out of being able to exercise rights.

They want to be able to use both.

They do not want feather-bedding, they want a foothold.

They do not want cotton-woolling, they want a chance to contribute.

That is the freedom they want.

That is the freedom we want them to have.

When you have read this speech and have written about your first reactions, move on to the following activities.

PUTTING ON A PERFORMANCE

Neil Kinnock's speech was written for a live audience, to be read aloud. It was also written knowing that sections would be televised, usually as 'soundbites' of no more than 30 seconds, which would stay in the minds of a nationwide audience. Which sections do you think a TV news editor would select to broadcast? Why? Make your own selection of five short 'soundbites'. Explain why you chose them.

Working in groups of about four to six, prepare a reading aloud of this speech to the rest of the class. Doing this will help you understand the sound and power of a speech, and how speakers communicate with their audience. Follow these stages:

- Divide the speech between the members of the group, and decide who will read which section.

- In smaller groups of two or three, discuss the situation, the audience, and the purpose of the speech. Where would Neil Kinnock be when he gave the speech? What audience is he speaking to? How do you know? What's his purpose in giving the speech? Again, how do you know?

- Look at the speech as a whole and decide what sections it falls into. Pick out some of the chains of ideas and words that run through the speech. Make sure you bring out the overall organisation in the way you read your section. Note the paragraphing, as well. Some of the paragraphs are very short. How will that help you to read the speech aloud? What does Neil Kinnock do at the start to capture the attention of his audience, and to signal what his speech will deal with? How does he establish his authority to speak on this subject?

- Now, still with your small group, look together at the sections each of you will read. Pick out the rhetorical techniques Neil Kinnock uses. Look first for the kinds of techniques you found in Old Major's speech (rhetorical questions, pronouns, lists, repetition, emotive language, building to a climax). Neil Kinnock uses other techniques, as well:

alliteration – repeating consonants at the start of words ('**c**ollective strength, **c**ollective **c**are').

sentence structure – writing short sentences ('I think of the youngsters I meet'); writing phrases ('Three, four, five years out of school.') or clauses ('And they say to me, 'Do you think we'll ever work?'') which stand alone, rather than being parts of full sentences.

rhythm – using alliteration and/or repetition to build up a regular pattern of stresses, which hold longer sentences together ('Did they lack talent – those people who could sing, and play, and recite, and write poetry').

anecdote – telling stories to illustrate a point. ('And I think of the old couple…')

argument – referring to his opponents' claims, so that he can contrast them with his own views. He criticises his opponents and praises his own side. ('Of course you hear the Tories talking about freedom. We'll be hearing a great deal about that from the same people who have spent the last eight years crushing individual freedoms under the weight of unemployment and poverty…' [contrasting with what he believes] 'How can they – and millions like them – have their individual freedom if there is no collective provision?')

- When you have picked out examples of these techniques, discuss with your group the effect the examples would have on the audience.

- Now prepare a reading aloud of your own section of the speech. Your partner, or partners, will coach you and give you advice on how your performance looks and sounds. If possible, watch videos or listen to audio tapes of great speakers like Nelson Mandela, Martin Luther King, or Winston Churchill. Note the way their voices rise and fall, speed up and slow down, stress words, build up rhythms and climaxes, and use pauses (often to leave space for applause). A video tape will show you how they use eye contact, gestures and body language, and build up a rapport with the audience. Think about these aspects of speech-making when you are practising your own reading. Use as many as possible to build up an effective rapport with your own audience.

- When you have practised in your small groups, rejoin your larger group and run through the speech until you are confident that you are using your voice, eye-contact, gesture, and body language effectively. Comment on each other's performances, and practise until you are happy with them.

- Finally, work with at least one other group, and perform the whole speech for each other. Give feedback on what went well and what could have been performed better. Copy the checklist below and use it to help you.

Speaker's	Notes
name	
rise / fall of voice	
variations in speed	
use of stress	
use of rhythm	
building climaxes	
use of pauses	
eye contact	
gesture	
body language	
rapport with audience	

WRITING YOUR OWN SPEECH

Use what you have learnt so far in this unit to write your own speech. The techniques you practice here will be useful to you not only later in this unit, but whenever you have to put across your ideas in a persuasive and organised way to a particular audience.

Think of a subject for your speech. (For example, you might be trying to persuade the bank manager to give you a loan to buy a vehicle; you might be persuading other residents in your neighbourhood to demonstrate against the widening of a main road; you might speak on behalf of a campaign against drug abuse.)

Now use the following steps to help you with putting together a speech.

- Think about the audience you are preparing your speech for. Who are they? What do they know about the subject you will be speaking about? What information do you want to give them? What specific reactions do you want from them?

- Gather information on your subject. You need this to provide evidence for what you say. Look again at the speech by Neil Kinnock. Pick one section, and look at how he gives evidence for his opinions, and makes it convincing for his audience. A lot of his evidence is based on his own experiences or on stories he has been told. How far do these anecdotes stand for facts or principles which are valid for a wide number of people?

- When you have gathered your evidence, group your ideas into paragraphs. What topic sentence will you have to introduce each paragraph? How will you link your paragraphs? What words and ideas will you chain through the speech?

- Think about planning the introduction. How will you attract your audience's attention, set out your interest and credentials, and let them know what is to come in the rest of the speech?

- Now think about planning the final paragraph. It has to be the point towards which you've been arguing for the whole of the speech. Look back at how Old Major and Neil Kinnock end their speeches. How do they bring the speeches to a conclusion? What effect would they have on the audience? What effect do you want from your conclusion?

- Before you write a draft of your speech, work with a partner and list the speech-making techniques you have learnt about in this chapter. Make an effort to get as many as you can into your speech.

- Write a draft, try it out on your partner, to see if they react as you wanted them to. Did they spot the techniques you were using?

- Write your final draft, in the light of the comments made by your partner.

FOR OR AGAINST?

A speech can be given 'live' to an audience who are actually present, or it can be recorded, to be delivered on different occasions to various groups of people. What follows are the transcripts of promotional videos. Each is the equivalent of a 'speech' being delivered.

Organise yourselves into 'home' groups of four. Half of the class should look at the Transcript 1, below, and complete the tasks on the next page. The other half should examine Transcript 2 on page 69 and complete the tasks on page 70.

TRANSCRIPT 1

THROUGH THE FARM GATE

And God said unto Noah:
'Every moving thing that liveth upon the face of the earth shall be meat for you; even as the green herb have I given you all things'.

Genesis 9 : 3

The landscape of Britain, the inspiration of poets and painters for thousands of years: undisturbed nature at its most perfect. If you think that, you're wrong. This landscape is entirely man-made – made, in fact, by hundreds of generations of farmers. Without them, the view we're looking at would be an uninterrupted sweep of dense forest, just as it was five thousand years ago, before the first primitive farmers came here.

Modern farmers have been on the receiving end of a lot of criticism in recent years, not just for the way they manage the landscape, as they always have, but because of the animal husbandry methods they use to provide the rest of us with the food we eat every day. This video aims to put the other side of the case, to tell you how farmers provide a densely populated island with a plentiful supply of tasty, nutritious food, safe to eat and at affordable prices. Come with us ... through the farm gate.

Farmers invest huge amounts of money in advanced technology and use sophisticated modern science to produce more and better food, at less cost to the shopper's pocket. The real price of food has come down. Twenty years ago it would have taken the average British worker twenty-four minutes to earn enough to buy these pork chops; today it takes only fifteen. The aim of all this investment, all this science and technology, is to help the farmer work in and with the natural environment, within the limits that nature imposes. Climate, for example, puts limits on what farmers can do. You can only raise pigs outdoors in parts of Britain where you don't expect extremes of heat and cold. You need well drained land, too. Altitude is another limiting factor. Hill farms are suitable for sheep and some types of cattle, but not for other farm animals, or most crops. Soil type and topography are a third constraint. You can't grow nutrient-hungry crops on poor soil; and on steep hillsides the only possible crops are grass and timber. Three quarters of the UK's farm land is permanently under grass, so the first rule farmers have to follow is that they must work within nature's constraints.

LOOKING CLOSELY

Each member of the 'home' group is going to investigate a different aspect of Transcript 1 and, working with members of other groups who are exploring the same area, you can pool your ideas and become 'experts' who can report back to your 'home' group.

HOME GROUP   EXPERT 4 GROUP

EXPERT ONE: What is the 'argument' of the speech? You will need to look closely at each sentence and note down, in order, the points that are made. Sometimes a point will be 'explicit' – directly stated. Sometimes it will be 'implicit' – suggested indirectly. Point 1 might be: *'Through the Farm Gate' – farmers have nothing to hide, they are inviting you to come in and see for yourself.*
Does the order of the points seem important? Would a different order have a different effect? Is this the best order?

EXPERT TWO: What is the speech arguing against? In a trial, you would listen to both sides of the case. Here, only one side is given. You can read 'between the lines' to see what points they are arguing against. Look closely at each sentence and note down the points in the opposing case, in order. Point 1 might be: *'Through the Farm Gate' no-one really knows what farmers are up to: farms are private places, with gates to keep the public out.*
Could you construct a convincing speech against this one by linking together these points 'between the lines'?

EXPERT THREE: What features of language can you find? You may want to look back to the techniques you have already identified earlier on. You might want to consider:

How is the listener addressed? Who are 'us' and 'you'?
What length sentence and phrase is used? Does it vary?
What effect does this have?
How are 'witnesses' used to give evidence? Look at quotations and statistics.
What technical terms are there? Why are they used?
Is there any emotive language used for impact? How effective is it?

EXPERT FOUR: The video itself. When you use a video to promote a point of view, you can use much more than the words.
Create a storyboard of five frames that you would use if you were the director of this video. Remember to include comments on music, other sound effects, and tone of voice as well as details of the shot. Make the first frame a title shot. Indicate which line in the commentary would be the cue for each of your shots.

When you have discussed ideas in your 'expert' group, return to your 'home' group and report your findings.

TRANSCRIPT 2

In your 'home' group of four, read the following speech carefully. It is part of the transcript of a video made by the Farm Animal Welfare Network.

HIDDEN SUFFERING

We often call hens, chickens, turkeys and ducks 'domestic fowl'. That's because for thousands of years human beings have kept these birds for eggs and meat, usually in quite small flocks.

But, over the past few decades, poultry keeping has undergone a drastic change. Worldwide, vast numbers of 'domestic fowl' are now raised intensively in what are often called 'factory farms', where the word 'domestic' hardly applies. In a factory farm, the old idea of stockmanship, where animals had a relationship with their keeper, no longer exists. Instead, the aim is to increase profits by processing the maximum number of birds in the minimum space and time, and with the smallest possible workforce. For the birds, this means cruelty, stress, deprivation, pain and eventually the terror of slaughter.

Battery hens are not seen as living creatures, but as egg laying machines. In this extreme confinement a battery hen can never walk, run or fly. There is no privacy for egg laying, no comfort, no relief from stress, just the never ending misery of standing or crouching day and night on the same tiny area of sloping wire. Many hens' feet become deformed, as a result of cruelly unsuitable cage floors. Almost every natural behaviour pattern is frustrated. Bored and desperate, hens are reduced to pecking the feathers or flesh of cage mates. In an attempt to minimise the damage from pecking, some farmers have their hens' beaks mutilated with a red hot blade to discourage this stress-related cannibalism. Yet, even after a year or more in the living hell of a battery unit, the hens' instincts remain intact. Birds released from cages build nests from wisps of straw in their first hour of freedom, or take their first dust bath, or enjoy the warmth of the sun. The cage system does nothing to breed out age-old behavioural needs. What it does is to produce a bird with bones so brittle that they break under stress, during catching, transport and slaughter.

Poultry, like people, need exercise and fresh air to keep fit and stay healthy. If cats or dogs were kept in these conditions, what would the reaction be? In many parts of the world their owners would be prosecuted.

There are alternatives to factory egg production. The free range system, when properly managed, allows hens to lead a busy and contented existence. But eggs are just one aspect of the way in which chickens are exploited for profit.

LOOKING CLOSELY

The second half of the class are looking at Transcript 2, which presents the opposite point of view. Each member of your 'home group' should investigate a different aspect of the speech and, working with members from other groups who are exploring the same area, pool your ideas and become 'experts' who can report back to your 'home' group.

Expert 1	Expert 2
Expert 3	Expert 4

HOME GROUP

Join other experts researching same topic

Report back to Home Group

Expert 4	Expert 4
Expert 4	Expert 4

EXPERT 4 GROUP

EXPERT ONE : What is the argument of the speech? You will need to look closely at each sentence. Note down, in order, the points that are made. Sometimes a point will be 'explicit' – directly stated. Sometimes it will be 'implicit' – indirectly suggested. Point 1 might be: *'Hidden Suffering' – What happens on farms is hidden away from us because animals experience so much pain.*
Does the order in which the points are made matter? What would be the effect of another order? Is this the best order?

EXPERT TWO : What is the speech arguing against? In an argument there are two sides to be heard. Here, you are only given one point of view. By reading 'between the lines', you can work out the points against which the speech is being made. Look carefully at each sentence and see if you can identify the hidden counter-argument. All of these points are 'implicit' – indirectly suggested. Point 1 might be: *'We often call hens, chickens, turkeys and ducks "domestic fowl".' – Farmers should care for their animals. 'Domestic' means to do with the home. These birds are really part of the family.* From these points hidden 'between the lines' can you work out what the opposing speech might have been like? Do you have to rearrange the points?

EXPERT THREE: What features of language can you find? You might want to look back to the techniques you identified earlier in this unit. You might consider:

Who is meant by 'we' in this speech?
What effect does this have?
Is there any use of alliteration? Does it help make the point?
What length are sentences and phrases? Does this vary?
Why?
What technical terms are used? For what purpose?
Is there any use of emotive language for emotional impact and what effect does this have on the listener?

EXPERT FOUR: The video itself. When you record a video to promote a point of view, you can use much more than the words alone. Create a storyboard of five frames that you would use if you were the director of this video. Remember to include comments on music, other sound effects, and tone of voice, as well as details of the shot. Make the first frame a title shot. Indicate which line of the transcript is the cue for each shot.

When you have discussed ideas in your 'expert' group, return to your 'home' group and report your findings.

COMPARING NOTES

You are going to look at the different ways in which the two speeches tried to persuade you. Your 'home' group should pair up with a group who have been investigating the other speech.

HOME GROUP A

Expert 1	Expert 2
Expert 3	Expert 4

HOME GROUP B

Expert 1	Expert 2
Expert 3	Expert 4

join together to present findings

Expert 1	Expert 2	Expert 3	Expert 4
Expert 1	Expert 2	Expert 3	Expert 4

• Look at one speech at a time. Each group should read their speech aloud. Then, one group at a time, each 'expert' should present his or her findings to the two groups. Use the help box for useful tips on presenting your information.

HELP

You will be talking to a group of seven other people. What do you need to remember if you are going to make it as easy as possible for the people listening?

Use notes to remind you but don't read word for word.

Give examples from the speech to show exactly what you mean.

Make eye contact – include everyone, don't just talk to one person.

Sound enthusiastic – it will help your listeners.

Can you think of any other good advice to help when you are talking to a group? Remember, when you are not giving your presentation, be an attentive audience – it helps the person who is talking.

FEEDING BACK TO EACH OTHER

Later on in this unit you will be making a speech to a larger group, trying to convert them to your point of view. What have you learnt from talking to this much smaller group as you have presented your findings? Thinking about this will help to prepare you for making your final speech as effective as possible.

In your 'home' group, or in your new group of eight, feed back to each member some ideas that might help them as a speaker.

What was the overall impression of their talk?

Which points were particularly well put?

Which points from the advice list were remembered?

Which piece of advice should they try to concentrate on?

Remember to be as positive as you can in your comments. Apart from being well prepared, a feeling of confidence is the best way to ensure a successful speech.

When all eight 'experts' have presented their findings, you will be ready to make a comparison of the techniques that the two videos are using to try to influence your views.

HOW DID THEY DO IT?

You have considered many views now on the ways in which each of these two speeches is trying to influence its audience. Each speech gives a different point of view in the farming 'debate', which has been frequently in the news for different reasons over the past few years. But are they using different techniques to make their point?

Think about what you have found out. It might help to read and hear the two 'speeches' one more time. Consider the following questions, remembering that it helps to give an example from the speeches when you make a point.

- How well have they chosen their titles? What is particularly effective about each one?

- How does each speech try to catch your attention right at the beginning?

- What attitude does each speaker seem to have towards you, the listener?

- What kinds of sentences do they each use – long, short, simple, complex, questions, statements, assertions?

- What different kinds of 'evidence' does each one use? How reliable do you think this evidence is?

- Does each speech have the same view of the past? What are the differences?

- How do they each use technical terms?

- What use does each speaker make of emotive language? Does this make you more or less likely to trust them?

- What do you think is the main purpose of each speech?

- What kind of shot, voice and sound effects would you need for each one?

- Which speech do you find more convincing and why?

This could be a discussion that forms part of your oral assessment or you could write up your own views as a piece of course work.

ARGUING A CASE

How many situations can you think of for the kind of speech which argues a point of view? They might include:

a school council meeting

a business board meeting

a major family discussion

a court case

a parliamentary debate

a demonstration

a rally

a fund-raising meeting

In all of these cases, speakers are trying to influence the listeners in one way or another. Think about the different reasons there might be for making a public speech, such as:

- to make you change your mind

- to confirm or re-affirm what you already think

- to make you reconsider your point of view

- to influence the way you behave

- to draw people together

- to make you understand someone else's position

Make a note of any others you can think of. Remember that speeches can be made for good and bad purposes.

The kind of discussion, where people with strong opinions take it in turns to argue their point, is known as a **debate**, and it can take place in any of the situations you have been thinking about, and for any of those purposes.

PLANNING AND CONDUCTING YOUR OWN DEBATE

In a group of four, you are going to plan, research and conduct a debate.

You will have to agree a subject between you. It must be something that you can find out more about if you need to, and about which you have strong feelings. For example:

animal testing?

compulsory AIDs testing?

nuclear power?

blood sports?

vegetarianism?

religious education?

school uniform?

assisted places to private schools?

A debate needs to focus on a 'motion' – the proposition which is put forward by one pair of speakers, and argued against by the other pair.

The motion is usually phrased as a statement of one side of the case. For the ideas listed the motions could be:

'Testing on animals is vital if medical science is going to save human lives.'

'Routine AIDs testing will ensure a healthy population.'

'Nuclear power is the only way to provide economical, reliable energy into the twenty-first century.'

'Fox hunting is a healthy way to take exercise and keeps a serious rural pest under control.'

'A vegetarian diet is the only safe and humane way to eat.'

'Only the religious education of our young people can produce a society with sound moral values.'

'A school uniform is the only way to instill a sense of discipline and community into our young people.'

'Our brightest young people must be offered the chance to succeed, which only private education can ensure.'

- In your group, decide on your subject, phrase your motion and decide which two of you are going to 'propose' and which two will 'oppose'.

PREPARING YOUR SPEECH

You have learnt a lot about the elements that make a persuasive speech. This is your opportunity to put all you have discussed into practice. You are working in a pair, as a team, to prepare your case.

Remember that you are competing with the pair who will be opposing you in the debate, not with each other!

STEP ONE
Each of you brainstorm all the ideas that occur to you as you think about the case you are going to argue. This might include:

major points
examples from news or literature
statistics
other evidence
anecdotes
conclusions that you want to draw

STEP TWO
Compare your two brainstorms. Decide which are really the same point being phrased differently, and which are separate points.

STEP THREE
Divide the points you now have into two groups, one for the first speaker, and one for the second speaker. Decide which of you is going to be the first and which the second speaker.

STEP FOUR
We have seen how important the order of your points can be. Each working on your own points, decide on your concluding point. It needs to be a strong one, as it is the last thought you will leave in your audience's mind.

STEP SEVEN
Once you and your partner have agreed the structure of your speech, it will be up to you to find the right words, phrases and tone to suit you. Take a postcard-sized piece of paper for each point, and, in clear writing, summarise each point at the top of its own piece of paper.

STEP SIX
Test your flow diagram out on your partner.

How strong is your opening? It needs to capture your audience's attention.
How logical is your argument?
Do your points lead smoothly into each other?
Are there any gaps that you need to deal with by moving a point or adding something?
How strong is your conclusion? It needs to sum up the whole of the case, and take you back to the motion.

STEP FIVE
We have seen how logical an argument must be. In a flow diagram, find the best order for your points, to make the most convincing case. You need to carry your audience with you step by step. Remember to anticipate the points the opposition are likely to make. Try to build answers to them into your own points.

STEP TEN
Taking note of your partner's comments, go back to the speech, and try to incorporate the advice. Make sure your notes are clear – you might need to write them out again when you have finalised the speech.

STEP NINE
Try out sections of your speech on your partner, who will make notes as you talk, focusing on things like:

How clear is your expression?
Are there any good phrases to keep in – these might include techniques such as alliteration, repetition, rhetorical questions?
Is the pace right?
How does your voice sound?
Do you make eye contact?
Is there a place where you need to pause to let a point sink in?
Is there any humour? Should there be?

STEP EIGHT
Taking each point one at a time, work on the best possible delivery of that point. Jot down any key words on your piece of paper. These are only to jog your memory, not to read from.

DRESS REHEARSAL

Since you are working as a team, you need to know exactly what to expect from your partner's speech. You also need to know how long it is going to last. You need to prepare together for the likely points your opposing pair might make, so that your second speaker isn't caught out by an unexpected comment. This last run-through is important. If you know what you are going to say, you will sound confident and relaxed, and that will make you sound more convincing.

YOU ARE READY TO FACE THE JURY

FOR THE JURY

How can you measure how successful a speech has been? You need to test out your speaking on a real audience. You need to know whether they agree with your point of view before you give your speech, and then check to see how many have changed their minds after listening to you. In the following activity you will have the chance to practice your:

note writing – as you prepare your speech

speaking – as you discuss your case with your partner, and as you consider the most effective ways of communicating your point of view

listening – as you take part in the audience, and ask questions of the main speakers.

In your 'home' group, you have now:

identified and agreed the issue of your debate

phrased the motion that you are going to argue

decided on the pairs of speakers to propose and oppose the motion.

- Think about the layout of the room. Everyone needs to be able to see the chairperson and the speakers. Speakers should be able to make eye contact with every member of the audience. Write the motion clearly, so that everyone can see it throughout the debate. A blackboard or overhead projector would be ideal. You are ready to begin.

- Choose a chairperson from the rest of the class. This is the person who will make sure that everything runs smoothly. Everyone else will be a member of the audience.

- The chairperson should read the motion aloud, so that everyone is clear about the issue that is going to be discussed. He or she should then ask the audience to consider the motion carefully, and then conduct a vote, where every member of the audience either:

Votes: **For** – agreeing with the motion; or

Against – disagreeing with the motion;

Or: **Abstains** – unable to decide between the two.

- Write the result of the vote clearly underneath the motion.

- The chairperson should introduce each speaker to the audience.

- All four speakers should have their chance to put their point of view. This is the order that you must follow:

FIRST will be one speaker from the pair who are proposing the motion. The pair will have worked together and agreed which points the first speaker will cover.

SECOND will be the first speaker from the pair who are opposing the motion. This pair will also work as a team and will have agreed the points to be made in the opening speech.

THIRD will be the second speaker proposing the motion. He or she will make the points agreed on by the pair in advance making sure to answer the points raised by the opposition.

FOURTH will be the second speaker opposing the motion, making points previously agreed on, with the aim of countering the third speaker's points.

- The chairperson will give members of the audience the chance to ask any questions or make additional points on either side of the debate.

- When everyone has spoken, one speaker from each pair must 'sum up' their case – a final chance to persuade the audience of their case.

- The chairperson will take a final vote from the audience, and see which team of speakers have persuaded most people to change their minds.

WHAT NEXT?

- Use the notes you made for your speech in the final activity and turn them into a *written* piece in which you argue your point of view. You should consider the changes you need to make to the structure and style of your writing in order to convey your argument. Remember to write in an appropriately *formal* style.

  Possible forms for your writing:

  - a 'comment' section from a newspaper

  - a magazine article

  - a pamphlet for distribution at a rally or protest

  - a 'letter to the editor'

Lord of the Flies

- Find examples of speeches in literature (like Old Major's *Animal Farm* by George Orwell). Use the techniques you have learned in this unit to analyse them. Some examples to find (but look as well for others not listed here):

  - Mr Collins' proposal of marriage to Elizabeth in Jane Austen's *Pride and Prejudice* (Ch. 19) beginning:

    'Believe me, my dear Miss Elizabeth, that your modesty, so far from doing you any disservice, rather adds to your other perfections.'

  - Ralph's speech to the assembly in William Golding's *Lord of the Flies* in which he tries to persuade the boys to work at a community (Ch. 5) beginning:

    'The thing is: we need an assembly.'

  - Billy Casper's 'speech' to his English class in which he tells the anecdote about tadpoles in *A Kestrel for a Knave* by Barry Hines.

  - Mr Rochester's proposal of marriage to Jane in Charlotte Brontë's *Jane Eyre* (Ch. 23).

  These are just examples; you should be able to find other examples where a character in a novel or play delivers a more formal speech to one or more others.

  For each speech you find, read it carefully, and summarise its purpose and impact on a chart like the one below:

SPEAKER	AUDIENCE	PURPOSE	CONTENT or ARGUMENT	EFFECT
Old Major (Animal Farm)	Other animals	To inspire revolutionary ideas	An account of a vision he has of a better, fairer, more equal life for animals on the farm	The animals rise up and overthrow Mr Jones, the farmer

UNIT FOUR

Serial Thriller

In this unit you will study the features of the popular genre of 'thrillers' in literature, television and film, and consider the issues raised by censorship of such materials.

You will develop your skills as:

SPEAKERS AND LISTENERS

by discussing controversial issues
by sharing some of your experiences of thrilling stories and frightening moments

READERS

by comparing and generalising about stories in the thriller genre
by studying writers' techniques for playing on readers' emotions and fascinations

WRITERS

by writing openings and extracts in the style of a thriller
by developing a thriller story of your own

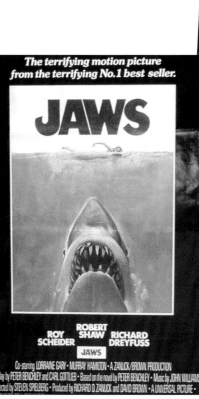

- The films advertised here have been extremely successful. So have the books. Why?

- What is it about the images that customers find so compelling?

- Think of all the films or books that have frightened you the most. What was the most frightening part of each? Which part did you enjoy most?

HOOKS...

At the beginning of a book or film, you do not have to know exactly what is happening – but you do have to *want* to know what happens next. To capture your interest, writers use 'hooks' – on which, like fish, we bite. Sometimes it is one sentence, sometimes a whole opening scene.

American programmes usually have a sequence before the opening credits called 'teasers' or 'hooks'. They grab the audience's attention and keep the viewer watching after the first break for advertisements. In Britain this break might be 15 to 20 minutes into the programme but in America it comes within 2 or 3 minutes of the start.

The popular cult series *The X-Files* uses every imaginable means to create suspense and tension. Each episode is carefully structured and builds to a thrilling climax. Look closely at this opening scene of the episode 'Duane Barry'. How is our attention 'hooked'? And how is tension built up?

1 Starry Sky. Pans down to ordinary house, lights on porch, wind rustling. Caption on screen: **Pulaski, Virginia, June 3 1985.**

2 Interior of house. Ground level shot. Television is on somewhere in the house but all is quiet. Camera seems to be looking at the layout. Dog comes into shot. Eats from bowl. Goes away. Camera follows. House is in the process of being extended. Plastic dust sheeting covers some walls. Camera enters bedroom behind dog. Dog settles at the bottom of the bed on which Duane Barry is sleeping on his back. Camera moves in close to sleeping man. He snores a little in his sleep.

3 Cut to television screen. Black and white film on.

4 Cuts back to dog looking at screen. Television turns to static. Dog raises its head.

5 Cut to television screen – no image.

6 Dog whimpers – seems frightened.

7 Shot of strange figures moving in the house.

8 Shot of man and dog. Seen through plastic sheeting, two indiscernable shapes seem to be watching.

9 Back to dog – whimpers – jumps off bed.

10 Duane Barry abruptly wakes up, startled.
'I can't breathe.'
Illuminated by an intense white light.

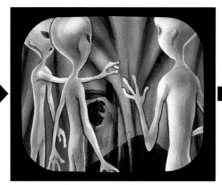

11 Cuts to and moves towards three alien figures
standing mysteriously behind sheeting.

12 Shot of Barry on bed, plus shapes silhouetted
behind the plastic sheeting. Light becomes
more intense.

13 Back to Barry who turns his head away from
the light.

14 Picks up Shot 11 and moves closer to aliens.

15 Shot from over bed – close-up of Barry's face.
'No, NO! Not again!' (Screams sustained
throughout the next sequence.) Camera pulls
away to ceiling – we see possibly eight white
alien figures surrounding bed.

16 Cut to outside of house with white light
pouring out of every window and door. Pans
up and we see a beam of intense white light
coming from an alien spaceship to the house.
Music reaches a climax with scream
sustained.

Into opening credit sequence.

(The X-Files: Duane Barry)

- How do you think this story will develop? How do you know?
- What clues have been left for the viewer to work out?
- What questions do you want answered after seeing this opening?
- What is the appeal of *The X-Files*?

- *The X-Files* has spawned a vast publishing industry, from books on the unexplained and novelisations of episodes, to original stories and graphic novels. Imagine you have been given the task of turning the opening sequence of this episode into novel form. This is called novelisation. Remember the reader will need to be 'hooked' as soon as possible.

The creator of *The X-Files*, Chris Carter, described the intention of the programme:

'to make people uneasy and scare them in ways that are believable and real … if you can believe it can happen to you in your neighbourhood, in your back yard, your house, it's scarier. Mostly we scare people by not showing them what they are afraid of, but by intimating, by hinting at it, by showing it in the shadows or just glimpsing it – my philosophy is less is more.'

- Look at a selection of television drama. Watch the opening two or three minutes. Try to predict what will come next.

- Now read the opening to Graham Greene's *Brighton Rock*. Where is the 'hook'? The writer paints a very detailed picture of Brighton, building the holiday atmosphere. Why?

Hale knew, before he had been in Brighton three hours, that they meant to murder him. With his inky fingers and his bitten nails, his manner cynical and nervous, anybody could tell he didn't belong – belong to the early summer sun, the cool Whistun wind off the sea, the holiday crowd. They came in by train from Victoria every five minutes, rocked down Queen's Road standing on the tops of the little local trams, stepped off in bewildered multitudes into fresh and glittering air; the new silver paint sparkled on the piers, the cream houses ran away into the west like a pale Victorian water colour; a race in miniature motors, a band playing, flower gardens in bloom below the front, an aeroplane advertising something for the health in pale vanishing clouds across the sky.

From *Brighton Rock* by Graham Greene

Sometimes the *style* of writing builds tension, as does the build up of detail (just as a lingering camera shot in a film might alert us to danger).

The night was dark. There was no moon. The land was as dark as the water, and only the white beach could easily be seen. The great fish moved silently through the water. The tail made short sweeps from side to side to push the fish along. The mouth was open just enough to let the water in to pass over the gills. From time to time a fin on the back of the fish moved to keep it on course. The eyes could not see through the dark water. The small brain did not pick up anything to interest it. The fish might have been asleep. But every one of its kind had known for millions of years that if it stopped moving it would sink to the bottom and die. For it was unlike most fish in two ways. First, there was no air-bag inside it to keep it afloat if it stopped moving. Second, its gills had no flaps to push the water through them, so without moving it could get no oxygen.

On the edge of the beach there was a house. The light from its windows shone on to the white sand. The front door to the house opened and a man and a woman went out on to the beach. They stood for a moment looking at the sea. Then they kissed, and ran down the beach towards the sea. The man was drunk, and nearly fell over. The woman laughed and took his hand. They ran on.

From *Jaws* by Peter Benchley

- The passage is written in short sentences. What is the effect?

- What do you think will happen next? Why do you think you think it? Do you think what happens next should happen quickly, or should there be a delay? Give reasons for your answer.

BUILDING TENSION

Imagine an elastic band being slowly twisted – it becomes more and more taut. Telling thriller stories is like tightening an elastic band. The writer keeps on twisting until the band eventually snaps.

In thrillers, we want to see what happens, but we are also scared to look. In a typical *X-Files* episode, the two main characters, Mulder and Scully, race against time to solve the mystery they are investigating. They have many obstacles put in their way by unreliable witnesses, by members of the FBI, and by the cunning person they are pursuing. Danger and difficulties stand in their way.

There are often tensions and uncertainties between the characters in thrillers. Mulder believes in paranormal explanations for the unsolved cases in the X-Files; Scully is more sceptical and practical, but does not have a closed mind. They pull away from each other in their views, but they pull together towards a solution. Also, they are both young, attractive and intelligent: the possibility of romance is tantalising. Why are the programme makers unlikely to allow a romance to be fully developed?

- • Can you think of films, programmes or stories that build up tension by:
  - – pitting the main characters against the clock?
  - – putting many obstacles between the main characters and their goal?
  - – exploiting tensions between two main characters?
  - – exploiting a possible romance: 'will they, won't they'?

As the tension mounts, the writer or director begins to drop clues about the imminent danger. Very often, the reader or viewer spots the risk before the characters.

After three murders in as many weeks, there were few in Woodham who did not expect a fourth. They just hoped it would not be them.

That night Mary left 'The Rod and Gun' early – at half past ten – to be home for the phone call from her sister Jane, a nurse in Saudi Arabia. Mist had crept in from the fens while she had been drinking, and the moment the pub door closed behind her the **cold/chill** caught her throat. A tremor **ran through/pierced/entered** Mary's sturdy frame, so her hand was tightening her collar before she had told herself not to be such a wimp. Wasn't it July? But her hand kept a tight **grip/strangle hold** on her coat collar as her manly stride took her **steadily/inevitably/ever closer** to the **dark/brooding/dense** wood that lay between the pub and her lovely house. From the distant sea she could hear the **dismal/lonely/faint** crash and crumple of the waves.

- • Which of the words in blue would you choose to build tension? Give reasons for your answers.

- • What other clues would alert the reader to imminent danger?

- • Now write your own opening paragraph you feel will hook the attention of your readers. Remember the opening sentence of this section: at the beginning of a book you do not need to know exactly what is happening, but you do have to *want* to know what happens next.

- • Review the points made about style. Work in a group and pass round your completed paragraphs. Point out what is good about each paragraph, and suggest improvements you think could be made.

MAKE THEM SUFFER!

Once a reader or viewer is hooked, it is a good idea to keep them that way. In fact, most of us enjoy being hooked: as we watch an exciting car chase, for instance, half of us wants the good guys to escape; the other half wants the thrills to go on…

The following scene from *Talking in Whispers* by James Watson is set in Chile in South America.

The country is under the brutal control of the Army, who are ruthlessly killing or jailing their enemies. Andres Larreta, the hero, decides to fight back by printing the truth about what is going on. The army has smashed most of the printing equipment owned by its enemies, but one press still exists in many parts, spread among friends. A plan is made, in which all the parts of the printing press will be taken by their owners to the left luggage lockers at Santiago Central Station. Andres, at enormous personal risk, will dress as a porter, collect the parts and make his getaway in a van parked outside the station owned by his friends Isa and Beto.

But things go wrong. Time runs out – and he has to contend with the unwanted help of a soldier:

Andres has opened the first locker. He recovers the parcel and lays it, with desperate calm, on the trolley. The second key proves difficult. Come on, blast you! Then he realises he is trying to insert it upside down. Idiot. Oaf.

The locker door swings open. Large, awkward parcel this; and heavy. Labelled WITH GREAT CARE. On to the trolley. Next locker – a canvas holdall, containing several items. Heavy as the girls' cases. Rattling a bit, too.

'Keeping you busy, are they?' It is the nosy soldier, right behind Andres.

'Always busy.' He has to decide – to stop and talk or to carry on. He goes to the next locker, opens it. Just a small parcel, but of an odd shape.

'Overstayed, have they?'

'Overstayed?'

'Well, gone over their time.'

'Oh yes, yes.'

'What happens if no-one comes to claim them?'

Locker number five – an item so small it hardly seemed to be worth leaving in such a spacious cubicle. 'My job's just to –'

'Anyone check out the contents of these things?'

'Oh yes.' Andres is running with sweat. He drags at his collar. He half turns. He wants to remind the soldier that there are plenty of better things a sentry can do with his time than spend it chatting to a junior porter.

He is to be spared more of the soldier's breath on his neck: a black van screeches into the station forecourt. 'Here's trouble – our pals the arm-twisters.' Clearly the soldier doesn't care for the Security any more than Andres does.

The rear doors of the van open. Three plain-clothes men descend. At the same moment, the officer of the Black Berets strides out through the gate of platform nine. Two policemen following him, escorting the girls Andres had helped only minutes ago.

The girls were handcuffed.

'What a waste!' mutters the soldier. 'There'll be no lipstick or high heels where they're being taken.'

Behind the prisoners comes the station supervisor. Andres opens locker number seven. The parcel seems to contain rollers. He adds it to his pile. He feels on his back the distant yet burning gaze of the supervisor.

As the girls are bundled violently into the Security van, the supervisor calls to Andres. 'You – porter!' The voice cuts through a station announcement of the departure of the train from platform nine.

'You're wanted,' calls the soldier. 'The Gaffer.'

Andres surveys his route to freedom. Thirty paces into sunlight, then left past the taxi rank. He surveys the route to captivity. He also sees a surge of passengers coming out from platform ten, crossing the path – and the vision – of the station supervisor.

It's got to be now.

- • How are we, as readers, 'made to suffer' by this extract? Do you think Andres will get all the parts of the printing press into his trolley and escape to the van without further problems? Or will other foreseen events delay him further? What problems do you think he might face?

This scene is thrilling and tense because:

1 The stakes are high.

2 There are 'close shaves' and near misses that threaten to ruin the plan.

3 There are unexpected events that surprise the reader.

4 The style of writing also heightens the tension through the use of

    short sentences and paragraphs

    the present tense

    changing narrative viewpoints (third to first person)

- • Find examples in the extract to illustrate each of the points above.

- • Can you spot other ways in which the scene is thrilling?

- • Take the following situation and use it to write your own suspense story.

You are on a railway station late at night waiting for the last train. There is one other person on the platform, a dark figure. Suddenly the lights are extinguished, a sudden rush of wind whips up and there is a strange howling sound…

SCARING YOUR SOCKS OFF

Most people enjoy being frightened, when they are safe in the knowledge that the threat is not real. Although we might watch a really frightening scene with a hand half over our eyes, we still watch it!

Imagine you were making a horror film where the killer had murdered a young man and left his body submerged in the bath. The murderer hides in the attic. The young man's girlfriend, Georgina, arrives at the front door. She pushes at the open door and enters …

At the moment, the scene develops like this: Georgina goes into the kitchen and calls out her boyfriend's name. There is no answer so she goes upstairs. She goes into the bathroom and finds the body in the bath. She screams.

The problem is that the scene is too short: the body is found too quickly, without suspense building up as well as it could.

- Look at the storyboard. Discuss how you might add to the suspense of your film. What scenes would you create to fill the gaps, and from what angle would they be shot?

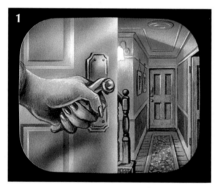

1

Shot of Georgina pushing at the front door. Move to focus on hand on door.

2

Hallway stretching beyond door frame. Move down hallway. Georgina: 'Don?'

3

[Crash!]

Camera moves quickly to right – scene through another doorway.

4

Camera 'looks around' – comes to focus on cat hiding under desk – eyes shining.

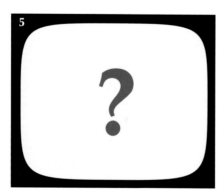

5

?

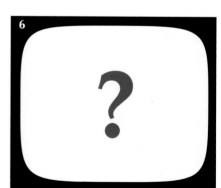

6

?

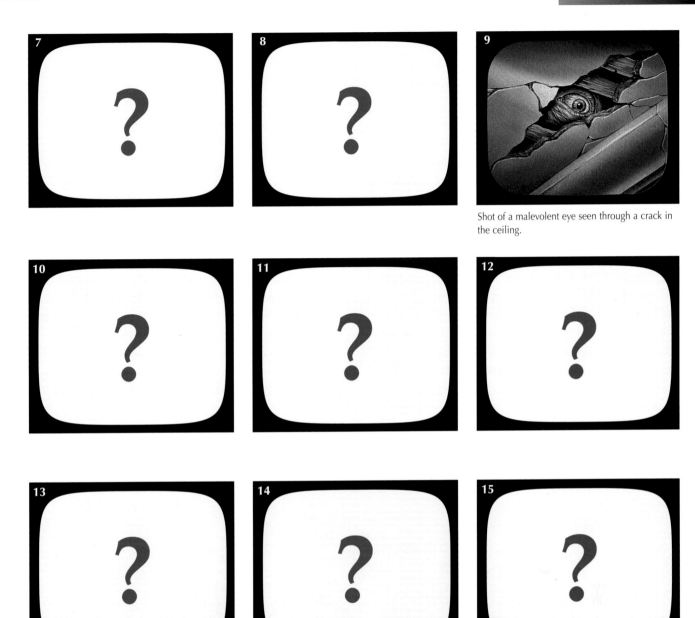

7

8

9

Shot of a malevolent eye seen through a crack in the ceiling.

10

11

12

13

14

15

16

Georgina screaming.

• Think about the background music you might use to heighten the suspense. (How has music been used in other films you have seen? For example, would *Jaws* be the same without the music?)

URBAN LEGENDS

An urban legend is an often retold story that allegedly has a basis in fact. Many involve encounters with psychopaths, and horrifying, gruesome experiences.

'The Hook' and 'The Hitchhiker' are two typical urban legends. You may have come across a version of one of these.

THE HOOK

Now believe me, this is a true story. A boy and his girlfriend drove to their favourite spot, quiet and secluded, where they could listen to some music on the car radio and get a little friendly. The music was abruptly interrupted by an announcer – a crazed one-handed killer with a hook in place of a hand had escaped from a local asylum, and listeners were warned to take extra care.

The girl was frightened and begged her boyfriend to drive her home. Annoyed that their romantic evening had been spoilt, he threw the car into gear and roared off.

When he pulled up outside his girlfriend's house, he got out and walked round the car to let her out. There on the door handle was a blood-covered iron hook.

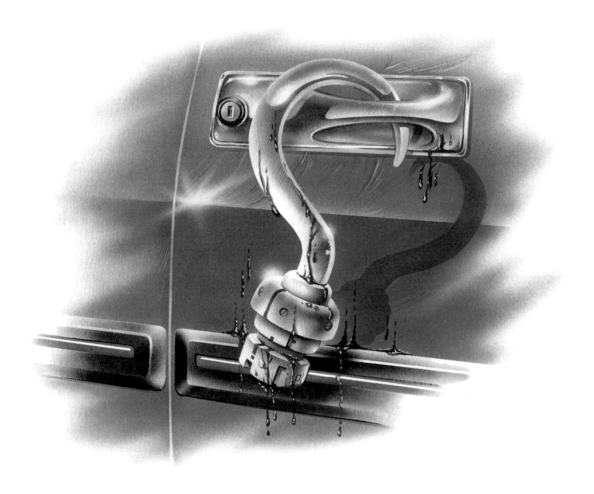

THE HITCHHIKER

Have I ever told you what happened to one of my girlfriend's best friends and her dad? They were driving home one evening along a country lane when they saw a young girl hitchhiking. She looked as if she could do with a lift, so they stopped and picked her up and she climbed in the back seat.

She told them that she lived in a house about five miles up the road. After that she didn't say anything, but just stared out of the window.

When the father saw the house he drove up to the door and turned around to tell the girl they had arrived – but she wasn't there!

They were totally baffled. They got out of the car and went up to the house to tell the girl's parents what had happened.

The couple told him they once had a daughter who answered the description of the girl they had supposedly picked up, but she had disappeared some years ago. The last time she was seen she was hitchhiking about five miles away on this very road. Today would have been her birthday.

You will notice that both stories are pared-down plots.

- What is the power they have over the listener? What is their fascination?

- Have you found similar storylines appearing in any films or books you know?

- What other urban legends do you know?

- In groups, retell either *The Hook* or *The Hitchhiker'*, or an urban myth of your own in your own words. Each member of the group should take responsibility for a section of the story. Add detail to the story in order to build up suspense.

For instance:

The music was abruptly interrupted by an announcer. A crazed one-handed killer had escaped from the local asylum …!

could become

Suddenly the music on the radio was interrupted by the flat tones of a news announcer. 'We interrupt this programme,' intoned the voice, 'to bring you a serious warning'.

'What?' The girl was suddenly alert.

'Listen!' hissed the boy.

'An escape has been reported from the High Security Prison. The escaped prisoner, a convicted murderer, can easily be identified: instead of a left hand, he has a steel hook.'

CLIFFHANGER 1 – PAST MASTER

The device of the 'cliffhanger ending' to generate suspense is not new. In the nineteenth century many books were published not as we find them today in book form, but as serials in monthly magazines. A gripping story with a cliffhanger ending each month would obviously guarantee good sales of the next issue – when Charles Dickens wrote *Oliver Twist,* the excitement in America was so great that there would be crowds on the quayside waiting for the ship bringing in the latest episode.

Few writers have mastered the art of the cliffhanger ending to a chapter better than Dickens, and when he came to write *Great Expectations* there were special reasons why he had to grip the attention of a wide public.

In 1850, Dickens set up a magazine called *Household Words* which ran with success for nine years but folded after he and his partners in the magazine had a disagreement. Dickens then set up a new magazine called *All the Year Round,* but the first stories in the magazine did not achieve

instant success and the project was faced with disaster. To save the magazine, Dickens began *Great Expectations* in December of 1860, completing it in June 1861.

Great Expectations tells the story of young Pip, an orphan boy brought up by his sister. There is a fine example of a cliffhanger ending in Chapter 4. In this chapter, a lunch party is in progress, and the grand finale of the meal is to be a home-made pork pie, a gift from one of the guests. Unfortunately, Pip has stolen the pork pie and given it to an escaped convict who threatened his life if he did not bring him food. The meal is almost over …

I foresaw what was coming, and I felt that this time I really was gone.

'You must taste,' said my sister, addressing the guests with her best grace, 'You must taste, to finish with, such a delightful and delicious present of Uncle Pumblechook's!'

Must they! Let them not hope to taste it!

'You must know,' said my Sister, rising, 'it's a pie; a savoury pork pie.'

The company murmured their compliments. Uncle Pumblechook, sensible of having deserved well of his fellow-creatures, said, – quite vivaciously, all things considered – 'Well, Mrs. Joe, we'll do our best endeavours; let us have a cut at this same pie.'

My sister went out to get it. I heard her steps proceed to the pantry. I saw Mr Pumblechook balance his knife. I saw re-awakening appetite in the Roman nostrils of Mr Wopsle. I heard Mr Hubble remark that 'a bit of savoury pork pie would lay atop of anything you could mention and do no harm,' and I heard Joe say, 'You shall have some, Pip.' I have never been absolutely certain whether I uttered a shrill yell of terror, merely in spirit, or in the bodily hearing of the company. I felt I could bear no more, and that I must run away. I released the leg of the table, and ran for my life.

But, I ran no further than the house door, for there I ran head foremost into a party of soldiers with their muskets: one of whom held out a pair of handcuffs to me, saying, 'Here you are, look sharp, come on!'

- In what sense in this a cliffhanger ending?

- How does Dickens build up the tension throughout this passage? Consider: the feelings of Pip who tells the story; the sequence of events; the descriptive details; the choice of words.

- Now find a copy of *Great Expectations* and read the opening of Chapter 5 down to '... scattered wits', and discuss your reaction to it.

- What piece of information has Dickens withheld to give more impact to the final paragraph? In your opinion, does Dickens cheat his readers to make sure they read the next episode, or is this part of the novelist's craft?

- Think of other novels that you have read. What piece of important information can you think of that the writer has withheld? How has this generated suspense?

CLIFFHANGERS 2 – ARE WE BEING CONNED?

Just as Dickens wrote cliffhanger endings to his chapters to ensure his magazine had a good readership, so modern writers use exactly the same technique. Many people see at least one 'cliffhanger ending' a night – at the end of a popular 'soap'.

Dickens and the scriptwriters of soap operas have the same aim: Dickens wanted to keep us reading, television scriptwriters want to keep us watching.

But do cliffhanger endings 'cheat' us, by leading up to an exciting ending that seems not so exciting when we watch the next episode (just as Dickens led us to believe that Pip was about to be arrested for stealing the pie – when in fact the soldiers had simply stopped to find a blacksmith to work on some handcuffs)?

- Watch your favourite soap for two episodes. Note down the 'cliffhanger ending' for each episode and write down how you think the situation will develop in the next episode. Later, compare your forecast with the actual outcome in the next episode.

- Share your findings with others in a group. Do you think cliffhanger endings cheat the audience by giving it false expectations? Or is giving false expectations part of the writer's craft?

HOW FAR CAN YOU GO?

Some films have come in for a great deal of criticism in the media and elsewhere for the alleged effects they had on viewers. From films like *Nightmare on Elm Street* to *Child's Play 3* – the film that some suggest planted evil ideas in the minds of two young children who murdered a toddler – there are a range of films that have been described as either 'sick' or 'brilliant' depending on your point of view.

What is undeniable is that these films attract large audiences, and some of that audience is very young – in a recent survey, 43% of 8 to 11 year olds had seen the film *Terminator* (Certificate 18). It seems there has always been a market for things that scare and shock us. In the safety of our front rooms watching a video or in a cinema, we can be thrilled but know that ultimately we are watching fiction, a piece of make-believe. Some psychologists believe watching frightening stories is a therapeutic exercise and not harmful in the way some critics argue.

In the nineteenth century the general public loved stories of grisly murders. The Gothic novel was very popular, as was melodrama in the theatre. Both often featured evil villains. While some people have few objections to violence in a pre-twentieth century context, they find modern treatments of similar stories unacceptable.

Here are some comments on the influence of film and television:

Parents are allowing children as young as eight to watch extreme sex-and-violence films at home. Some are being traumatised by the shocking scenes and end up having nightmares. And psychiatrists fear that many of them will be 'emotionally brutalised' by the experience.

Paul Nathanson, Media Correspondent, *Mail on Sunday*

Violence on television does not encourage young people to be aggressive, according to a controversial new report.

Its author, sociologist David Gauntlett, says that despite years of research into a possible link there is no proof that violent scenes on television and video prompt real crime.

The Express

Of course television has an influence. Like newspapers, movies, novels, parents, peers, heroes, work, non-work, genes and so on. No-one denies that. What Gauntlett does deny, authoritatively, is the repeated assertion that acts of violence on television cause acts of violence in society.

Melvin Bragg, *The Independent*

A child watching Tom drop a ton weight on Jerry knows that Jerry will get up again only because he is cartoon. He equally knows that if a ton weight is dropped on him, it will cause severe pain and damage. Children can tell what is fantasy and the evidence is that cartoon action, or violence, has no influence at all.

Dr Guy Cumberbatch, Aston University

When I grow up I've got to get used to them … so my brother said I've got to start watching horror films more often.

Gavin, aged 9

The survey (1988) reveals an alarming new fact – that two million people actually get a kick from watching programmes with a violent content.

The twitchy two million (about 6% of the viewing public) admitted they felt 'quite violent' after watching crime shows.

The Daily Star

Lots of our children would appear to be extraordinarily stable, capable, innovative, enthusiastic citizens and they watch appalling things and can brush them off with great ease. They can distinguish perfectly well between fact and fiction – indeed they would be more disturbed by graphic news coverage of Rwanda than they ever would be by Freddy Krueger.

Professor Jack Sanger

WHAT DO YOU THINK?

Research tells us that one third of 8 to 11 year olds have seen films rated 15 to 18. If you have seen something rated beyond your age, did it disturb you?

- Discuss what you know and feel about censorship.

Which are more troubling – violent images or sexual images?

Which are more troubling – extremes on film or in books or on television?

Can you justify any distinctions you make?

What practical problems are raised by a decision to censor?

What ethical problems are raised by a decision to censor?

Suggest solutions and find out how censorship is enforced in the different media.

CLIMAX

The climax of a story ends the suspense. The moment arrives when good and evil confront each other. It is very exciting, full of action, and everything depends on the outcome. It might be:

- an attack
- a combat
- a chase
- an explosion
- a frantic race against time

- Can you think of examples of each of these climaxes?
- Can you think of other types of climatic endings?

On the next page is an extract from the climax of a prize-winning novel called *The Ghost Road* by Pat Barker. The main character, Prior, is a soldier in the first world war waiting for the signal to attack the enemy trenches.

Read the passage carefully.

Concentrate on nothing but the moment, Prior told himself, moving forward on knees and elbows like a frog or a lizard or like – like anything except a man. First the right knee, then the left, then the right, then the left again, and again, and again, slithering through fleshy green grass that smelled incredibly sharp as scrabbling boots cut it. Even with all this mist there was now a perceptible thinning of the light, a gleam from the canal where it ran between spindly, dead trees.

There is to be no retirement under any circumstances. That was the order. They have tied us to the stake, we cannot fly, but bear-like we must fight the course. The men were silent, staring straight ahead into the mist. Talk, even in whispers, was forbidden. Prior looked at his watch, licked dry lips, watched the second hand crawl to the quarter hour. All around him was a tension of held breath. 5.43. Two more minutes. He crouched further down, whistle clenched between his teeth.

Prompt as ever, hell erupted. Shells whined over, flashes of light, plumes of water from the drainage ditches, tons of mud and earth flung into the air. A shell fell short. The ground shook beneath them and a shower of pebbles and clods of earth peppered their steel helmets. Five minutes of this, five minutes of the air bursting in waves against your face, men with dazed faces braced against it, as they picked up the light bridges meant for fording the flooded drainage ditches, and carried them out to the front. Then, abruptly, silence. A gasp for air, then noise again, but further back, as the barrage lifted and drummed down on to the empty fields.

Prior blew the whistle, couldn't hear it, was on his feet and running anyway, urging the men on with wordless cries. They rushed forward, making for the line of trees. Prior kept shouting, 'Steady, steady! Not too fast on the left! It was important there should be no bunching when they reached the bridges. 'Keep it straight!' Though the men were stumbling into quagmires or tripping over clumps of grass. A shell whizzing over the German side exploded in a shower of mud and water. And another. He saw several little figures topple over, it didn't look serious, somehow, they didn't look like beings who could be hurt.

Bridges laid down, quickly, efficiently, no bunching at the crossings, just the clump of boots on wood, and then they emerged from beneath the shelter of the trees and out into the terrifying openness of the bank. As bare as an eyeball, no cover anywhere, and the machine-gunners on the other side were alive and well. They dropped down, firing to cover the sappers as they struggled to assemble the bridge, but nothing covered *them*. Bullets fell like rain, puckering the surface of the canal, and the men started to fall. Prior saw the man next to him, a silent, surprised face, no sound, as he twirled and fell, a slash of scarlet like a huge flower bursting open on his chest. Crawling forward, he fired at the bank opposite though he could hardly see it for the clouds of smoke that drifted across. The sappers were still struggling with the bridge, binding pontoon sections together with wire that sparked in their hands as bullets struck it. And still the terrible rain fell. Only two sappers left, and then the Manchesters took over the building of the bridge. Kirk paddled out in a crate to give covering fire, was hit, hit again, this time in the face, went on firing directly at the machine-gunners who crouched in their defended holes only a few yards away. Prior was about to start across the water with ammunition when he was himself hit, though it didn't feel like a bullet, more like a blow from something big and hard, a truncheon or a cricket bat, only it knocked him off his feet and he fell, one arm trailing over the edge of the canal.

- Try reading the passage aloud. It is a very dramatic passage, full of action and nervous excitement. Can you hear this as you read? What is it about the writing that communicates the action and nervous excitement?

- Go through the passage listing the words that emphasise the drama, excitement and horror of the battle, for example:

    hell erupted

    flung

    shook

    bursting in waves

    gasp for air

- Go through the passage and work out what actually happened and write this down as a plain, detached description.

    At the signal, the soldiers started to advance under heavy fire, carrying the light bridge ready to cross the flooded area. After five minutes …

- At the first reading, it is difficult to work out what actually happens because we see the battle through Prior's frightened eyes. We have seen how the writer communicates the emotions of battle in the choice of words. Now look at how it is done through the structure of sentences and of the whole piece. Note down your conclusions.

- There are very few adjectives in this passage. Why might this be?

- Try to find some – at which points do they occur?

- Look for **similes** in the passage (there are three) – what effects do they have on the pace of the narrative, and why do you think the writer chose to use each one?

Simile – a comparison between two very different things made in order to point out a similarity. A simile can be recognized by the use of 'like' or 'as' linking the descriptions.

her eyes are as blue as the sky

or her eyes are blue, like the sky

- The story is told in the third person narrative and yet we see it through Prior's eyes. How is it that we see it this way?

- Find a moment of climax in another novel and see if you can find any of the techniques you have studied used there. Are there any different techniques employed?

- Find a moment of climax in a video or television programme of your own choice and work out how film and television directors create an exciting climax. In particular, pay attention to the use of sound and the pace of the shots.

In stage drama, the audience will often feel that they have lived through events with the characters. Feelings run high in a good play. It is as though the audience have a 'virtual' experience. At the end, they might well feel better for this. Their wound-up emotions are relieved as they survive safely whatever terror or tragedy has happened on stage. This feeling of relief, of getting all the pent-up motion off your chest, is known as **catharsis.**

In the plays you have seen or studied, which ones left you feeling relieved? Were there any that made you feel lucky to be returned to your normal life? Were there any that made you feel differently about the world?

Catharsis is usually associated with tragedy, horror stories and thrillers. Why is this do you think?

JUST DESERTS

Endings are important. Traditional happy endings will:

> bring the story to rest
>
> reward or punish characters
>
> reveal all
>
> pass judgement on all that has happened

- What is the typical happy ending in:
  - A love story?
  - Horror stories about monsters?
  - Disaster movies – crashes, earthquakes, fires, etc?
  - Spy thrillers – such as James Bond films?
  - Police and detective dramas?
  - Supernatural threats?

- What messages do these traditional endings seem to give about: crime, love, marriage, the supernatural, taking risks, foreigners, goodness in people, villains, age?

  > e.g. Crime = crime doesn't pay; truth and justice always triumph; no matter how clever the bad guy is, the good guy is always that bit better.

- Not all stories have a traditional happy ending. Thrillers often end on an unsettling note. Can you think, for example, of stories which have a:
  - sadder but wiser ending?
  - sting-in-the-tail surprise ending?
  - question mark ending – is it really over?
  - bitter-sweet ending – something lost, – something gained?
  - to-be-continued ending?

How do you react to such endings? Can you think of an ending which left you feeling dissatisfied or cheated? Why?

Have you ever re-read or re-watched a story you already know? Did you read it differently because you knew the ending? Where is the interest and excitement?

- Write the brief final chapter of this story:

Alter ego

The hero has been fighting throughout the book with his monstrous alter ego: the dark side of his nature, which was separated from him in a laboratory accident. His alter ego takes the form of a monster which the hero recognises as being part of his own nature.

Finally, they are locked in a life or death struggle in a hostile environment, and equally matched in strength and resolve.

> Picture the alter ego. Sketch it.
>
> Picture the environment. Sketch it.
>
> Consider the kind of ending you want from the list above.
>
> Work out how it will come about.
>
> Consider how you will tell the story – as an observer, a detached narrator, or as one of the participants?
>
> Now write your ending.

WHAT NEXT?

Here are a number of topics for discussion or for written assignments:

1. What is a thriller?

HELP

Give examples from different types of literature: film, books, drama, etc.
Describe the typical features of the thriller.
Give examples to illustrate the effective build-up of tension, climax and ending.

2. *Either:* Choose a thriller and use three passages in it to show how the writer is effective in hooking the interest of the reader, building suspense and creating thrills.

   Or: Choose three openings to thrillers and show how the writers have gone about the task of hooking the interest of the reader.

HELP

Choose the passages.
Go through each one carefully picking out suspense-building techniques:
   choice of vocabulary
   setting
   atmosphere
   pace
   structure and rhythm of sentences
   repetition
   how it is told

Consider how best to structure your essay, probably working through each one, drawing out comparisons and contrasts as you go.

3. Take any television drama or soap opera that you regularly watch and enjoy – what are its typical features? Use examples to illustrate these and to explain its winning formula.

   (See Help box top right)

HELP

Choose a programme.
Identify those characters and setting that are stable from episode to episode.
Identify elements of the plot which are repeated from week to week, even if the characters change.
Identify what it is about the shape or structure of the programme that is common to each episode.
Identify other recurring or common features.
   Where do elements vary from week to week?
   What emphases vary from week to week?
   What are the common themes to which the programme return again and again?
   Which elements could you not bear to lose?

Keep a note of examples as you go.
Consider how best to organise your thoughts into an essay. For example:
   introduction to the programme
   stable elements
   typical episode features
   variables
   most appealing features

4. Take two plays you have studied and show how dramatists build up tension. How much of the suspense is owed to the script and how much to the acting?

HELP

The best way to approach this is to take a scene in which tension is developed from each play and discuss it in some detail, referring to choice of vocabulary, context, setting, atmosphere, pace, structure and rhythm of lines, use of repetition, and so on. Then look at it from a director's point of view, seeing how you can exploit the script by using delivery, lighting, costume, movement and timing. If you can comment on a particular production, that would be easiest.

UNIT FIVE

Heroes and Heroines

In this unit, you will investigate how characters are created in literature and examine how writers use heroes and heroines. You will develop your skills as:

SPEAKERS AND LISTENERS

by discussing, in pairs and in groups, whether particular heroes and heroines conform to stereotypes

by reading extracts aloud to discover the tone of a description

READERS

by studying the development of character in a range of pre-20th and 20th century fiction

by analysing the ways in which language is used to create the desired response from the reader

WRITERS

by keeping a 'character file' in which you note down your ideas and keep track of character development

by trying out for yourself some of the techniques used by writers

by applying what you have learned and completing a written assignment

THE WRITER AS PUPPET MASTER

In all stories, writers create and manipulate their characters just as a puppeteer pulls the strings of a puppet in order to bring it to life. They invent features and characteristics which clothe the characters; they make them move by pulling the strings; and they give them voice through dialogue and interaction with other characters. In this unit, you will be looking at how writers do this, at the different ways characters can be presented and developed and the reasons why these manipulations take place.

Writers use characters in all sorts of different ways; as heroes, as heroines, as supporting characters, and sometimes simply as devices to help the development of the story or theme.

• Working in groups, discuss the way the Walt Disney team visually construct their hero, Captain John Smith, for the film *Pocahontas*. The picture on the bottom left is an actual likeness of the captain. The picture above is Disney's version. What has been changed by the 'authors' and why do you think they have done it?

• How do these changes affect your impression of what the film is about? In particular, what do they tell you about the qualities that are needed in a hero, the kinds of relationships that he is likely to form and the themes explored in the film?

Although Captain John Smith actually existed, the version of him created by Walt Disney for *Pocahontas* is only a representation of reality. The puppet-master has worked the strings for his own particular purpose.

• Imagine that you are going to create a character based on yourself to play the central role in a book or film. Choose the genre you wish to use (cowboy, thriller, romance, for example) and consider how you would represent different aspects of your personality. If you are shy, for example, and don't say much when you are with other people, how might you turn this to advantage as a character in a western? Discuss your ideas with another member of your group.

CHARACTERS AS CARICATURES

The idea of presenting characters as distortions of reality can most clearly be understood by looking at the way satirists draw cartoons or the way some writers use caricature. In both cases, the creator chooses to emphasise only certain aspects, often to make people laugh, or to reinforce particular ideas which are crucial to the context.

- Look carefully at the cartoons of Tony Blair and John Major, drawn by Heath for the *Independent*.

- You would probably have no difficulty recognising either politician, but compare the cartoons with the photographs. What aspects of their features have been distorted? What image has been created?

YOUR CHARACTER FILE

As you read through this unit, you are going to analyse a lot of different fictional characters. You will need to use a standard format to compare your findings. Use these headings to assemble your thoughts and discoveries about the way writers create characters:

Title and type of extract

Characteristics

Effect

Purpose

This will be referred to as your 'character file', and should help you to keep a full set of notes.

In *Nicholas Nickleby,* Charles Dickens introduces a character called Wackford Squeers, a Yorkshire schoolmaster. His school, Dotheboys Hall, and Nicholas's experiences there, are the subject of the first part of the novel. As you read the extract, what impression do you gain of this character? Can you predict what his school might be like?

Mr. Squeers's appearance was not prepossessing. He had but one eye, and the popular prejudice runs in favour of two. The eye he had was unquestionably useful, but decidedly not ornamental: being of a greenish-gray, and in shape resembling the fanlight of a street door. The blank side of his face was much wrinkled and puckered up, which gave him a very sinister appearance, especially when he smiled, at which times his expression bordered closely on the villainous. His hair was very flat and shiny save at the ends, where it was brushed stiffly up from a low protruding forehead, which assorted well with his harsh voice and coarse manner. He was about two or three-and-fifty, and a trifle below the middle size; he wore a white neckerchief with long ends, and a suit of scholastic black; but his coat sleeves being a great deal too long, and his trousers a great deal too short, he appeared ill at ease in his clothes, and as if he were in a perpetual state of astonishment at finding himself so respectable.

Derek Francis as Squeers, BBC

Like the cartoons of Tony Blair and John Major, this is a caricature. The only difference is that Dickens has used words rather than pictures.

In order to understand how the description works, you will need to look closely at the way in which it has been constructed.

• Imagine that you have been asked to provide a very accurate description of Mr Squeers of the kind that the police ask for when they are interviewing witnesses. Write down, in no more than 100 words what you would say. Remember, your aim is to create a kind of photograph in words so that Mr Squeers could be instantly recognised by a member of the public.

• Compare your account with Dickens's. What difference is there between the two versions? List the key phrases that you have had to leave out, making a note of the effect they have on the reader.

• Think of the description of Mr Squeers as a sketch being produced by a cartoonist. Make a note of the order in which the artist has built up the image. He starts, for example, by drawing Mr Squeers's eye and then … what? As the picture develops, what does each new brushstroke contribute to what has gone before?

• What does your analysis tell you about the attitude that Dickens is adopting towards the character of Mr Squeers, and what kind of response would you expect the reader to have? Add your conclusions to your character file.

CHARACTERS AS HEROES AND HEROINES

This is Janet.

2

This is John.

3

Many of the most interesting characters you will meet in your study of literature will be those that the writer has created as the hero or heroine of the book. What exactly do we mean by these terms? What are the key characteristics that make these characters special, that make them 'heroes' or 'heroines'.

• Using pieces of plain A4 paper, and working in a group, write down your answers to the questions above, by listing the most important attributes of any hero or heroine. Using the layout on the right, think first about the use of the words 'hero' and 'heroine' in the media, and then consider the meanings when applied to characters in literature.

MEDIA	
Hero	Heroine

• Once you have completed your lists, consider the following questions:

Are the qualities of a hero significantly different to those of a heroine?

Are these differences directly linked to gender?

What criteria would you use to assess whether a particular character really was a hero or a heroine?

LITERATURE	
Hero	Heroine

These sheets can be added to your character file, and the list of ideas applied to any work of literature you are reading. It should help you to understand exactly what writers are doing with the idea of heroes and heroines as they create their characters.

Some of the first instances in which we come across heroes and heroines are in the stories we are told as children. In traditional fairy tales, the characters fulfil their roles in very simple, direct ways. The story of *Snow White* makes use of a stereotypical hero, heroine and villain. In the first written version, *Snow-drop* by the Brothers Grimm, the little princess and her step-mother are described at the very beginning of the tale:

And so the little girl [the princess] grew up: her skin was white as snow, her cheeks as rosy as the blood, and her hair as black as ebony; and she was called Snow-drop. But the queen died; and the king soon married another wife, who was very beautiful, but so proud that she could not bear to think that anyone could surpass her. She had a magical looking-glass, to which she used to go and gaze upon herself, and say,

> 'Tell me, glass, tell me true!
> Of all the ladies in the land,
> Who is the fairest? Tell me who?'

And the glass answered,

> 'Thou, queen, art fairest in the land.'

But Snow-drop grew more and more beautiful; and when she was seven years old she was bright as the day, and fairer than the queen herself. Then the glass one day answered the queen, when she went to consult it as usual,

> 'Thou, queen, may'st fair and beauteous be,
> But Snow-drop is lovelier far than thee!'

When she heard this she turned pale with rage and envy; and called to one of her servants and said, 'Take Snow-drop away into the wide wood, that I may never see her more.'

Snow-drop, of course, is saved by the dwarfs, whose interventions also help her to survive two more attempts on her life. Only after the third, the poisoned apple, do they place her in the glass coffin, where the hero finds her:

And thus Snow-drop lay for a long, long time, and still only looked as though she was asleep; for she was even now as white as snow, and as red as blood, and as black as ebony. At last a prince came and called at the dwarfs' house; and he saw Snow-drop, and read what was written in golden letters. Then he offered the dwarfs money, and earnestly prayed them to let him take her away; but they said, 'we will not part with her for all the gold in the world'. At last, however, they had pity on him, and gave him the coffin: but the moment he lifted it up to carry it home with him, the piece of apple fell from between her lips, and Snow-drop awoke, and said, 'Where am I?'. The prince answered, 'Thou art safe with me.' Then he told her all that had happened, and said, 'I love you better than all the world: come with me to my father's palace, and you shall be my wife.' And Snow-drop consented, and went home with the prince.

Left: Snow White, Disney; above: Snow-drop, from Household Tales by the Brothers Grimm, illustrated by Mervyn Peake

However, some more recent writers of children's stories have transformed these traditional roles.

THE PAPER BAG PRINCESS

Robert H. Munsch

Elizabeth was a beautiful princess. She lived in a castle and had expensive princess clothes. She was going to marry a prince named Ronald.

Unfortunately, a dragon smashed her castle, burned all her clothes with his fiery breath, and carried off Prince Ronald.

Elizabeth decided to chase the dragon and get Ronald back.

She looked everywhere for something to wear but the only thing she could find that was not burnt was a paper bag. So she put on the paper bag and followed the dragon.

He was easy to follow because he left a trail of burnt forests and horses' bones.

Finally, Elizabeth came to a cave with a large door that had a huge knocker on it.

She took hold of the knocker and banged on the door.

The dragon stuck his nose out of the door and said, 'Well, a princess! I love to eat princesses, but I have already eaten a whole castle today. I am a very busy dragon. Come back tomorrow.'

He slammed the door so fast that Elizabeth almost got her nose caught.

Elizabeth grabbed the knocker and banged on the door again.

The dragon stuck his nose out of the door and said, 'Go away. I love to eat princesses, but I have already eaten a whole castle today. I am a very busy dragon. Come back tomorrow.'

'Wait,' shouted Elizabeth, 'Is it true that you are the smartest and fiercest dragon in the whole world?'

'Yes,' said the dragon.

'Is it true,' said Elizabeth, 'that you can burn up ten forests with your fiery breath?'

'Oh, yes,' said the dragon, and he took a huge, deep breath and breathed out so much fire that he burned up fifty forests.

'Fantastic,' said Elizabeth, and the dragon took another huge breath and breathed out so much fire that he burned up one hundred forests.

'Magnificent,' said Elizabeth, and the dragon took another huge breath, but this time nothing came out.

The dragon didn't even have enough fire left to cook a meat ball.

Elizabeth said, 'Dragon, is it true that you can fly around the world in just ten seconds?'

'Why, yes,' said the dragon and jumped up and flew all the way round the world in just ten seconds.

He was very tired when he got back, but Elizabeth shouted, 'Fantastic, do it again!'

So the dragon jumped up and flew around the whole world in just twenty seconds.

When he got back he was too tired to talk and he lay down and went straight to sleep.

Elizabeth whispered very softly, 'Hey, dragon.' The dragon didn't move at all.

She lifted up the dragon's ear and put her head right inside. She shouted as loud as she could, 'Hey, dragon!'

The dragon was so tired he didn't even move.

Elizabeth walked right over the dragon and opened the door to the cave.

There was Prince Ronald.

He looked at her and said, 'Elizabeth, you are a mess! You smell like ashes, your hair is all tangled and you are wearing a dirty old paper bag. Come back when you are dressed like a real princess.'

'Ronald,' said Elizabeth, 'your clothes are really pretty and your hair is very neat. You look like a real prince, but you are a toad.'

They didn't get married after all.

- What sort of heroine is *this* princess? What sort of hero is Ronald?

Think about: Appearance, Characteristics, Actions, Role in the plot, and Status. It is particularly important to consider the status of these characters. What power or control do they have over the events in the story? What happens to them, and what do they make happen?

SNOW-DROP	
Hero	Heroine

THE PAPER-BAG PRINCESS	
Hero	Heroine

These two fairy stories show how our view of what makes a hero or heroine changes over time. The story *The Paper Bag Princess* is very different from that of *Snow-drop*, but so is the way in which it is told.

- Re-read *The Paper Bag Princess* carefully. Make a note of all the phrases or words that could never have appeared in a traditional fairy story such as *Snow-drop*.

- What is different about the way in which Robert Munsch has told his story?

- What difference is there between traditional and modern ways of viewing heroes and heroines?

LITERARY HEROINES

Many novelists have been interested in exactly these questions, and have explored issues of gender, status and control through the heroines they have created. The authors of the next two extracts, William Thackeray and Jane Austen, recognise that the reader has expectations of heroines, and openly acknowledge this when they introduce their female characters. In *Vanity Fair*, Amelia Sedley is a character destined not to be the heroine of Thackeray's novel:

> What, then, should a heroine's appearance be?

> What is Thackeray's opinion of this character?

But as we are to see a great deal of Amelia, there is no harm in saying, at the outset of our acquaintance, that she was a dear little creature; and a great mercy it is, both in life and in novels, which (and the latter especially) abound in villains of the most sombre sort, that we are to have for a constant companion so guileless and good-natured a person. As she is not a heroine, there is no need to describe her person; indeed I am afraid that her nose was rather short than otherwise, and her cheeks a great deal too round and red for a heroine; but her face blushed with rosy health, and her lips with the freshest of smiles, and she had a pair of eyes which sparkled with the brightest and honestest good-humour, except indeed when they filled with tears, and that was a great deal too often; for the silly thing would cry over a dead canary-bird; or over a mouse, that the cat had haply seized upon; or over the end of a novel, were it ever so stupid; and as for saying an unkind word to her, were any persons hard-hearted enough to do so – why, so much the worse for them.

> Look at this photograph of Francis Dee who played Amelia Sedley in 1935. Does she look like the character Thackeray portrays?

In *Northanger Abbey* Jane Austen opens with a description of Catherine Morland, her main female character. The description is couched entirely in terms of her qualifications to be considered a heroine. By 1818, when this novel was published, people clearly had fixed ideas about what a heroine in a novel should be like.

No one who had ever seen Catherine Morland in her infancy, would have supposed her born to be an heroine. Her situation in life, the character of her father and mother, her own person and disposition, were all equally against her. Her father was a clergyman, without being neglected, or poor, and a very respectable man, though his name was Richard – and he had never been handsome. He had a considerable independence besides two good livings – and he was not in the least addicted to locking up his daughters. Her mother was a woman of useful plain sense, with a good temper, and what is more remarkable, with a good constitution. She had three sons before Catherine was born; and instead of dying in bringing the latter into the world, as anybody might expect, she still lived on – lived to have six children more – to see them growing up around her, and to enjoy excellent health herself. A family of ten children will be always called a fine family, where there are heads and arms and legs enough for the number; but the Morlands had little other right to the word for they were in general very plain, and Catherine, for many years of her life, as plain as any. She had a thin and awkward figure, a sallow skin without colour, dark lank hair, and strong features; – so much for her person; and not less unpropitious for heroism seemed her mind. She was fond of all boys' plays, and greatly preferred cricket not merely to dolls, but to the more heroic enjoyments of infancy, nursing a dormouse, feeding a canary-bird, or watering a rose-bush. Indeed she had no taste for a garden; and if she gathered flowers at all, it was chiefly for the pleasure of mischief – at least so it was conjectured from her always preferring those which she was forbidden to take. – Such were her propensities – her abilities were quite as extraordinary. She never could learn or understand anything before she was taught; and sometimes not even then, for she was often inattentive, and occasionally stupid. What a strange, unaccountable character! – for with all these symptoms of profligacy at ten years old, she had neither a bad heart nor a bad temper; was seldom stubborn, scarcely ever quarrelsome, and very kind to the little ones, with few interruptions of tyranny; she was moreover noisy and wild, hated confinement and cleanliness, and loved nothing so well in the world as rolling down the green slope at the back of the house … it was not very wonderful that Catherine, who had by nature nothing heroic about her, should prefer cricket, baseball, riding on horseback, and running about the country at the age of fourteen, to books – or at least books of information – for, provided that nothing like useful knowledge could be gained from them, provided they were all story and no reflection, she had never any objection to books at all.

Jane Austen is poking fun at some novels and novelists. Part of her purpose is to surprise and amuse her readers by the creation of Catherine Morland, somebody who does not fit the stereotype.

• Working in pairs, re-read the passage with the following two questions in mind:

In what ways does Catherine upset the reader's expectations about what a heroine should be like?

What do you think is the effect that Jane Austen creates by acknowledging these expectations and then refusing to conform to them?

• Now you have studied these heroines and the way writers manipulate their characters, summarise your ideas using one of the following suggestions:

Draw your own version of a 'perfect' heroine and an unconventional one. Around these drawings place words which describe their attributes (features, personality and behaviour).

Create a collage of pictures from magazines to express the same ideas. Under the headings 'Perfect' and 'Unconventional', make a list of the attributes of the heroes and heroines that you have selected.

Add the work from this section to your character file.

LITERARY HEROES

When we study the way heroes are represented, we find similar patterns, expectations and conventions. From the intrepid rescuer in fairy tales to the superheroes of the twentieth century, we all recognise the conventional ideas of a hero. Novelists, as puppet masters, all rely upon these basic expectations of what a hero will be like.

As you work through this part of the unit, you will be asked several questions. Listed below are different ways in which you might work. Select from this list whichever way of working suits you and the class:

1 Working alone or with a partner, write down your answers and add them to your character file.

2 Discuss the answers in pairs.

3 In small groups, discuss your ideas and jot them down on a large sheet of paper.

4 Read some of the extracts aloud to each other, adapting your voice to the character.

● Read the two extracts below. One is taken from a novel considered by many to be a classic, the other from a formula romance. Each of them deals with the first time the heroine of the book meets the hero.

Which of these do you think is a classic? Can you explain why?

What are the similarities and differences between the two pieces?

Make a list of the features the writer has included to create a 'typical' hero. Do either of the two descriptions depart from this conventional idea?

From the information given to you about these two characters, what do you expect to happen in the story?

Half a lifetime of being taller than most of her sex, and as tall as most men she knew, had invested her with an inbuilt measuring mechanism, and she could say without fear of contradiction that this man was himself at least six foot three. He also, she noted, had thick, dark hair and a pair of deep blue eyes and some lines beside his mouth which invested him with a world-weary rather cynical look; he was tanned, and beneath much more reputable jeans than hers and a grey sports shirt he looked to be supremely fit and streamlined. Finally, he appeared to be in his late thirties.

Something of daylight still lingered, and the moon was waxing bright: I could see him plainly. His figure was enveloped in a riding cloak, fur collared and steel clasped; its details were not apparent, but I traced the general points of middle height and considerable breadth of chest. He had a dark face, with stern features and a heavy brow; his eyes and gathered eyebrows looked ireful and thwarted just now; he was past youth, but had not reached middle-age; perhaps he might be thirty-five. I felt no fear of him, and but little shyness. Had he been a handsome, heroic-looking young gentleman, I should not have dared to stand thus questioning him against his will.

Some authors make it more difficult for the reader to tell whether a character will turn out to be the hero. In the next two extracts it is not so easy to judge.

When Farmer Oak smiled, the corners of his mouth spread till they were within an unimportant distance of his ears, his eyes were reduced to chinks, and diverging wrinkles appeared round them, extending upon his countenance like the rays in a rudimentary sketch of the rising sun.

His Christian name was Gabriel, and on working days he was a young man of sound judgement, easy motions, proper dress, and general good character. On Sundays he was a man of misty views, rather given to postponing, and hampered by his best clothes and umbrella: upon the whole, one who felt himself to occupy morally the vast middle space of Laodicean neutrality which lay between the Communion people of the parish and the drunken section – that is, he went to church, but yawned privately by the time the congregation reached the Nicene creed, and thought of what there would be for dinner when he meant to be listening to the sermon. Or, to state his character as it stood in the scale of public opinion, when his friends and critics were in tantrums, he was considered rather a bad man; when they were pleased, he was rather a good man; when they were neither, he was a man whose moral colour was a kind of pepper-and-salt mixture.

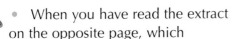

• When you have read the extract on the opposite page, which introduces Farmer Oak in Thomas Hardy's *Far From the Madding Crowd*, consider the following questions:

Does Farmer Oak have any features in common with the other heroes you have just read about?

What has been added to this description of the character to make him more interesting, unusual and convincing?

Would you describe Farmer Oak as a simple or a complicated character? Why?

Adding dialogue to the description of a character allows the reader an insight into the character interacting with someone else. This creates a different perspective for the reader, giving the character a voice and an attitude.

Two men emerged from the path. The first man was small and quick, dark of face, with restless eyes and sharp, strong features. Every part of him was defined: small, strong hands, slender arms, a thin and bony nose. Behind him walked his opposite, a huge man, shapeless of face, with large, pale eyes, with wide, sloping shoulders; and he walked heavily, dragging his feet a little, the way a bear drags his paws. His arms did not swing at his sides, but hung loosely and only moved because the heavy hands were pendula.

The first man stopped short in the clearing, and the follower nearly ran over him. He took off his hat and wiped the sweat-band with his forefinger and snapped the moisture off. His huge companion dropped his blankets and flung himself down and drank from the surface of the green pool; drank with long gulps, snorting into the water like a horse. The small man stepped nervously beside him.

'Lennie!' he said sharply. 'Lennie, for God's sakes don't drink so much.' Lennie continued to snort into the pool. The small man leaned over and shook him by the shoulder. 'Lennie. You gonna be sick like you was last night.'

The passage on the left introduces a character called George Milton in John Steinbeck's *Of Mice and Men*.

• Compare the description of the 'first man' (George Milton) with the typical representations of the heroes you have encountered in this unit.

How is he similar or different?

How would you describe his personality from the way he speaks to his partner, Lennie Small?

Is there anything heroic about him at this stage?

In novels, dialogue gives an added insight into a character. However, in plays, impressions of characters are gained almost entirely through their dialogue and their actions. Discuss the different ways a playwright can use to portray a character. You might wish to consider the hero or heroine of a play you are studying. In what other ways might the audience's impression of a character be affected?

THE NARRATIVE POINT OF VIEW

In reaching judgements about the hero or heroine of a book, it is always important to bear in mind *how* the character is being presented. This can be referred to as the 'narrative point of view'. In some of the extracts you have read so far, the narrative point of view has been very obviously the author's point of view, such as in *The Paper Bag Princess*. In *Jane Eyre,* the point of view is Jane's and not necessarily the author's. In the extract from *Of Mice and Men,* the narrative point of view is not obvious – the characters' appearances are described, but the impression of George Milton's personality is to be gained from the use of direct speech allowing the character to speak in his own right.

Read the next two extracts in which the author depicts the character of the hero in unusual ways.

If you really want to hear about it, the first thing you'll probably want to know is where I was born, and what my lousy childhood was like, and how my parents were occupied and all before they had me, and all that David Copperfield kind of crap, but I don't feel like going into it. In the first place, that stuff bores me, and in the second place, my parents would have about two haemorrhages apiece if I told anything pretty personal about them. They're quite touchy about anything like that, especially my father. They're *nice* and all – I'm not saying that – but they're also touchy as hell. Besides, I'm not going to tell you my whole goddam autobiography or anything. I'll just tell you about this madman stuff that happened to me around last Christmas before I got pretty run-down and had to come out here and take it easy.

From *The Catcher in the Rye* by J. D. Salinger

Mr. Darcy soon drew the attention of the room by his fine, tall person, handsome features, noble mien; and the report which was in general circulation within five minutes after his entrance, of his having ten thousand a year. The gentlemen pronounced him to be a fine figure of a man, the ladies declared he was much handsomer than Mr. Bingley, and he was looked at with great admiration for about half the evening, till his manners gave a disgust which turned the tide of his popularity; for he was discovered to be proud, to be above his company, and above being pleased; and not all his large estate in Derbyshire could then save him from having a most forbidding, disagreeable countenance, and being unworthy to be compared with his friend. What a contrast between him and his friend! Mr. Darcy danced only once with Mrs. Hurst and once with Miss Bingley, declined being introduced to any other lady, and spent the rest of the evening in walking about the room, speaking occasionally to one of his own party. His character was decided. He was the proudest, most disagreeable man in the world, and everybody hoped that he would never come here again. Amongst the most violent against him was Mrs. Bennet, whose dislike of his general behaviour was sharpened into particular resentment by his having slighted one of her daughters.

From *Pride and Prejudice* by Jane Austen

Right: Laurence Olivier as Mr Darcy, 1946

• In order to appreciate how the author is working, try answering the following questions:

What reliable information do you have about either of the characters?

What does Salinger want the reader to think about Holden Caufield, the character, in the first extract? Do you have any evidence for your answer?

What is the narrative point of view of the character, Mr Darcy, in the second extract?

Do you trust the description of his appearance offered by the other guests?

Can you tell from these extracts whether either of these characters will be the hero of the book in which they appear? What evidence do you have?

DEVELOPING CHARACTERS

Authors maintain our interest in the hero or heroine of a novel by developing that character gradually. We get to know the character in the same way as we would get to know a person, learning more about their thoughts and personality the more we come into contact with them.

Read through this second extract from *Of Mice and Men*, where George is introducing himself and his friend Lennie, to the ranch owner. They are hoping to work for him.

Gary Sinise as George and John Malkovich as Lennie in Of Mice and Men, *1992*

George scowled meaningfully at Lennie, and Lennie nodded to show that he understood. The boss licked his pencil. 'What's your name?'

'George Milton.'

'And what's yours?'

George said: 'His name's Lennie Small.'

The names were entered in the book. 'Let's see, this is the twentieth, noon the twentieth.' He closed the book. 'Where you boys been working?'

'Up around Weed,' said George.

'You, too?' to Lennie.

'Yeah, him too,' said George.

The boss pointed a playful finger at Lennie. 'He ain't much of a talker, is he?'

'No, he ain't, but he's sure a hell of a good worker. Strong as a bull.'

Lennie smiled to himself. 'Strong as a bull,' he repeated.

George scowled at him, and Lennie dropped his head in shame at having forgotten.

The boss said suddenly: 'Listen, Small!' Lennie raised his head. 'What can you do?'

In a panic, Lennie looked at George for help. 'He can do anything you tell him,' said George. 'He's a good skinner. He can rassel grain-bags, drive a cultivator. He can do anything. Just give him a try.'

The boss turned to George. 'Then why don't you let him answer? Why you trying to put over?'

George broke in loudly: 'Oh! I ain't saying he's bright. He ain't. But I say he's a God damn good worker. He can put up a four-hundred-pound bale.'

Darcy was introduced to us on page 114 as an enigmatic hero: one who possesses the outward features of a hero but whose personality is open to debate. It is this doubt in the reader's mind which creates the desire to read on and discover the truth. Again, Darcy's personality is revealed through another character's observations about him.

It was not often that she could turn her eyes on Mr. Darcy himself; but whenever she did catch a glimpse, she saw an expression of general complaisance, and in all that he said, she heard an accent so far removed from hauteur or disdain of his companions, as convinced her that the improvement of manners which she had yesterday witnessed, however temporary its existence might prove, had a least outlived one day. When she saw him thus seeking the acquaintance, and courting the good opinion of people with whom any intercouse a few months ago would have been a disgrace; when she saw him thus civil, not only to herself, but to the very relations whom he had openly disdained, and recollected their last lively scene in Hunsford Parsonage, the difference, the change was so great, and struck so forcibly on her mind, that she could hardly restrain her astonishment from being visible. Never, even in the company of his dear friends at Netherfield, or his dignified relations at Rosings, had she seen him so desirous to please, so free from self consequence, or unbending reserve, as now.

- In the first extract about George on page 113, he was seen to have many unattractive features. Does this second extract change your view of him in any way?

- Make a list of the features George displays which would disqualify him from being called a 'hero'. Given this list, can you speculate on any way in which George might be considered a hero?

- What impression do you now have of Mr Darcy's character?

- Do you trust this account more or less than the previous extract about Darcy? Discuss why.

WRITING ABOUT CHARACTERS

You have met many different heroes and heroines in this unit and looked closely at the way writers create and control them, making them conform to or depart from stereotypes. You should now be able to apply what you have learned in a written assignment.

WRITING A CHARACTER STUDY

In some examinations, questions such as the following might be asked. These could be applied to any book:

- Does the heroine of the book you are studying conform to conventional expectations?

- Do you feel that the hero of the novel you are studying is a convincing character? Write about his personality and the way it develops.

- Compare the treatment of heroes or heroines by two different writers.

HELP

▶ Remind yourself about the way in which authors create characters by reviewing your character file.

▶ Brainstorm any initial ideas you might have in response to the question you have decided to tackle.

▶ Sift through these ideas and select those which are most appropriate to the question.

▶ Think more deeply about the function of your chosen character. Why do they behave in certain ways?

▶ Choose significant quotations from the text to back up your ideas.

▶ Organise this material into a logical structure which directly answers the question.

▶ Follow the drafting process.

DRAFTING

You should be familiar with the idea that you need to re-draft your work if it is to be any good. Nobody can produce high quality work without going back over what they have written, checking it out and making improvements.

What is sometimes forgotten is that there are two reasons for re-drafting. It can help you make your work more accurate, but it also gives you the chance to make sure that you are communicating more clearly. Look at the list below. Which activities are about improving accuracy and which are about communicating more clearly?

Correcting your spelling

Re-writing the introduction

Improving your hand-writing

Inserting paragraphs

Rephrasing a sentence so that the meaning is clear

Putting the paragraphs in a different order

Inserting full stops

Adding a new section

Changing key words

Most people re-draft only in order to ensure that their work is well presented. That is important, but it is no use producing beautifully accurate rubbish. Be prepared to re-write your work much more radically. Here are some key questions that you need to consider if you want to improve your ability to communicate clearly:

- Is your meaning unambiguous? Might the reader understand something other than you intended? Re-read your work as if it was written by somebody else.

- Have you repeated yourself? Check each sentence to see whether it adds something fresh to what has gone before.

- Could you have said it more simply? Look at the grammar that you have used. Do you need to turn the sentence around so that the emphasis is different and the meaning clearer?

- Does the first sentence of each paragraph sum up what follows in the rest of the paragraph? A good test of this is to read only the first sentence of each paragraph and see if your assignment still makes sense.

- Is the language that you have used precise? Does it say exactly what you mean?

Questions like these will force you to revise your work much more thoroughly, and that will, at first, seem a bit tedious. The good news is that it will turn you into a much better writer.

CREATING YOUR OWN CHARACTER

Imagine that you are creating the hero or heroine for a novel or short story of your own.

- Write the first meeting with the character and two later extracts as we discover more about them. Remember some of the techniques that are available to writers as they develop characters:

  direct description by the author as narrator of the story

  observation and comments by other characters

  dialogue

  first person narrative

HELP

Consider the way some writers have described the process of creating characters. For Susan Hill, author of *I'm the King of the Castle*, characters emerge from a place and develop around a theme.

'… the setting affected me – places always do, and my antennae were pricked, taking in every detail of the countryside, the weather, the whole atmosphere. There wasn't a story though. The place has often come first for me. And then one day two young boys aged eleven or so went by the gate … it was out of them that my two characters began to grow. Where the dark side of the story came from, the hostility between the boys, the bitter misery and suffering of the victim Kingshaw, the evil – for I think it is evil – of Hooper, I am unsure. It is a novel about cruelty and about the power of evil, which can possess even a young child: about a victim and a tormentor. But most of all it is about isolation and the lack of love. It is a dark book though it emerged from beautiful places and happy scenes.'

In a television discussion of his play *Man of the Moment*, Alan Ayckbourn suggested that his characters emerge straight from a theme, perhaps greed or power, and then develop according to the storyline. He did not want to allow his character, Vic Parks, an attractive villain, to become too attractive to the audience, so he wrote in scenes showing Vic being particularly cruel to vulnerable characters.

WHAT NEXT?

As you continue your exploration as a reader, use the understanding gained from this unit to deepen your appreciation of writers and characters in other texts you might read in the future. You now have an awareness of the conventions writers often employ to reveal a character, and as a skilful reader you should be able to recognise and assess whether a character is truly a hero or heroine in the terms of a particular text. You could do this with:

- Scout in *To Kill a Mockingbird* by Harper Lee.

- Cassie in *Roll of Thunder, Hear My Cry.*

- Macbeth or Lady Macbeth in Shakespeare's *Macbeth.*

- Proctor or Elizabeth Proctor in *The Crucible* by Arthur Miller.

- Frankie Mae in *Frankie Mae and other stories,* compiled by Ann Mann and Hilary Rich.

- Ralph in *Lord of the Flies* by William Golding.

- George Milton in *Of Mice and Men* by John Steinbeck.

- Rochester in *Jane Eyre* by Charlotte Brontë.

'I often think that the purpose of the novelist is simply to …
make some people realise that they are not, after all, alone.'

Dead Man Walking

This unit is about how real life issues are reported on and written about in the media, and how the same issues are treated in fiction. As you work through the unit you will develop your skills as:

SPEAKERS AND LISTENERS

by discussing the facts, the fiction and your own ideas about the death penalty
by working in a group to produce a piece of media course work
by planning and presenting a piece of oral course work

READERS

by comparing and contrasting different forms of writing about the death penalty
by analysing the language, content and style of different accounts
by appreciating the 'point of view' of particular writers

WRITERS

by researching an aspect of the topic and writing your own information text
by writing in a specific style with a particular target audience in mind
by exploring an argument and expressing your point of view in a written course work assignment

As you work through the unit you should build up a personal set of notes to use towards the end of the unit when you plan your course work assignments.

An extract from

THE BALLAD OF READING GAOL

by Oscar Wilde

He did not wear his scarlet coat,
    For blood and wine are red,
And blood and wine were on his hands
    When they found him with the dead,
The poor dead woman whom he loved,
    And murdered in her bed.

He walked amongst the Trial Men
    In a suit of shabby grey;
A cricket cap was on his head,
    And his step seemed light and gay;
But I never saw a man who looked
    So wistfully at the day.

I never saw a man who looked
    With such a wistful eye
Upon that little tent of blue
    Which prisoners call the sky,
And at every drifting cloud that went
    With sails of silver by.

I walked, with other souls in pain,
    Within another ring,
And was wondering if the man had done
    A great or little thing,
When a voice behind me whispered low,
    "That fellow's got to swing."

Dear Christ! the very prison walls
    Suddenly seemed to reel,
And the sky above my head became
    Like a casque of scorching steel;
And, though I was a soul in pain,
    My pain I could not feel.

I only knew what hunted thought
    Quickened his step, and why
He looked upon the garish day
    With such a wistful eye;
The man had killed the thing he loved,
And so he had to die.

Oscar Wilde (1856–1900) was sentenced in 1895 to two years hard labour, for homosexual practices. 'The Ballad of Reading Gaol' was published in 1898 and was written from his experiences in prison.

- In pairs, read 'The Ballad of Reading Gaol'. Think of how you could perform a reading of this to the class. Think carefully about the voice in the poem and the tone, or way, those voices speak.

- Explain what is happening in the story of this poem, then summarise your thoughts or feelings about the extract.

- Which words or phrases are the most powerful to you? What effect do they have?

PUNISHABLE BY DEATH

All of the following 'crimes' are punishable by death somewhere in the world today.

arson   political offences   robbery   rape   murder

religious activities   aiding escape of an arrested person   illegal currency dealing

embezzlement   being mercenary   theft   taking bribes

taking part in illegal strikes or demonstrations   treason   profiteering   sabotage

incitement to looting   adultery   prostitution   kidnapping

training in order to achieve the aims of communism   hoarding   defacing wall posters

spying   causing breaches of military discipline   smuggling   terrorism

overcharging   planning to overthrow the government

causing damage to state property   setting up a trade union   drug trafficking

fraud   refusal to take part in an initiation ceremony

- In pairs discuss which crimes are worse crimes than others. You may need to use a dictionary to find out what some of them are.
- Write a list of the 'Five Worst Crimes'.
- Do you believe that the death penalty should exist for any of these crimes? If so, which one(s)? Be prepared to explain why.

- Which of these are crimes against the government?
- Which are crimes against the individual?
- Do you think these two types of crime should have the same punishment?

Read the two extracts from this eye-witness account by Charles Dickens (1812–1870).

A VISIT TO NEWGATE

In the first apartment into which we were conducted – which was at the top of a staircase, and immediately over the press-room – were five-and-twenty or thirty prisoners, all under the same sentence of death, awaiting the results of the recorder's report – men of all ages and appearances, from a hardened offender with a swarthy face and grizzly beard of three day's growth, to a handsome boy, not fourteen years old, and of a singularly youthful appearance even for that age, who had been condemned for burglary. There was nothing remarkable in the appearance of these prisoners. One or two decently-dressed men were brooding with a dejected air over the fire; several little groups of two or three had been engaged in conversation at the upper end of the room, or in at the windows; and the remainder were crowded round a young man seated at a table, who appeared to be engaged in teaching the younger ones to write. The room was large, airy and clean. There was very little anxiety or mental suffering depicted in the countenance of any of the men; – they had all been sentenced to death, it is true, and the recorder's report had not yet been made; but, we question there was a man among them, notwithstanding, who did not know that although he had undergone the ceremony, it never was intended that his life should be sacrificed. On the table lay a Testament, but there were no tokens of its having been in recent use.

A few paces up the yard, and forming a continuation of the building, in which are the two rooms we have just quitted, lie the condemned cells. The entrance is by a narrow and obscure staircase leading to a dark passage, in which a charcoal stove casts a lurid tint over the objects in its immediate vicinity, and diffuses something like warmth around. From the left-hand side of this passage, the massive door of every cell on the story opens; and from it alone can they be approached.

There are three of these passages, and three of these ranges of cells, one above the other; but in size, furniture and appearance, they are all precisely alike. Prior to the recorder's report being made, all the prisoners under sentence of death are removed from the day-room at five o'clock in the afternoon, and locked up in these cells, where they are allowed a candle until seven next morning. When the warrant for a prisoner's execution arrives, he is removed to the cells and confined in one of them until he leaves it for the scaffold. He is at liberty to walk in the yard; but, both in his walk and in his cell, he is constantly attended by a turnkey who never leaves him on any pretence.

We entered the first cell. It was a stone dungeon, eight feet long by six wide, with a bench at the upper end, under which were a common rug, a bible, and prayer-book. An iron candlestick was fixed into the wall at the side; and a small high window in the back admitted as much air and light as could struggle in between a double row of heavy, cross iron bars. It contained no other furniture of any description.

• What indications are there that this was written in the nineteenth century? Make a list of the words or phrases which are your clues. Which of these are:

▶ old-fashioned words which you recognise but are no longer in regular use? What are their meanings?

▶ words or items that you are not familiar with at all? Find out their meanings.

▶ phrases whose order of words is different to the way we write today? How would you write them?

Dickens was writing about a very famous prison in London. Can you imagine what it looked like inside from his description?

• Sketch either the press-yard or the entrance to the condemned cells. Quote words or phrases from the text as labels for your sketch.

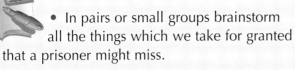

• In pairs or small groups brainstorm all the things which we take for granted that a prisoner might miss.

Do this as a spider diagram:

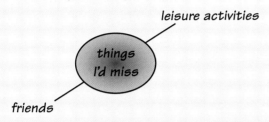

which you could extend to show different groups:

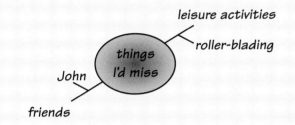

or as a list:
    sight –
    touch –
    hearing –
    taste –
    smell –

RESEARCH TOPIC – *HOW DIFFERENT IS THE MODERN PRISON OF TODAY?*

• Where could you get information about prisons? Make a list and devise an action plan for collecting all the information you can from each of your sources. For example:

The media

Think of television programmes (or films) with scenes in a prison, such as

The Governor

Prisoner Cell Block H

Dangerfield

Porridge

What are the cells like? Size? Shape? Door? Are they similar or different to Newgate?

Organise your collected data carefully to avoid confusion, drawings may help.

• Which of the items in your brainstorm do you consider yours as a right and which are luxuries? Consider the following:

**holidays   religion   entertainment
transport   money   education
clothes   accommodation
food & drink   friendship & love**

Which of these do you consider to be unimportant to you personally? Identify which are essential / important / desirable.

• Imprisonment caters for the *essential* requirements of an individual but discuss the extent to which important and desirable items are withheld by prison.

You could go on to give an oral presentation of your findings to your group or class, or you could write an essay answering the questions you have researched.

THE UNIVERSAL DECLARATION OF HUMAN RIGHTS

In December 1948 the United Nations General Assembly adopted *The Universal Declaration Of Human Rights.* They laid down how controlling forces, such as government, should behave towards their citizens, based upon the simple principle that all people have the same basic rights. This is only a statement but has been used on numerous occasions to force or embarrass companies, leaders and organisations as well as governments into respecting the rights of groups or individuals. The points on the right, called 'articles', are only a summarised selection of a much longer document. A full copy can be obtained from Amnesty International. (Amnesty International is a charity organisation which fights for human rights on behalf of individuals and groups of people.)

All human beings are born free and equal in dignity and rights.

Everyone has the right to life, liberty and security.

No-one should be subjected to torture, to cruel, inhuman or degrading treatment or punishment.

No-one should be subjected to arbitrary arrest, detention or exile.

Everyone has the freedom of opinion and expression.

Everyone has the right to freedom of assembly and association.

Everyone has the right to full security in society.

Everyone has the right to a standard of living adequate for health and well being.

Everyone has the right to participate freely in the cultural life of the community.

Everyone has duties to the community and a duty to respect the rights and freedoms of others.

- Look back at the list of crimes around the world for which the death penalty is the punishment on page 123. How many of these are in direct contravention of articles in *The Declaration of Human Rights?* What do you think about this?

BRESLAU PRISON, DECEMBER 1917

Here I am lying in a dark cell upon a mattress hard as stone; the building has its usual churchyard quiet, so that one might as well be already entombed; through the window there falls across the bed a glint of light from the lamp which burns all night in front of the prison. At intervals I can hear faintly in the distance the noise of a passing train or close at hand the dry cough of the prison guard as, in his heavy boots, he takes a few slow strides to stretch his limbs. The grind of the gravel beneath his feet has so hopeless a sound that all the weariness and futility of existence seems to be radiated thereby into the damp and gloomy night. I lie here alone and in silence, enveloped in the manifold black wrappings of darkness, tedium, unfreedom and winter – and yet my heart beats with an immeasurable and incomprehensible inner joy, just as if I were moving in the brilliant sunshine across a flowery mead. And in the darkness I smile at life, as if I were the possessor of a charm which would enable me to transform all that is evil and tragical into serenity and happiness. But when I search my mind for the cause of this joy, I find there is no cause, and can only laugh at myself – I believe that the key to the riddle is simply life itself, this deep darkness of night is soft and beautiful as velvet, if only one looks at it in the right way. The grind of the damp gravel beneath the slow and heavy tread of the prison guard is likewise a lovely little song of life – for one who has ears to hear.

MISSISSIPPI'S CHAMBER

He eased to his feet and stretched his back. His bed consisted of a piece of foam, six feet by two and a half, four inches thick, otherwise known as a mattress. It rested on a metal frame fastened securely to the floor and wall. It was covered with two sheets. Sometimes they passed out blankets in the winter. Back pain was common throughout the Row, but with time the body adjusted and there were few complaints. The prison doctor was not considered to be a friend of death row inmates.

He took two steps and leaned on his elbows through the bars. He listened to the wind and thunder, and watched the drops bounce along the windowsill and splatter on the floor. How nice it would be to step through that wall and walk through the wet grass on the other side, to stroll around the prison grounds in the driving rain, naked and crazy, soaking wet with water dripping from his hair and beard.

The horror of death row is that you die a little each day. The waiting kills you. You live in a cage and when you wake up you mark off another day and you tell yourself that you are now one day closer to death.

Sam lit a cigarette and watched the smoke float upward toward the raindrops. Weird things happen with our absurd judicial system. Courts rule this way one day and the other way the next. The same judges reach different conclusions on familiar issues. A court will ignore a wild motion or appeal for years, then one day embrace it and grant relief. Judges die and they're replaced by judges who think differently. Presidents come and go and they appoint their pals to the bench. The Supreme Court drifts one way, then another.

At times, death would be welcome. And if given the choice of death on one hand, or life on death row on the other, Sam would quickly take the gas. But there was always hope, always the slight glimmering promise that something somewhere in the vast maze of the judicial jungle would strike a chord with someone, and his case would be reversed. Every resident of the Row dreamed of the miracle reversal from heaven. And their dreams sustained them from one miserable day to the next.

Sam had recently read that there were almost twenty-five hundred inmates sentenced to die in America, and last year, 1989, only sixteen were executed. Mississippi had executed only four since 1977, the year Gary Gilmore insisted on a firing squad in Utah. There was safety in those numbers. They fortified his resolve to file even more appeals.

COMPARING THE TWO ACCOUNTS

- In pairs, consider the following questions and note down your conclusions. (Make a note of any relevant quotes.)

  How much factual information are you given in each account of life in prison?

  What emotions do the characters display?

  How does each convey their feelings about the value of life?

- Next, take a text each. Work out individually a set of points with which you could define your text as the most effective. Talk through your points with your partner, discussing each one.

- One of these passages was written by a real prisoner and one was written by an author based on information he had been given. Which one is which? List the reasons – even the dubious ones – for your decision.

- In your opinion, which extract is *really* the more effective piece of writing, and why? (Use quotations from the extracts to support your argument.)

Read this page. Which of these facts do you find the most surprising and which the most shocking? Does this information influence your personal opinion at all? You may find the information recorded here useful for your course work assignment on page 134.

FACTS FACTS FACTS FACTS FACTS FACTS FACTS FACTS FACTS FACTS FACTS FACTS FACTS

Over 20 countries now give the death penalty for drugs offences.

In 1990, China executed more than 500 people in a crack down on crime.

2029 executions in 26 countries took place in 1990.

1964 saw the last two male hangings in the UK.

The death penalty still exists in the UK for high treason, piracy and, if you are a member of the armed forces, for treason and spying.

In England in the eighteenth century, the death penalty was the punishment for at least 50 offences including stealing, shoplifting and poaching.

Death by electrocution, poisonous gas and lethal injection of poison are all methods used in the USA but no other country.

Death from shooting is virtually instantaneous **if** the person is shot as very close quarters through the skull.

Electrocution produces visible destructive effects as the body's internal organs are burned.

Beheading by sword sometimes requires several blows to sever the neck.

In 1990–92 in the USA, 260 people per year were sentenced to death. In 1991 the number of murders was about 25,000. Thus only about 1% of murderers got the death penalty.

The last public execution in the USA took place in Kentucky in 1936. It was estimated that it attracted 15,000 observers.

Amnesty International polls conducted in six states in America consistently showed that citizens prefer life imprisonment to death when offered the choice between the two alternatives.

In Saudi Arabia execution is by beheading in public. In the first four months of 1995 there were 90 such executions – nearly 70% of those executed were foreigners.

During the apartheid era in South Africa, hundreds of people were executed each year by hanging – over 1,500 death sentences were passed between 1978 and 1987.

Ruth Ellis, a 28-year-old model, was the last woman to be hanged in this country in 1955.

FACTS FACTS FACTS FACTS FACTS FACTS FACTS FACTS FACTS FACTS FACTS FACTS FACTS

Read the following, think very carefully about each statement, and decide which statements you agree with. Jot down your thoughts and be prepared to discuss your choice and reasons with a partner.

OPINIONS OPINIONS OPINIONS OPINIONS OPINIONS OPINIONS OPINIONS OPINIONS

THE CASE FOR ABOLISHING THE DEATH PENALTY FOR MURDER

We all have the right to life, as cited in *The Universal Declaration of Human Rights*.

Knowing you may die for your crime is not a deterrent – the threat of death doesn't stop people from driving dangerously or under the influence of alcohol.

The judicial system is imperfect, and innocent people are often sentenced for crimes they didn't commit.

The process of waiting for the death penalty to be enforced makes the penalty itself premeditated and cold-blooded.

It is impossible to show that killing is wrong if that is the punishment given for such crimes.

No-one has the right to take away the life of another person.

Redemption is better than revenge.

Life imprisonment is a suitable punishment and answers most of the public's demands.

THE CASE FOR RETAINING THE DEATH PENALTY FOR MURDER

Those who have committed a crime which goes against *The Declaration of Human Rights* cannot then expect to defend themselves by that Declaration.

The death penalty acts as a form of deterrent, making possible murderers re-consider their actions.

Society needs to be secure and free from murderers.

Taxpayers' money should not be spent on supporting those who have committed inhumane acts against that community.

The state/country must show its disapproval of serious law breakers.

It is not fair for the victim's family that a murderer should go on living.

We should not risk dangerous criminals being released at some stage in the future in case they commit the same crime again.

By having the death penalty the lives of your friends and family, or your own life, could be saved one day.

OPINIONS OPINIONS OPINIONS OPINIONS OPINIONS OPINIONS OPINIONS OPINIONS

THE EXECUTION

In this section of the unit you will look at two short extracts and analyse the content, the language, the point of view, and your impressions. At the end of this section you will write a magazine article based on the information you have read and on your own point of view.

Read the first extract carefully at least twice.

"How many men have died in Mississippi's chamber?" he asked.

"It was first used here in 1954, or thereabouts. Between then and 1970, they killed thirty-five men. No women. After Furman in 1972 it sat idle until Teddy Doyle Meeks in 1982. They've used it three times since then, so that's a total of thirty-nine. I'll be number forty."

He began pacing again, now much slower. "It's a terribly inefficient way to kill people," he said, much like a professor in front of a classroom. "And it's dangerous. Dangerous of course to the poor guy strapped in the chair, but also to those outside the chamber. Those damned things are old and they all leak to some degree. The seals and gaskets rot and crumble, and the cost of building a chamber that will not leak is prohibitive. A small leak could be deadly to the executioner or anyone standing nearby. There are always a handful of people standing in the little room just outside the chamber. There are two doors to this little room, and they are always closed during an execution. If any of the gas leaked from the chamber into the room, they'd croak right there on the floor.

Not a bad idea, come to think of it.

"The witnesses are also in a great deal of danger, and they don't have a clue. There's nothing between them and the chamber except for a row of windows, which are old and equally subject to leakage. They're also in a small room with the door closed, and if there's a gas leak of any size these gawking fools get gassed too.

"But the real danger comes afterward. There's a wire they stick to your ribs and it runs through a hole in the chamber to outside where a doctor monitors the heartbeat. Once the doctor says the guy is dead, they open a valve on top of the chamber and the gas is supposed to evaporate. Most of it does. They'll wait fifteen minutes or so, then open the door. The cooler air from outside that's used to evacuate the chamber causes a problem because it mixes with the remaining gas and condenses on everything inside. It creates a death trap for anyone going in. It's extremely dangerous, and most of these clowns don't realise how serious it is. There's a residue of prussic acid on everything – walls, windows, floor, ceiling, door, and, of course, the dead guy.

"They spray the chamber and the corpse with ammonia to neutralise the remaining gas, then the removal team or whatever it's called goes in with oxygen masks. They'll wash the inmate a second time with ammonia or chlorine bleach because the poison oozes through the pores in the skin. While he's still strapped in the chair, they cut his clothes off, put them in a bag, and burn them. In the old days they allowed the guy to wear only a pair of shorts so their job would be easier. But now they're such sweethearts they allow us to wear whatever we want."

From *The Chamber* by John Grisham

Before you answer the following questions, think about how to organise your notes so that you can refer to them later.

- • What is happening in this extract? Who is doing most of the talking? Explain how you know.

- • Discuss or record your reaction to this piece of writing.

- • Record the main points made in this extract:

  a) about the procedures of judicial execution.

  b) about the dangers of judicial execution.

- • Would you say that the information given in this extract is likely to be factually accurate or not? Why/why not?

- • Explain what you think the writer of this extract wants to convey to the reader. Is the writer in favour of the death penalty or not? (*Note:* The writer is not the speaker in the extract.)

- • Where do you think the extract comes from? What clues are there in the text?

Sister Helen Prejean, a Catholic nun, befriended Pat Sonnier, the murderer of two teenage girls, after being invited to write to him on death row. Her book, *Dead Man Walking*, is subtitled 'An eyewitness account of the Death Penalty in the United States'. Read the following extract carefully.

Pat is in the chair now and guards are moving quickly, removing the leg irons and handcuffs and replacing them with the leather straps. One guard has removed his left shoe. They are strapping his trunk, his legs, his arms. He finds my face. He says, "I love you." I stretch my hand toward him

"I love you, too."

He attempts a smile (he told me he would try to smile) but manages only to twitch.

A metal cap is placed on his head and an electrode is screwed in at the top and connected to a wire that comes from a box behind the chair. An electrode is fastened to his leg. A strap placed around his chin holds his head tightly against the back of the chair. He grimaces. He cannot speak anymore. A greyish green cloth is placed over his face.

Millard says, "Father forgive them, for they know not what they do."

Only the warden remains in the room now, only the warden and the man strapped into the chair. The red telephone is silent. I close my eyes and do not see as the warden nods his head, the signal to the executioner to do his work.

I hear three clanks as the switch is pulled with pauses in between. Nineteen hundred volts, then let the body cool, then five hundred volts, pause again, then nineteen hundred volts. "Christ, be with him, have mercy on him," I pray silently.

I look up. His left hand has gripped the arm of the chair evenly but the fingers of his right hand are curled upward.

The warden says over the microphone that we will wait a few minutes for the doctor to make the "final check". Then the prison doctor, who has been sitting with the witnesses, goes to the body in the chair and lifts the mask and raises the eyelids and shines the light of a small flashlight into the eyes and raises up the clean white shirt and puts his stethoscope against the heart and listens and then says to the warden that, yes, this man is dead. Warden Maggio looks up at the clock and announces the time of death: 12.15 a.m. His eyes happen to look into mine. He lowers his eyes.

The witnesses are lead from the room. As we walk through the lobby, I go over to the old priest and ask him to give me communion for "both of us", as Pat had requested. I go to where the witnesses are gathered to sign the papers. Everyone is silent. All you can hear is the papers being shuffled across the white tablecloth and the scrawling of ballpoint pens as people put their signatures on three copies of the official state papers.

- What does Sister Helen Prejean think about the death penalty? How do you know? Make a note of your conclusions, supporting them with quotations.

THE CHAMBER and DEAD MAN WALKING

Look carefully again at the two pieces of writing. Add to your notes, answering the following questions.

1 How does the language differ in each extract?

Look carefully at the actual words used. Which one sounds more like everyday (colloquial) speech? What type of writing does the other extract remind you of?

Dead Man Walking has very short sentences at times. When has the author chosen to use short sentences and how do these affect your reading?

Analyse the sentences in the extract from *The Chamber.* Does it make use of short sentences?

What does this add to your understanding of or feelings about these two extracts?

One extract is written in the present tense, the other is in the past tense. Was this apparent while you were reading? What impressions do you gain as a reader from the use of each tense?

2 How much factual detail is included in each extract?

Particular details have been selected by the author – what impact do these details have?

How much do we learn about people's feelings?

3 From whose point of view is each extract told?

Are you shown the situation from the point of view of the author or a character? What difference does this make to you as a reader?

4 What impression of the two prisoners do you get? Explain how the writer achieves this.

5 Discuss with a partner which extract is more or less effective as an account of an execution. Explain carefully and by referring to particular parts of the extracts.

FACING THE GALLOWS

• First, read just the headline and the sub-headline of the news article from the *Daily Mail* (opposite).

How is this headline different to usual newspaper headlines? How do you react to the two statements?

• Now read the whole article. When you have read it, go back to the highlighted sections. Rewrite each one in two forms:

1. to reinforce the obvious point

2. to emphasise the underlying meaning

For example: 'That was all the prison guards said'.

1 The prison guards said, 'You are going to be hanged in three days time'.

2 Even though Scripps asked them many questions about his hanging, the guards refused to give him any more information.

• What does the reporter, Paul Harris, think about John Scripps? What is the newspaper's point of view on this particular execution?

• How does the article build up the drama of the event?

The very last Scripps heard was the sharp pull of a lever and the swing of a trap door

From PAUL HARRIS IN SINGAPORE

They shook John Scripps awake at nine o'clock on Tuesday morning and told him he was going to be hanged in three days. That was all the prison guard said.

No attempt at explanation or condolence – but no pretence either that as a convicted murderer, Scripps's execution in Singapore was anything other than routine.

At Changi prison they nearly always hang on Fridays. Scripps, who killed South African tourist Gerard Lowe in a hotel room, chopped up his body and dumped the parts in Singapore harbour – had been expecting it to happen.

But after six months on Death Row it still took a while to sink in. Scripps had refused to be weighed and fitted for the gallows, so the dynamics of the rope and the drop were estimated rather than exact.

In a prison where they have hanged at least 152 people in 20 years, they seldom get it wrong.

Yesterday as dawn broke outside his windowless cell, John Martin Scripps – petty thief, burglar, heroin-smuggler and suspected serial killer – prepared himself to earn a brief mention in criminal history.

He was about to become the first Briton to hang for murder in more than 30 years, his only moment of dubious achievement in a largely dismal life.

Scripps, 36, was determined not to waste it. Like some would-be tough guy in an old movie, he had told his family the last time they saw him: 'I'm not going quietly.'

He would go naked and screaming in protest to the gallows, he insisted. More in arrogance than dignity, he pledged that his performance in the face of hanging would 'make sure it's one they remember'.

The tap on the shoulder came around 5am, from two prison officers and a Roman Catholic priest. Scripps was told to dress in his own clothes. He refused. He was offered a last breakfast.

When the time came, he was taken along the corridor with prison officers either side of him.

The walk from his cell to the gallows can be counted in seconds but is an eternity for those who make the journey.

He put up a struggle and shouted something about coming back as a spirit. No-one took much notice.

The execution room has one door in and one door out – to the gallows.

With a hood on his head and his hands tied behind his back, Scripps was led the final few steps.

The noose was already at the right height and he walked straight into it. The hangman made a final adjustment.

No clemency now, no mercy, no escape. Only a prayer from the priest with a small black book held tightly in both hands.

Then, within seconds, the last sound Scripps would hear – the sharp pull of a lever and the swing of the trap door beneath him.

At 6.37am precisely, his brief moment of fame was over.

They hanged him with two Singapore-Chinese drug traffickers. Outside the jail, as cars and buses passed by in the soft, humid drizzle, one of the families burned joss-sticks for their condemned relative.

The prison officers checked the dead men's names one by one in the record book and went back to work. It was strictly business, Singapore style.

In the end Scripps's dramatic performance made no difference. The priest who administered the last rites was the only public witness.

'He put up a brief struggle,' said Father Eugene Vaaz. 'If he hadn't, then perhaps it would have been easier for him.'

Scripps, gaunt and pale from his months inside, told the priest that he didn't want any of his organs donated for medical services because he wanted his family to see him intact afterwards.

His mother Jean Scripps and sister Janet Scripps spent much of the afternoon and evening sitting with the body in its casket at a private location in Singapore. They will fly him back to England for a funeral and cremation.

Course work assignment

Choose one of the following tasks or essays as a course work assignment. You can carry out either **original/personal writing** or **non-fiction writing to inform, explain or describe.**

1   Write a diary for an imaginary prisoner based on the information in 'Ballad of Reading Goal', 'A Visit to Newgate', 'Breslau Prison' or *The Chamber.*

2   Record your personal thoughts and opinions about the death penalty using specific references to the extracts you have read.

3   Use what you have learned from the newspaper article and the extracts from *The Chamber* and *Dead Man Walking* to write a magazine article which discusses the procedures of executing a prisoner on Death Row. Before you begin, read the advice in the Help box.

HELP

The article should:

*   **be targeted at a specific audience**

    – name the magazine and think about who buys it. What style of writing is appropriate?

*   **be structured**

    – start with an introductory paragraph outlining the general subject

    – arrange the information about execution in a logical, chronological order

    – include all essential information in the first half of the article, people may not read all of it

    – come to a point (of view?) at the end

*   **convey your point of view**

    – emphasise the information which is strongest for your opinion

    – use language which will emphasise the feelings you want to encourage in the reader, even when giving factual information

MEDIA ANALYSIS

Sister Helen Prejean's story was portrayed in the film *Dead Man Walking* in 1996. Here are four reviews of the film.

DEAD MAN WALKING

TIM ROBBINS' DEVASTATING DEATH Row Drama is so even-handed in probing sore issues of the capital punishment debate and so deliberately free of polemic or easy sentiment that it is all the stronger: both gut-wrenchingly emotive and genuinely thought-provoking. Based on the real experiences and insights of Sister Helen Prejean, a Catholic nun in Louisiana whose community service took her into the state penitentiary's death house, the film explores moral truth, the consequences of murder, and the human need for revenge.

Sister Helen (Sarandon) replies to a letter from lonely, frightened Matthew Poncelet (Penn), a condemned rapist and murderer awaiting execution. Despite her own misgivings and outside pressure to distance herself from him, she becomes his visitor, spiritual adviser and friend. For nun and killer it is a remarkable journey. Poncelet is not charming or even likeable, nor is he a victim of injustice. His crime was heinous. He is repellent, bigoted trash. But Sister Helen is a woman centred on faith in God and humanity. Confronting his demons, she hopes to move him to take responsibility for his life, to face death with honesty.

Sarandon, as ever, is superlative. Penn is *beyond* superlatives. Unflinchingly he presents a cold, hard, despicable individual, then rips him inside out until the monster is revealed to be a human being. Their dual achievement is the true intimacy they develop despite the prison barriers of wire and window, Robbins skilfully working with the space between them.

Beyond these two and Sister Helen's fight for Poncelet's soul, Robbins gives enormous weight to the victims of the crime. The ordeal of the young couple murdered is glimpsed and, finally, remembered. The pain, grief and rage for vengeance in those who mourn them are dutifully respected.

It may be regarded as a failing that Robbins' apparent lack of certainty in the ethical conflict laid out prevents him verbalising an unequivocal pro or con answer. Instead, he very effectively forces the viewer to ask, with no little distress, is it ever right to kill? ★★★★

From *Empire,* April 1996

DEAD ON TARGET
FILM OF THE WEEK

For sheer audacity in this age of the easy thrill and the feelgood film, Tim Robbins's *Dead Man Walking* probably deserved an Oscar rather more than *Braveheart*, Mel Gibson's admittedly entertaining Highland fling. It's not exactly a plea against capital punishment but a film which suggests that official killings tend to be as innately barbarous as those committed by individuals.

Based on the memoirs of Sister Helen Prejean, a Catholic nun, it recounts the story of her awkward relationship with Matthew Poncelet, a prisoner on Death Row. He is accused of the savage murder of a courting couple and the hideous rape of the girl.

He claims innocence, but few believe that it was his companion who did the deed, and it isn't surprising. He is a low-life, not a sympathetic character, and the nun, who does social work among the poor of New Orleans, is told she is out of her depth when she replies to his request for a visit.

Supporting his plea for a pardon, though unconvinced by his story, she engages a lawyer to represent the man at the Pardon Board hearing and persuades his reluctant mother to attend.

Upon this structure, Robbins builds a film that carefully eschews the usual Hollywood sentimentality. It is directed with much more certainty than *Bob Roberts*; Robbins's engaging but uneven first film. It is also shot with real distinction by Roger Deakins, the British cinematographer, has an intelligent and effective music score and, above all, has at its centre two remarkable performances by Susan Sarandon and Sean Penn.

Sarandon's Oscar, a long time coming, was well deserved. She makes Sister Helen something less than a saint and never entirely certain of herself. She is, for instance, riven with doubt when the parents of the murdered couple accuse her of being more concerned with comforting the killer than helping them through an equally terrible time. And she finds the prisoner as suspicious of her motives as she is of his. She wants to save a soul even if it doesn't much want to be saved. But she doesn't know how to go about it honestly.

Robbins's screenplay emphasises her dilemmas with sophistication, as does his direction, which carefully underlines the essential divide between the two. But it still takes a very considerable actress – which we know Sarandon to be – to accomplish her part without mawkishness and to achieve, in the final cathartic prison sequences, the right balance between a natural horror of the proceedings and the charitable determination to comfort, offering herself as "the face of love", even to evil.

Sean Penn, in the sort of part that suits his introspective but incandescent style of acting, is equally good as the condemned man – again because Robbins allows his character to seem other than a clichéd version of an emotionally deprived psychopath. He is repellent until he forces himself to tell the truth and then, despite neo-Nazi leanings, possessed of a kind of hopeless courage which will not be defeated. And he makes the final moments of the film – as he is clinically prepared for death in a prison that looks like a triumph for bureaucracy, rather than a hellhole – into a tour de force of a sort.

The film perhaps makes the mistake of too many flashbacks – it might have been better had we never seen either the crime as he imagines it or as it actually took place. There's enough subtlety in it without that kind of emotional underlining.

But *Dead Man Walking* is the kind of work that suddenly shows us that the American cinema is not always predicated towards an easy fluency that sets up problems, examines them and then takes the easy way out.

There's still someone out there who, though clearly trying to make a film people will want to see, wishes to do as little as possible to seduce them and as much as possible to make them think.

From *The Guardian*, 28 March 1996

When Sister Helen Prejean (Susan Sarandon), a nun who works with the (mainly black) local poor, first visits the Louisiana State Penitentiary in response to a letter from Death Row inmate Matthew Poncelet (Sean Penn), asking for help in an appeal against his impending execution, she's barely prepared for the ethical, emotional and spiritual turmoil she's letting herself in for. With politicians and radio fundamentalists advocating tougher measures, the chances of a stay of execution are slim for an unrepentant, poor white trash racist who insists he only watched, rather than participated in, the rape and murder of a teenage couple six years earlier. And if his appeal is denied, will Helen have the strength not merely to continue as his spiritual adviser, but to guide her arrogant, hate-filled charge towards some sort of redemption?

Inspired by the real-life Prejean's experiences, Tim Robbins' film may not be especially original (in some respects it resembles an American version of Kieslowski's 'A Short Film About Killing'), but it is a brave, intelligent and very moving exploration of the issues surrounding capital punishment. Though it finally takes a firm stand against institutionalised murder, Robbins' tough, balanced script never succumbs to special pleading; Poncelet (superbly played by Penn in bouffant hair and goatee) is a very nasty piece of work, while the vengeful grief of the victims' families are depicted with sympathy and respect. And while the message is made clear by the variety and pertinence of the questions it raises – the film never degenerates into dry thesis, thanks largely to the excellence of the vivid performances (Sarandon complements Penn perfectly, with strong support from Robert Prosky, Scott Wilson, R Lee Erney et al). Exemplary stuff.

From *Timeout*, 27 March 1996

A captive audience

★★★★★ Masterpiece
★★★★★ Dead Man Walking (15)

Dead Man Walking is the best film about execution I've ever seen. It drags you through all the little tortures that go through a man's mind as he realises he's going to be killed. It also shows you the grief of the victims' families being horribly rekindled as the killer's execution day comes closer. And then there are the shadowy, terrifying scenes of the original rapes and murders. There's not much light relief here (I counted two moments of deadpan humour). It's so perfectly disturbing, in fact, that it makes you feel it's you, and

not a celluloid character, who will die by lethal injection at the end. It's the most powerful film I've seen since *Schindler's List*.

'Dead Man Walking' are the words a prison guard must call out just when the condemned man leaves the holding cell and begins his walk down the corridor towards the execution chamber. You might be thinking, 'I've seen that kind of thing before.' You might even be thinking, 'I've seen Mel Gibson hung, drawn and quartered.' But you've seen nothing like this.

Sean Penn is the only actor I've ever seen who plays a condemned man convincingly. Normally, they say a few brave words and get strung up. But that can't be normal, can it? You'd be frightened out of your wits. When you're in Death House, a week before your

execution, Death Row looks like a holiday camp. When you're on your last day, saying goodbye to your family, the early stages of the Death House seem like happy childhood memories. When you're strapped to the trolley with a lethal needle in your arm, that moment when the guard calls out 'Dead man walking' is part of your idyllic past. Sean Penn conveys all of this. It's an amazingly fine piece of acting.

Tim Robbins, who directed this film, tells you the story of this condemned man (based on real-life killer Elmo Patrick Sonnier) through the eyes of a nun who visits him during his last few days. The nun is played by Susan Sarandon, who won an Oscar for the role. Sarandon arrives at Death Row. She's shocked at the brutality. Then

she meets the victims' families, and she's shocked because they can't stand her. Then she gets to know them and she's torn apart by their pain as they reconstruct the days after their children disappeared. Here, Robbins uses his camera documentary-style, keeping it on people for long stretches; he manages to wring meaning out of throat-clearings and brave smiles.

And the time is ticking away, moving you closer to the moment you're dreading more and more. I've never dreaded a screen death so keenly. It's extremely disturbing and thought-provoking. And if you think there's anything humane about the lethal injection, think again. Do you have any idea what it's like? I'd rather be shot, anyway.

From *Night & Day*, Mail on Sunday, 31 March 1996

- In a group of four, divide the reviews between you so you each concentrate on one of them. Look carefully at your own review, and decide what audience you think it is aimed at – adults? young people? film fans? Jot down any words or phrases which give clues about who the audience might be.

Then briefly jot down, in the chart format below, what your review tells you about the following things:

Review	storyline/plot	acting	director	the 'real' events

- Now compare your chart with the charts of others in your group. Does each review cover the same points and give the same factual information? How much of the story does each review give away? Do they all seem to share the same ideas about the film? Talk about how they differ, and why.

- Which review do you find the most persuasive, either in encouraging you to see the film, or to avoid it? Using the notes and your charts to help you, write a few paragraphs commenting on your expectations of the film based on the evidence of the reviews. Then add a concluding paragraph summarising the differences between the reviews.

- Now choose a film or TV drama you have seen recently which also deals with a difficult or controversial topic. Write a review of 250 words for a magazine, a tabloid or a broadsheet newspaper, thinking carefully about the following:

  ▶ your readers

  ▶ your choice of language

  ▶ factual information about the film/drama

  ▶ your own opinion of the film/drama

  ▶ the audience most likely to enjoy the film drama

Imagine you have been asked to design a new poster promoting *Dead Man Walking*. Your poster must give a strong sense of:

the controversial nature of the film

the prison environment

the relationship between Poncelet (the prisoner) and Sister Helen

- Using the research you have completed so far, sketch a rough draft of your design, including title, credits and a slogan which summarise the film. Don't worry about brilliant artwork – a matchstick-person sketch will do. Then write

an analysis of your design which explains the following points:

▶ the visual elements you intend to emphasise

▶ reasons for your choice of images, colour and layout

▶ the style of lettering you have chosen for the title and slogan

▶ the audience you are hoping to attract, and why you think your poster will work

▶ the research (from work in this unit, and from your own analysis of other film posters) which you have drawn on to develop your design

FROM WORDS TO IMAGES

The film *Dead Man Walking* was based on the account by Sister Helen Prejean. The Director's task was not easy. He had to find ways of visually showing not only the story, action and events of the plot, but also:

▶ the feelings and emotions of the characters

▶ background information the viewer needs to make sense of the story

▶ particular points of view or comments about the story

He had to do this through his use of the camera, sound-track and lighting, and through the sequence and pace of his chosen camera shots – in other words, his use of editing.

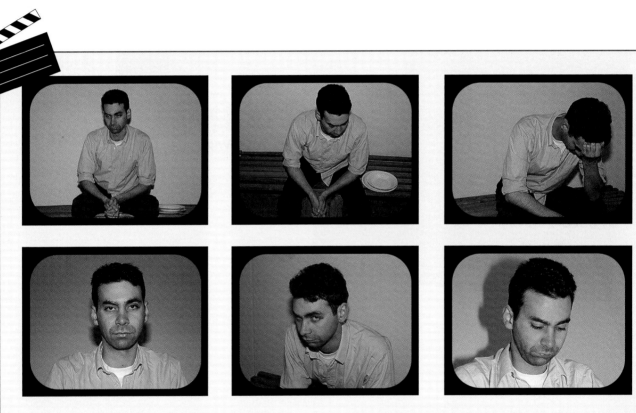

- If you were directing a film about a prisoner on Death Row, which shot/s would you use to give the atmosphere that this man is:

  an important character in the film

  a minor character in the film

  depressed

  isolated and lonely

  imprisoned in a small space

  powerless

  sinister

- Try experimenting by combining one or more of the images on the next page, with two or more of the prisoner pictures to create a story without words. Then suggest a soundtrack – words, music or sound-effects – to build up atmosphere.

- See how many different variations you can create, using a maximum of five shots each time. Each one will create a different atmosphere, or tell a slightly different story. Write a short paragraph about each sequence, explaining the effect and story you think it might convey.

CREATING A STORYBOARD

A storyboard is sometimes used by a Director to work out ideas visually before filming. It is a way of breaking down each scene of a film into a sequence of sketches showing exactly what the camera will see in each shot, together with details of the soundtrack.

Shot no.	Vision	Shot description / Camera Movement	Sound

As well as drawn images for each shot, the storyboard should also include the following:

- ▶ instructions for type of shot
- ▶ camera movement – such as **zoom in** or **out, pan left** or **right, tilt up** or **down, tracking shot** (following the action)
- ▶ spoken dialogue
- ▶ sound effects and/or music
- ▶ particular lighting instructions

These are all the elements which will eventually build up atmosphere and tell the story from a particular point of view. For example:

TEXT

He eased to his feet and stretched his back. His bed consisted of a piece of foam, six feet by two and a half, four inches thick, otherwise known as a mattress. It rested on a metal frame fastened securely to the floor and wall. It was covered with two sheets. Sometimes they passed out blankets in the winter. Back pain was common throughout the Row, but with time the body adjusted and there were few complaints. The prison doctor was not considered to be a friend of death row inmates.

He took two steps and leaned on his elbows through the bars. He listened to the wind and thunder, and watched the drops bounce along the windowsill and splatter on the floor. How nice it would be to step through that wall and walk through the wet grass on the other side, to stroll around the prison grounds in the driving rain, naked and crazy, soaking wet with water dripping from his hair and beard.

IDEAS FOR SHOTS TO STORYBOARD

1 Establishing shot, close-up of man's face, zoom out to reveal prison cell.

2 Focus on man as he sits up an swings legs to floor. We hear his breathing only.

3 He stands and stretches, long shot to emphasise the smallness of the cell. Pan around to cell bars.

4 Camera moves towards bars as if it is the man. We see his two hands grip the bars and then relax and move through the gaps. Close up. No sound except for the wind.

5 Close up of his face through the bars to sound of wind and rain (getting louder).

6 Mid-shot of window.

7 Close up of his face ...

- Select one of the following extracts you have read in this unit. From:

  'The Ballad of Reading Gaol'

  'A Visit to Newgate'

  'Breslau Prison'

  The Chamber

  Dead Man Walking

- Copy the extract and jot down your ideas for possible storyboard shots, as in the example above.

  Then use your ideas to produce a storyboard with full instructions for sound, lighting, and camera movement. Again, don't worry about drawing skills – your sketches should be simple and clear, and you can add notes to indicate extra elements like where the light is coming from, the direction of the camera movement, and so on.

- When you have completed your storyboard, write a detailed, shot-by-shot evaluation of what you have chosen to include, and why. If you have had to change or leave out any details from the original, or introduce new images of your own, explain why you have done so. Finish your evaluation with a paragraph explaining what you think your version will add to the original, what you think works well, and what you have had difficulty with. You should aim to write one or two sides of A4.

ORAL ASSIGNMENT

Now that you have a much better informed point of view about the issue of the Death Penalty, complete one of the following tasks as an oral assignment.

1 Use the information you have gathered so far for a presentation to the class. This should include two or three different sections for example: what you thought about the death penalty at the beginning of this unit; facts and opinions which influenced you; what do you think about the death penalty now. This could be a group presentation.

2 Discuss whether or not states in the USA should be encouraged to abolish the death penalty for all or some crimes.

3 Terrorism is an act of violence which is politically motivated. The act is sometimes aimed at government targets, sometimes at randomly selected civilians. Terrorism is often carried out by extreme left or right wing groups whose intention is to draw mass attention to their cause. The disruption to society and the fear created by these acts are their means of forcing governments to listen to their demands.

List the acts of terrorism that you know have taken place during the last year. Should the death penalty be re-introduced in this country for acts of terrorism?

4 'First, I am totally against the death penalty by any means. It is my belief that society should set the standard of non-violence and show by example its commitment to this. In saying this I accept that we have violent individuals in our midst who have to be dealt with. Indeed, I am one. In 1967 I was sentenced to life imprisonment with a recommended minimum of fifteen years. I was aged 23. At that time I was brutalised by prison staff and on three occasions almost lost my life. The situation became so bad that I was eventually kept naked inside a cell and given one book per week to read. I was kept like this for six and a half years. This sort of treatment made me more resentful and filled me with hatred for prison officers and the public in general; the latter because they locked people like me up for being violent but turned a blind eye when prison officers brutalised prisoners.

This situation only erupted in further violence and made the situation worse. Having played the ultimate in the punitive line the authorities were left helpless. It was at this point that the prison authorities took another direction. They opened a place called the Special Unit and asked for volunteer staff. They were quite courageous people who did not want violence – either to use it or to have it used on them. As a result of this much more progressive regime I began to find I had other abilities. I became a sculptor, a writer, and learnt a whole new set of skills. But more than this I learned a lot more about me and why people get into trouble.

As a result of this I am now working in the poverty-ridden streets I came from and doing work that prevents many youngsters getting into trouble. So if I had been hanged it would have been for a crime that I did not commit and second, perhaps many of the youngsters I work with and have helped may have ended up on murder charges.'

From A Sense of Freedom by Jimmy Boyle

Discuss the points made by Jimmy Boyle about punishment and rehabilitation.

WHAT NEXT?

Re read the extract from 'The Ballad of Reading Gaol' at the beginning of this unit. This next extract from the poem follows on immediately from that. Read it at least twice on your own, then consider what the writer might be saying about the death penalty.

Yet each man kills the thing he loves,
    By each let this be heard,
Some do it with a bitter look,
    Some with a flattering word,
The coward does it with a kiss,
    The brave man with a sword!

Some kill their love when they are young,
    And some when they are old;
Some strangle with the hands of Lust,
    Some with the hands of Gold:
The kindest use a knife, because
    The dead so soon grow cold.

Some love too little, some too long,
    Some sell, and others buy;
Some do the deed with many tears,
    And some without a sigh:
For each man kills the thing he loves,
    Yet each man does not die.

He does not die a death of shame
    On a day of dark disgrace,
Nor have a noose about his neck,
    Nor a cloth about his face,
Nor drop feet foremost through the floor
    Into an empty space.

READING LIST

The Chamber by John Grisham

Dead Man Walking by Helen Prejean

A Taste of Freedom by Jimmy Boyle

Stolen Years by Paul Hill

The Green Mile by Stephen King

The Man Died by Wole Soyinka

Biko by Donald Woods

When the State Kills – Amnesty International

Reportage edited by Geoff Barton

Solo 3 – Monologues for Drama in English by John Goodwin and Bill Taylor

VIEWING LIST

Fourteen Days in May

Dance With a Stranger

Live! On Death Row

The Shawshank Redemption

Too Young To Die

The Reading Odyssey

The aim of this unit is to enable you to develop your awareness of the way writers use and explore similar themes. You will be studying the different types of text, and will be learning to compare styles, approaches and ideas.

In working through this unit, you will develop your skills as:

SPEAKERS AND LISTENERS

by discussing the treatment of themes in extracts from different genres
by reading speeches aloud and reading in role
by giving a short presentation to your group

READERS

by studying extracts of non-fiction, media texts, pre-twentieth century and twentieth century prose, poetry, and drama
by comparing the treatment of a theme in different genres
by researching material of your own, such as postcards, songs, poems, advertisements

WRITERS

by recording your ideas in an easy-to-use reference chart
by writing to advertise, inform and persuade readers of a newsletter
by completing a written piece of course work

YOUR READING ODYSSEY

Everybody's choice of reading is personal. Their 'reading journey' is unique. Nonetheless, part of the pleasure that is to be had from reading is the discovery that somebody else has read the same book as you and feels the same way about it.

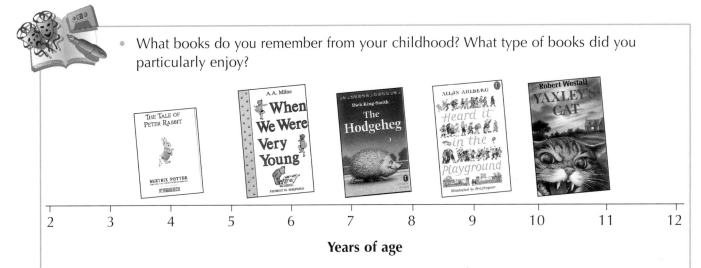

- What books do you remember from your childhood? What type of books did you particularly enjoy?

Years of age

- Design your own time line of reading – your 'reading history'.

- Compare your reading history with a friend's. What do they have in common?

When films or books share similar characteristics or features, they can be said to belong to the same 'genre'. Science fiction, romance, horror, travel writing, are all examples of genre.

- Take another look at your own reading history. Which books could be said to form part of the same genre?

What is interesting as we gain experience as readers is that we begin to recognise patterns and links. We begin to have preconceptions about what might be going to happen, based on our past reading, and we get better at predicting what might happen next. As a test of this, see how good you are at guessing from its title what a book is going to be about.

- Which genre do you think each of the titles above might belong to? What aspects of the genre do they highlight?

- Invent some of your own titles, each of which seem to suggest a particular genre. Swap with another group, and see if they can guess the genre and the possible contents.

In this unit you are going to explore the way two particular themes, *islands* and *romance*, are used in a variety of genres.

PRECIOUS STONES FOR PRECIOUS MOMENTS

Four hundred years after they were discovered by Portuguese navigators, the Seychelles remain the most beautiful and unspoiled islands in the world. These 115 granitic and coral islands, set like gems in the turquoise waters of the Indian Ocean, enjoy a comfortable, tropical climate year round. There's a wide choice of hotels to suit all tastes and budgets, from luxury suites to beach bungalows, all blending perfectly with their natural surroundings. With the prospect of a beach to yourself, countless opportunities for island-hopping, and some of the best diving and yachting imaginable in the company of the friendly Creoles, no wonder this is the world's most sought-after holiday destination. For more information on planning your holiday of a lifetime, please contact your Seychelles Tourist Office.

Seychelles
TREASURE EVERY MOMENT

ISLANDS

Writers have always been interested in islands. From classic texts like *Treasure Island* to blockbuster films like *Jurassic Park,* they exercise an enduring fascination.

• Using your skills of prediction, and your knowledge of books from your reading history, what do you associate with the concept of an island? Jot down your initial ideas, so that you can compare them with the discoveries you will make as you work through this unit.

ISLAND – THE MYTH

Writers expect readers to make certain associations. They build on our preconceptions (what we know and expect based on our past experience). Some writers reinforce the stereotype, the fantasy – the advertisement on the opposite page uses a variety of media techniques to promote a particular view of island holidays.

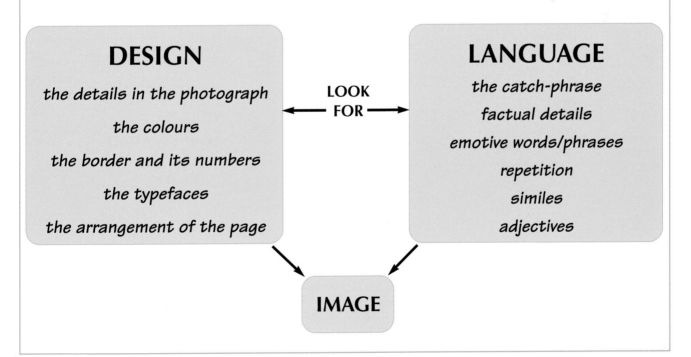

READING BETWEEN THE LINES

• In pairs, study the design and the language used in the advertisement. What is being suggested by each detail and each phrase used? What associations are readers expected to make? What 'image' is being created?

DESIGN

the details in the photograph

the colours

the border and its numbers

the typefaces

the arrangement of the page

LOOK ⟷ FOR

LANGUAGE

the catch-phrase

factual details

emotive words/phrases

repetition

similes

adjectives

IMAGE

Consider the similarities and differences in the use of the island idea as you read this extract from *Richard II* by William Shakespeare. Here, one of the characters expresses his ideas about his country, his land…

This royal throne of kings, this scepter'd isle,
This earth of majesty, this seat of Mars,   ◄——— *What is being emphasised here?*
This other Eden, demi-paradise;   ◄——— *the Roman god of war*
This fortress, built by nature for herself,   ——— *like heaven*
Against infection, and the hand of war;
This happy breed of men, this little world;   ◄——— *sounds like a special race of people*
This precious stone set in the silver sea,
Which serves it in the office of a wall,   *?*
Or as a moat defensive to a house,
Against the envy of less happier lands;
This blessed plot, this earth, this realm, this England.

• How is the concept of an island used in the advert for the Seychelles and in the extract from *Richard II?* Can you identify the similarities and differences between them?

• Record your findings on a grid, set out in columns, like the one shown here.

CONCEPTS	Seychelles advert	Richard II	
Excellence	✔	✔	
Perfection	✔	✔	

• What else would you include? Add other columns to your grid as you study each of the extracts in this unit.

ISLANDS – UTOPIA?

In 1516, Sir Thomas More wrote *Utopia*, a book describing an imaginary island with a perfect social and political system. This idea is still very much alive, as a recent article in *The Independent* showed:

BRAVE NEW WORLD?

By Emma Cook

Like latter-day Pilgrim Fathers, a band of Britons plans to cross the Atlantic and build Utopia. They've even put in an offer for an island. But can Tony Craig and his followers realise their dream before it all turns sour?

TONY CRAIG is on fire. He hasn't slept for weeks, and now he's darting round the living-room of his Welsh farmhouse, pouring out a nervous stream of exhaustive (and exhausting) ideas about the modern-day Utopia he's going to create; a Utopia that you too can join – if you've got £150,000 ready cash.

For this 45-year-old retired antique dealer has had a dream: a dream of creating a new world based on trust and harmony; a dream of a thriving community where crime is non-existent, where children are safe and the elderly well cared for, where sleaze, corruption, abuse, violence and greed have been left behind along with traffic jams, loud music and taxation. And, after a nine-year search, he and his wife, Lyn, think that they may have found the place in which their dream can become a reality: a 17 square mile uninhabited island off the coast of Panama for which they have made an offer of $25 million. All they need now is 400-odd families ready to share the cost. "We'll be out there working together," Tony is enthusing, "aiming for the same goal and building up something between us. We won't lack direction or have idle hands – it'll be so therapeutic." He is sprightly, boyish-looking and full of nervous energy. Dressed in crisp white shirt and wide red tie, he resembles a brash city slicker but talks like a student idealist; a dreamer in businessman's clothing. "You see," he goes on, "in our society, we're all prisoners in our own homes. It's now normal to have bars up at our windows. That won't happen on the island. We'll know each other, we'll help one another out."

Failure is much on Tony's mind, for the plan for his own community is turning into a logistical nightmare. He needs more people to help him realise his ambition, but many of those who want to join are either unwilling to take the initiative or doubt his management skills. Caught in limbo, he's unwilling to delegate, but desperate not to be the leader. The strain is beginning to show. "I don't want to be some sort of Ayatollah," he wails. "They always get burnt down in flames. I can't get agreement on anything." He paces the floor, unable to sit or stand still for a second. "How," he cries, "can I be all things to all people?"

THE CRAIGS' PROBLEMS seemed to have come to an end three months ago when, after a long quest, Tony, Lyn and their five-year-old son Ryan set foot on San Jose, an island just off the Pacific coast of Panama.

As tropical paradises go, San Jose is as clichéd as a Bacardi commercial but no less stunning for that: palm trees, turquoise seas, white sands, lagoons and dense green forest, uninhabited and up for sale. As such, it fits the bill for the 1,000 people who responded to a small ad the Craigs placed in the *Sunday Times* last Christmas, asking for other families to join them in their search for Utopia. Now the $25m asking price has to be found, and, at present, there is a core group of about 150 committed "members". The original idea was that each family would pay £50,000 towards the purchase of the island, and a further £100,000 towards building and infrastructure costs; it currently looks as though most of the money will go on buying the island. None the less, the members hope to create a commercially profitable, non-political, non-religious democracy with its own constitution and even its own currency.

Love, equality and peace are, according to those involved, the building blocks for their new community (tentatively called the Island of Trust).

Independent on Sunday, 17 December 1995 [abridged]

- What does the article tell you about the ideas and attitudes of Tony Craig?

- What possibilities are offered by his island dream, and what could be the problems and dangers?

POSSIBILITIES?		PROBLEMS?
1. Less crime		1. Sharing
2.		2. Leadership
3.		3.
4.		4.
5. Escape from	Pearl Islands / San Jose Island / Island del Rey	5.
6.		6.
7.		7.

- Imagine you are able to buy your own island, and decide to set up a community on it. What would your 'Utopia' be like? How might you try to overcome some of the potential problems?

- Write a newsletter to potential community members describing your ideas and trying to encourage them to join you.

- Share your newsletters around the class. Question each other about the ideas that have been included. What have you discovered about the potential of the island idea, and the possible dangers?

Tony Craig wrote a newsletter, giving details of his progress in securing the island, and sent it to his aspiring islanders:

I was overlooking one of the most beautiful beaches I had ever seen. It looked like a garden. Turquoise and emerald waters lapped a shore of white powdery sand. It didn't stop there, this crescent cove was fringed by perfect palms. Black boulders were set upon the beach. It was as though a Japanese gardener had positioned them to balance nature's perfection.

The *Independent* journalist described this as 'sugary prose'. How would you describe it?

In *The Tempest,* by Shakespeare, one of the characters expresses similar ideas to Tony Craig's when he describes what he would do if he were king of an island.

GONZALO:
Had I plantation of this isle, my lord, –

And were the king on't, what would I do?

In the commonwealth I would by contraries
Execute all things; for no kind of traffic
Would I admit; no name of magistrate;
Letters should not be known; riches, poverty,
And use of service, none; contract, succession,
Bourn, bound of land, tilth, vineyard, none;
No use of metal, corn, or wine, or oil;
No occupation; all men idle, all;
And women too, but innocent and pure;
No sovereignty, –
All things in common nature should produce
Without sweat or endeavour: treason, felony,
Sword, pike, knife, gun, or need of any engine,
Would I not have; but nature should bring forth,
Of its own kind, all foison, all abundance,
To feed my innocent people.

From *The Tempest,* Act 2, Scene 1

What does he wish to avoid?

What does he wish to have?

* Compare Gonzalo's ideas of Utopia with Tony Craig's. How are they similar and how are they different?

* To what extent do you think a Utopia is possible or desirable?

ISLANDS – REALITIES?

Even though travel writers write about real places, they often play on our preconceptions of the ideal when describing beautiful islands. Nicole Swengley writes about her journey to the Marquesas islands in the South Pacific:

Even before boarding I felt as if I'd stepped straight into a Robert Louis Stevenson story. The *Aranui's* Polynesian stevedores are straight out of *Treasure Island:* red bandannas, gold earrings, whale-tooth necklaces glimmering against gold-brown tattooed bodies. One grabbed my bag, tossed it on to his shoulder as if it were feather-light, and ran up the boarding ladder in bare feet. I followed at a more sedate pace trying not to slip on the rungs.

Two days later we reached the Marquesas. My first glimpse of the islands left a lasting impression of emerald mountains mysterious, brooding, inviting – rising jaggedly from the bluest of cobalt seas. Even a short walk inland is heady stuff. The eye is arrested by purple and cerise bougainvillaea, rosy oleander, yellow and red hibiscus, thrusting pink ginger, pale frangipani, pure white *tiare* (gardenia), unbelievably vivid flame trees and the weighty green globes of the breadfruit trees that brought Captain Cook to this remote area.

And the Marquesas really are remote. Further from a major landfall than any other group of islands on earth, they jut out into the open Pacific just south of the Equator about 800 miles north-east of Tahiti. Air services are limited and local flights are full six months in advance. It takes seven hours to fly from Papeete, Tahiti's capital, and seven days by copra boat. No wonder the islands are way off the usual tourist track.

From 'A Passage to the South Pacific' by Nicole Swengley, in the *Independent on Sunday*, 23 June 1996

Paul Theroux describes the same islands, but from a very different angle, making reference to the way in which they have been exploited:

The island of Fatu-Hiva was without doubt the most beautiful of the Marquesas, not just for its great vistas, and the wild horses scrambling on the slopes, the sheerest cliffs, the greenest ledges, and the beautiful bay. It was its greenness, its steepness, its emptiness; the way daylight plunged into it only to be overwhelmed by the darkness of its precipitous valleys, and the obvious dangers of its entire shoreline gave it the look of a fortress or a green castle in the sea.

About that water. Seeing those cataracts often made me thirsty. One day in Nuku Hiva I went to a bar and asked for a drink of water. A half-liter of Vittel was opened for me, and I paid – $2.50. It was unthinkable that I should want the vile water from the pipes of Taiohae, and no one questioned the absurdity of buying this little bottle of Vittel from halfway around the world. That it is available at all is something of a miracle; that it might be necessary is a condemnation of this lovely baffling place.

The French praise and romanticize the Marquesas, but in the 1960s they had planned to test nuclear devices on the northern Marquesan island of Eiao, until there was such an outcry they changed their plans and decided to destroy Mururoa instead. It is said that the French are holding Polynesia together, but really it is so expensive to maintain that they do everything as cheaply as possible – and it is self-serving, too. Better to boost domestic French industries by exporting bottled water from France than investing in a fresh water supply for each island. That is what colonialism is all about.

When France has succeeded in destroying a few more atolls, when they have managed to make the islands glow with so much radioactivity that night is turned into day, when they have sold the rest of the fishing rights and depleted them of fish (already in Tahiti the surrounding islands have been over-fished), when it has all been thoroughly plundered, the French will plan a great ceremony and grandly offer these unemployed and deracinated citizens in T-shirts and flip-flops their independence. In the destruction of the islands, the French imperial intention, its *mission civilisatrice* – civilizing mission – will be complete.

From *The Happy Isles of Oceania* by Paul Theroux

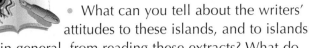

- What can you tell about the writers' attitudes to these islands, and to islands in general, from reading these extracts? What do the writers find attractive and what enrages them?

- Go back to the grid you started to help you identify what the advert about the Seychelles and the speech from *Richard II* have in common. You should have left enough space to extend it by including the other extracts you have studied since.

ISLANDS – AS METAPHORS

The previous pages have dealt with real islands – The Seychelles, England, The Marquesas – but the concept of an island has also been used as a metaphor, a way of describing relationships and feelings, using an image which we all find powerful.

In the 1960s, the singer and songwriter Paul Simon wrote:

A winter's day in a deep and dark December,
I am alone.
Gazing from my window to the street below,
On a freshly fallen silent shroud of snow,
I am a rock;
I am an island.
Don't talk of love, I've heard that word before,
It's sleeping in my memory,
I won't disturb the slumber of feelings that have died,
If I'd never loved I never would have cried,
I am a rock; I am an island.
For a rock feels no pain,
And an island never cries.

In the 1600s, the poet John Donne wrote:

No man is an Island, intire of it selfe; every man is a peece of the Continent, a part of the maine; if a Clod bee washed away by the Sea, Europe is the lesse, as well as if a Promontorie were, as well as if a Mannor of thy friends or of thine owne were; any mans death diminishes me, because I am involved in Mankinde; And therefore never send to know for whom the bell tolls; It tolls for thee.

From *Meditation XVII* by John Donne

- How is the idea of an island being used by these two writers?

ISLAND – CASTAWAYS

Many books, films and real adventures have been based around the idea of survival on a desert island. In 1719, Daniel Defoe's *Robinson Crusoe* was published. In this book the hero keeps a journal of his years on a desert island.

Read the extract from Robinson Crusoe's journal on the next page.

THE JOURNAL

September 30, 1659.—I, poor miserable Robinson Crusoe, being shipwrecked, during a dreadful storm, in the offing, came on shore on this dismal unfortunate island, which I called the Island of Despair, all the rest of the ship's company being drowned, and myself almost dead. I now began to consider seriously my condition, and the circumstance I was reduced to; and I drew up the state of my affairs in writing; not so much to leave them to any that were to come after me, for I was like to have but few heirs, as to deliver my thoughts from daily poring upon them, and afflicting my mind. And as my reason began now to master my despondency, I began to comfort myself as well as I could, and to set the good against the evil, that I might have something to distinguish my case from worse; and I stated it very impartially, like debtor and creditor, the comforts I enjoyed against the miseries I suffered, thus:

Evil.	*Good.*
I am cast upon a horrible desolate island, void of all hope of recovery.	But I am alive, and not drowned, as all my ship's company was.
I am singled out and separated, as it were, from all the world to be miserable.	But I am singled out, too, from all the ship's crew to be spared from death; and He that miraculously saved me from death, can deliver me from this condition.
I am divided from mankind, a solitaire, one banished from human society.	But I am not starved and perishing on a barren place, affording no sustenance.
I have not clothes to cover me.	But I am in a hot climate, where if I had clothes I could hardly wear them.
I am without any defence or means to resist any violence of man or beast.	But I am cast on an island, where I see no wild beasts to hurt me, as I saw on the coast of Africa; and what if I had been shipwrecked there?
I have no soul to speak to, or relieve me.	But God wonderfully sent the ship in near enough to the shore, that I have gotten out so many necessary things as will either supply my wants, or enable me to supply myself even as long as I live.

Having now brought my mind a little to relish my condition, and given over looking out to sea, to see if I could spy a ship; I say, giving over these things, I began to apply myself to accommodate my way of living, and to make things as easy to me as I could.

• Why do you think the idea of the castaway has captured the imagination of so many writers?

In the novel *Lord of the Flies* by William Golding, the first chapter begins:

The boy with the fair hair lowered himself down the last few feet of rock and began to pick his way towards the lagoon.

• Now you have seen the way in which writers make use of islands, what can you say about the possible subject matter and themes of Golding's book from this opening sentence?

ROMANCE

Perhaps the most popular genre, at least in terms of books sold, is that of the romantic novel.

We all have our own ideas of what the word 'romance' means based on things we have read, watched or experienced.

Over the next four pages, you will find all sorts of romantic images, used in a wide variety of genres, such as a play, a gothic novel, advertisements, poems, magazines. You may want to add to this collection by finding material of your own such as photographs, cards or songs. As you read through the section, new ideas will probably occur to you.

- Brainstorm all the words and ideas that you associate with romance.

- Look at the verses and images on these two pages. Considering these and your brainstorm, try to identify the main elements of romance.

The Rose

Some say love it is a river
That drowns the tender need
Some say love it is a razor
That leaves your soul to bleed
Some say love it is a hunger
An endless-aching need
I say love it is a flower
And you its only seed

It's the heart afraid of breaking
That never learns to dance
It's the dream afraid of waiting
That never takes the chance
It's the one who won't be taken
Who cannot seem to give
And the soul afraid of dying
That never learns to live

When the night has been too lonely
And the road has been too long
And you think that love is only
For the lucky and the strong
Just remember that in the winter
Far beneath the bitter snow
Lies the seed that with the sun's love
In the spring becomes the rose

by Amanda McBroom, for Fanfare Music Inc

Has your dream man got you all in a tizz? Have you been hit by the love bug? Restore our faith in boykind with all your slushiest, soppiest stories. Send 'em in to: True Romance, Sugar. And don't forget you piccies, or we can't print your story!

A Red, Red Rose

O my luve's like a red, red rose,
That's newly sprung in June;
O my luve's like the melodie
That's sweetly played in tune.

As fair art thou, my bonnie lass,
So deep in luve am I;
And I will luve thee still, my dear,
Till a' the seas gang dry:

Till a' the seas gang dry, my dear,
And the rocks melt wi' the sun!
I will luve thee still, my dear,
While the sands o' life shall run.

And fare thee weel, my only luve!
And fare thee weel a while!
And I will come again, my luve,
Though it were ten thousand mile.

Robert Burns

Since We Met I've Been Floating On Air...

My life was full, or so I thought, until we met and fell in love. I had no idea what I was missing...

A bow-shot from her bower-eaves,
He rode between the barley-sheaves,
The sun came dazzling thro' the leaves,
And flamed upon the brazen greaves*
    Of bold Sir Lancelot.
A redcross knight for ever kneel'd
To a lady in his shield,
That sparkled on the yellow field,
Beside remote Shallot.

From 'The Lady of Shallot' by Alfred Lord Tennyson
*Leg armour

Now look at the advertisement on the next page. Its rests on the assumption that romantic dreams and notions are something shared and understood by all the readers of the magazine.

"The perfect present," he whispered "the past".

Victoria station, platform 2, 9.45a.m. Romance is in the air. The train waits patiently on the platform, as the early morning sun glints on the immaculate umber and cream livery of the British Pullman carriages.

The steward welcomes you on board and escorts you to your table. George Mortimer Pullman used to refer to his carriages as "Palaces on Wheels," and so they are.

For the next few hours, you will travel in a style you thought had gone forever; in an England you thought had long disappeared.

"Where are we actually going?" asks the woman at the next table. The man with her smiles: "It's a surprise" he says.

As you sip a perfectly chilled glass of champagne, the English countryside passes by your window.

Later, lunch. A single red rose on the table suggests that it will be no ordinary day; and the cuisine and wine confirms it.

"Remember where we first met?" asks the man at the next table.

"July 22nd. The Pump Room. Bath. Of course I do." she says.

"The string quartet was playing Mozart and Mozart lost," he smiles.

The steward walks by the table. "Bath station in 5 minutes."

"Happy anniversary," the man whispers

VENICE SIMPLON ORIENT-EXPRESS

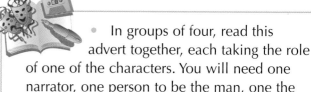

- In groups of four, read this advert together, each taking the role of one of the characters. You will need one narrator, one person to be the man, one the woman, and one the steward.

- Discuss what the necessary elements of romance seem to be, according to the writer of this advertisement. You should pay particular attention to:

The setting: Which details are important, and why? Look at the picture and the text.

The relationship: Who is in control here? What role does the man have, and what role the woman?

BECOMING A CRITICAL READER

As you study the extracts in this part of the unit you will begin to recognise the romantic elements used by each writer. You will be searching for answers to a key question: What exactly are the writers doing with the idea of romance? Do they repeat and reinforce the same notions, or are they trying to change our ideas of the possibilities provided by the theme?

Begin your search by creating the chart below, and by recording on it the discoveries you have made so far. This will help you to identify the similarities and the differences between the writers' approaches, and to understand the reasons for them. Use it to analyse each of the passages that follow.

ROMANCE

TEXT Name. Type. Audience.	SETTING Place. Surroundings. Objects. Surface details.	RELATIONSHIPS Male and female roles. Conventions & rules of behaviour. Power. Control.	EMOTIONS What feelings are described or suggested? What creates the feelings? Are they convincing do you think?
1. Orient Express Advert. Non-fiction. Appeals to ... ? 2. The Challenge of Love			

How, then, do some fiction writers deal with very romantic moments: moments when their male and female characters meet, reveal their feelings of mutual attraction, or even propose?

In the story 'The Challenge of Love', published in *My Weekly* magazine, Piers and Janey finally admit their true feelings:

What does the description of Piers and his actions show you about his role here?

What phrases are used to describe emotions? Do they seem convincing?

Who controls the conversation?

She shivered, suddenly conscious that it had grown dark, and that a sharp, chill breeze had risen from the sea. She wished that she had brought a jumper, but in her headlong dash from the hotel, she had not thought about anything but Piers.

She started as she saw the tall, shadowy figure looming up out of the darkness, and then recognition dawned.

"Where have you been?" Piers' voice was rough, and without warning he swept up Janey in his arms, holding her so tightly that she gasped for breath. "I've been worried out of my mind. Don't you ever do that to me again!" His eyes blazed down at her, with an anger that was borne out of anxiety and fear. His hold relaxed, and very gently, he placed a hand under Janey's chin and titled her face up to his. "Janey, I love you so much." His voice was muffled, as if he were in physical pain.

Janey stared at him, not daring to believe his words, and then as she read the truth in his eyes, she felt herself go weak. Her eyes swam with tears of joy, she felt as if she were drowning in her love for him. Wonderingly, she touched his face, exploring the contours of his mouth as she had so longed to do.

"I think I fell in love with you that evening when you were so furious about Becky. You seemed so convinced that I was some heartless, uncaring brute." He paused to kiss her tenderly. "I didn't realise how I felt for a long time, though." He grinned. "After all, it was a totally new experience for me."

"Of course you'll have to give up working at the airport when you're Mrs Piers Duncan," Piers said some time later. "Or I shouldn't be able to concentrate."

In *Hobson's Choice* written by Harold Brighouse and published in 1916, there is a rather different proposal. Here, Maggie, the daughter of the owner of a shoe shop in Lancashire, is interested in Willie Mossop, a shoemaker …

MAGGIE: Do you know what keeps this business on its legs? Two things: one's the good boots you make that sell themselves, the other's the bad boots other people make and I sell.
We're a pair, Will Mossop.

WILLIE: You're a wonder in the shop, Miss Maggie.

MAGGIE: And you're a marvel in the workshop. Well?

WILLIE: Well, what?

MAGGIE: It seems to me to point one way.

WILLIE: What way is that?

MAGGIE: You're leaving me to do the work, my lad.

WILLIE: I'll be getting back to my stool, Miss Maggie. (*Moves to trap.*)

MAGGIE (*stopping him*): You'll go back when I've done with you. I've watched you for a long time and everything I've seen, I've liked. I think you'll do for me.

WILLIE: What way, Miss Maggie?

MAGGIE: Will Mossop, you're my man. Six months I've counted on you and it's got to come out some time.

WILLIE: But I never—

MAGGIE: I know you never, or it 'ud not be left to me to do the job like this.

WILLIE: I'll – I'll sit down. (*He sits in arm-chair, mopping his brow.*) I'm feeling queer-like. What dost want me for?

MAGGIE: To invest in. You're a business idea in the shape of a man.

WILLIE: I've got no head for business at all.

MAGGIE: But I have. My brain and your hands 'ull make a working partnership.

WILLIE (*getting up, relieved*): Partnership! Oh, that's a different thing. I thought you were axing me to wed you.

MAGGIE: I am.

WILLIE: Well, by gum! And you the master's daughter.

Quentin Tarantino, an American film director and screenwriter, reveals his characters, their relationships and emotions in a unique way through his scripts. The following extract is from the screenplay of his film *True Romance*.

CLARENCE: Tell me about yourself.

ALABAMA: There's nothing to tell.

CLARENCE: C'mon. What're ya tryin' to be? The Phantom Lady?

ALABAMA: What do you want to know?

CLARENCE: Well, for starters, what do you do? Where're ya from? What's your favorite color? Who's your favorite movie star? What kinda music do you like? What are your turn-ons and turn-offs? Do you have a fella? What's the story behind you takin' a cab to the most dangerous part of town alone? And, in a theater full of empty seats, why did you sit by me?

Alabama takes a bit of pie, puts down her fork, and looks at Clarence.

ALABAMA: Ask me again. One by one.

CLARENCE: What do you do?

ALABAMA: I don't remember.

CLARENCE: Where are you from?

ALABAMA: I might be from Tallahassee. But I'm not sure yet.

CLARENCE: What's your favorite colour?

ALABAMA: I don't remember. But off the top of my head, I'd say black.

CLARENCE: Who's your favorite movie star?

ALABAMA: Burt Reynolds.

CLARENCE: Would you like a bite of my pie?

ALABAMA: Yes, I would.

Clarence scoops up a piece on his fork and Alabama bites it off.

CLARENCE: Like it?

ALABAMA: Very much. Now, where were we?

CLARENCE: What kinda music do you like?

ALABAMA: Phil Spector. Girl group stuff. You know, like 'He's a Rebel'.

CLARENCE: What are your turn-ons?

ALABAMA: Mickey Rourke, somebody who can appreciate the finer things in life, like Elvis's voice, good kung fu, and a tasty piece of pie.

[LATER – THAT NIGHT]
And, um, I guess I want a second date.

CLARENCE: Thank you. I wanna see you again too. And again, and again, and again. Bama, I know we haven't known each other long, but my parents went together all throughout high school, and they still got a divorce. So, you wanna marry me?

ALABAMA: What?

CLARENCE: Will you be my wife?

When Alabama gives her answer, her voice cracks.

ALABAMA: Yes.

CLARENCE: *(a little surprised)* You will?

ALABAMA: You better not be teasing me.

CLARENCE: You better not be teasin' me.

They seal it with a kiss.

• Read the play and film script extracts in pairs, each taking a role, in order to explore the different ways the characters might speak, move and interact and the different ways the writers use spoken language in these proposal scenes.

• Now discuss the similarities and the differences between the presentation of romantic moments in all the pieces in this section. What ideas of romance, love, marriage and possible relationships between men and women are suggested by each writer? Is each writer using the theme in a traditional way, or is he or she changing it? Add your discoveries to your chart.

Left: Brenda De Banzie and John Mills in Hobson's Choice, *1954*

In *Sense and Sensibility* (1811), Jane Austen's heroine, Elinor, has suffered many disappointments before Edward, the man she loves, finally proposes. How does the writer choose here to describe this climatic moment?

His errand at Barton, in fact, was a simple one. It was only to ask Elinor to marry him; and considering that he was not altogether inexperienced in such a question, it might be strange that he should feel so uncomfortable in the present case as he really did—so much in need of encouragement and fresh air.

How soon he had walked himself into the proper resolution, however, how soon an opportunity of exercising it occurred, in what manner he expressed himself, and how he was received, need not be particularly told. This only need be said—that when they all sat down to table at four o'clock, about three hours after his arrival, he had secured his lady, engaged her mother's consent, and was not only in the rapturous profession of the lover, but, in the reality of reason and truth, one of the happiest of men. His situation, indeed, was more than commonly joyful. He had more than the ordinary triumph of accepted love to swell his heart and raise his spirits. He was released, without any reproach to himself, from an entanglement which had long formed his misery, from a woman whom he had long ceased to love—and elevated at once to that security with another, which he must have thought of almost with despair, as soon as he had learned to consider it with desire. He was brought, not from doubt or suspense, but from misery to happiness; and the change was openly spoken in such a genuine, flowing grateful cheerfulness as his friends had never witnessed in him before.

Emma Thompson and Hugh Grant in Sense and Sensibility, *1996*

You have now seen how some writers use the genre to challenge familiar notions of romance, to go beyond our expectations, to surprise us or to transform our ideas. As a critical reader, you should be able to recognise the variety of techniques used to do this, the unique ways in which writers explore such a powerful theme.

Look finally at Charlotte Brontë's presentation of the proposal scene in *Jane Eyre*.

The heroine, Jane Eyre, who is narrating the story, has fallen in love with her employer, Mr Rochester. Only when it seems she might have to leave his home, do they reveal their true feelings for each other.

William Hurt and Charlotte Gainsbourg in Jane Eyre, *1996*

'Jane, be still; don't struggle so, like a wild frantic bird that is rending its own plumage in its desperation.'

'I am no bird; and no net ensnares me; I am a free human being with an independent will, which I now exert to leave you.'

Another effort set me at liberty, and I stood erect before him.

'And your will shall decide your destiny,' he said. 'I offer you my hand, my heart, and a share of all my possessions.'

'You play a farce, which I merely laugh at.'

'I ask you to pass through life at my side—to be my second self, and best earthly companion.'

'For that fate you have already made your choice, and must abide by it.'

'Jane, be still a few moments: you are over-excited: I will be still too.'

A waft of wind came sweeping down the laurel-walk, and trembled through the boughs of the chestnut: it wandered away—away—to an indefinite distance—it died. The nightingale's song was then the only voice of the hour: in listening to it, I again wept. Mr. Rochester sat quiet, looking at me gently and seriously. Some time passed before he spoke; he at last said:

'Come to my side, Jane, and let us explain and understand one another.'

'I will never again come to your side: I am torn away now, and cannot return.'

'But, Jane, I summon you as my wife: it is you only I intend to marry.'

I was silent: I thought he mocked me.

'Come, Jane—come hither.'

'Your bride stands between us.'

He rose, and with a stride reached me.

'My bride is here,' he said, again drawing me to him, 'because my equal is here, and my likeness. Jane, will you marry me?'

- Use your chart, and prepare with a partner your responses to these questions.

What do you notice about the roles of the man and the woman here?

What different and complex feelings are described?

How does this compare in style, and emotion, with the other extracts you have studied?

- Add this extract to your chart.

WHAT NEXT?

ROMANCE

Is there such a thing as true romance?

Oral work

- In a group, prepare a presentation for your class, expressing your views on this question. Use your collage, your chart, and some of the extracts to support your views. Which writers convince you one way or the other?

Written course work

- Use the same question to compose a piece of writing which explores writers' views, as well as your own, on this subject.

The following poems by Wendy Cope might help you to formulate your own ideas.

FLOWERS

Some men never think of it.
You did. You'd come along
And say you'd nearly brought me flowers
But something had gone wrong.

The shop was closed. Or you had doubts –
The sort that minds like ours
Dream up incessantly. You thought
I might not want your flowers.

It made me smile and hug you then.
Now I can only smile.
But, look, the flowers you nearly brought
Have lasted all this while.

DEFINING THE PROBLEM

I can't forgive you. Even if I could,
You wouldn't pardon me for seeing through you.
And yet I cannot cure myself of love
For what I thought you were before I knew you.

ISLANDS

Wide reading and oral work

- In a group, find some of the novels listed below which explore or use the theme of islands. Take a book each, research and consider:

    - How is the idea of an island used in the book?

    - How is the island described?

    - What is the writer's view of the concept of an 'island' – paradise or hell on earth?

        Treasure Island by R. L. Stevenson

        Lord of the Flies by William Golding

        Robinson Crusoe by Daniel Defoe

        Castaway by Lucy Irvine

        Jurassic Park by Michael Crichton

        The Lost World by Michael Crichton

        Coral Island by R. M. Ballantyne

- Prepare a presentation for your class, perhaps with some prepared readings.

Written course work

- *How do different writers use the idea of an 'island'?*

    From your work on this unit and your wide reading, write an essay or article in which you consider this question. Base your writing on the work you have done during this unit and on your wider reading.

The Witch Hunt

In this unit you will explore a wide range of thought-provoking material and re-work it into different forms and styles. You will develop your skills as:

SPEAKERS AND LISTENERS

by presenting information to a group and giving feedback

by taking part in drama activities which explore the issues raised by the material

by discussing themes

READERS

by practising a choral reading

by closely studying a range of non-fictional evidence for meaning

by looking at some ways in which the theme of witchcraft is used in fiction

WRITERS

by planning and presenting a wide range of formal styles of writing including letters, articles, pamphlets and a treatise

by devising a storyboard

by planning a documentary

You will need to keep a dictionary handy while you work through this unit as some of the language may be unfamiliar to you.

• Your first task is to write the opening chapter of an information book about witches for younger children of about 10 to 12 years of age. On the next three pages you will find a wealth of information and images about witchcraft in medieval Europe. Start here – with an account of what people believed in the middle ages.

Some of the material is quite complex. To make it more suitable, you will need to read it, select and omit information, simplify it and re-organise it so that it is accessible to a younger reader.

WITCHES

In Europe in the middle ages (roughly twelfth century to sixteenth century), over 100,000 people, mainly women, were either burned at the stake or hanged for being witches.

According to surveys, this witchcraze was the 'greatest European mass killing of people by people not caused by war'. Simply being accused of witchcraft often meant persecution, degrading treatment, torture, trial and sometimes death.

What Did People Believe About Witchcraft?
Here is what one writer says about belief in witchcraft (from *A History of Witchcraft* by Jeffrey B. Russell):

The scholastics firmly established the tradition that witches were more likely to be women than men. The master of the witch assembly was supposed to be, not an inferior demon, but the devil himself, the prince and the principle of evil. As an angel, the Devil was sexless, but also as an angel, he could take on either male or female form as he chose. But in theology, literature, and art, he almost invariably appeared as masculine. This is the result of an odd sexual bias. As the principle of evil and age-old adversary of the Lord, the Devil was a figure of great power, almost divinity. The Judaeo-Christian tradition was unable to attach such divinity to a female figure. Like God himself, then, the Devil was almost universally

For all those who died – stripped naked, shaved, shorn.
For all those who screamed in vain to the Great Goddess, only to have their tongues ripped out by the root.
For those who were pricked, racked, broken on the wheel for the sins of their Inquisitors.
For all those whose beauty stirred their torturers to fury; and for those whose ugliness did the same.
For all those who were neither ugly nor beautiful, but only women who would not submit.
For all those quick fingers, broken in the vice.
For all those soft arms, pulled from their sockets.
For all those budding breasts, ripped with hot pincers.
For all those midwives, killed merely for the sin of delivering man to an imperfect world.
For all those witch-women, my sisters, who breathed freer as the flames took them, knowing as they shed their female bodies, the seared flesh falling like fruit in the flames, that death alone would cleanse them of the sin for which they died – the sin of being born a woman who is more than the sum of her parts.

Anonymous, sixteenth century

perceived as male. From this it followed that the Devil's sexual activity at the sabbat was that of a male, and though homosexuality was not precluded, he almost invariably cohabited with women. Hence the belief in the preponderance of woman at the sabbat.

The Devil was usually thought of as male, so witches who submitted to him sexually were generally considered female.

A strange picture of witchcraft was drawn by writers of the fifteenth and sixteenth centuries during the witch-craze.

The sun has gone down, and honest people are asleep. The witches, including some men but mostly women, creep silently out of their beds, making sure that they do not disturb their husbands or wives. They are preparing for the sabbat. Those who live near the meeting ground will go on foot; those who live farther away will go to a private place, rub their bodies with an ointment that enables them to levitate, and fly off on animals, fencerails, brooms, or stools. At the meeting, which takes place in a cellar, cave, or deserted heath, they meet ten to twenty of their fellow witches. If a neophyte is there, an initiation ceremony precedes the ordinary business of the meeting. The novice will be bound to the cult in such a way that he or she will find it difficult to withdraw. Accordingly, she is obliged to swear to keep the secrets of the cult, and she further seals herself to the group by promising to kill a young child and bring its body to a subsequent meeting. She orally renounces the Christian faith and seals her apostasy by stamping on, or excreting on, a crucifix or a consecrated host.

Next she adores the male master of the cult, the Devil or his representative, by offering him the obscene kiss on the buttocks.

When the initiation has been completed, the assembly takes part in feasting and drinking. The witches enact a parody of the eucharistic feast, bringing in the bodies of children whom they have previously murdered. The infants may be stolen from Christian families, or they may be the offspring conceived by the witches at previous orgies. The children are offered up in sacrifice to the Devil. The witches may boil the children's bodies, mix them with loathsome substances, and render them into the levitating ointment. Or they may consume the children's body and blood in ritual parody of the Lord's Supper.

After the feast the torches are extinguished, or the candelabras are overturned by a black dog or cat. The orgy commences. Cries of 'Mix it up' are heard, and each person takes the one next him in lascivious embrace. The encounters are indiscriminate: men with men, women with women, mothers with sons, brothers with sisters. When the orgy is concluded, the witches take ritual leave of their master and return home replete to join their sleeping spouses.

The ritual murder of children, often accompanied by cannibalism, was one of the most common charges levelled against the witches. If the children were not eaten, they were often supposed to have been boiled in a cauldron and their fat used to help confect the magical salve.

Such a scene never occurred, but this is what was almost universally believed to happen at a witch's sabbat. What people believe to be true influences their actions more than what is objectively true, and the conviction that this picture was accurate brought about the execution of hundreds of thousands of people.

Accusing and Confessing

Being accused of witchcraft meant that you would probably be tortured to confess your 'crime'.

Swimming a witch. One of the common tests of witchcraft was to throw the witch into deep water. If the water, God's creature, rejected her and she floated, she was guilty. If she sank, she was innocent. Two men hold her with ropes so as to draw her up again if she sinks.

The final results of a witchcraft trial were horrific. Public executions in the forms of burnings or hangings are quite disturbing topics. How will you help your younger readers to understand these facts without being disturbed by them?

• When you have finished your opening chapter, present your work to some Year 7 students and ask for feedback.

Writers need to know whether they are working on the right lines before investing more time and effort in a project.

The next task is designed to help you think more deeply about witchcraft and to try your hand at writing for a more sophisticated reader, the kind who might want explanations and theories as well as facts.

• Imagine that you are a journalist for a Sunday newspaper. For the colour supplement, you have been asked to write an article which informs readers not only about the witchcraze but also about why it happened. You have already decided on an eye-catching title: 'Why did medieval Europe execute so many women?'

In order to write the article, you will need to make up your own mind about why it happened. First, however, look carefully at some of the theories that have been advanced by other people. Working in groups of about three or four, read the following theories together, and then follow the advice in the help box on page 170 to compose your article.

WHY DID MEDIEVAL EUROPE EXECUTE SO MANY WOMEN?

With so many people dead and such terrible fear surrounding the accusations, many people have since wondered about the reasons for this mass killing. Why did such cruelty and brutality occur? Here are some theories about the causes of what has since become known as the 'witchcraze'.

There are five main theories about European witchcraft:

1. Witchcraft never existed

There is a view that witches didn't really exist but were a convenient way for the church to impose its authority. If people are persuaded of the existence of evil, then they are much more likely to behave themselves. A modern theorist who seems to support this view is Peter Stanford who said in a recent article in the *Independent on Sunday:* 'The Devil is one of the best ideas Christianity ever came up with.'

He argued that witchcrazes occur because 'the idea of a group of people who are outwardly normal but acting out taboos and fantasies is enduring'. In other words, people in all societies are very willing to believe in conspiracy theories, to imagine that they may be being manipulated by mysterious forces beyond their control.

2. Witchcraft is an ancient religion

Historian Margaret Murray believes that European witchcraft is an ancient fertility cult devoted to the worship of Dianus and was, therefore, at odds with the medieval church. According to this theory, witchcraft is relatively harmless in itself but was demonised by the church in order to make sure that it did not come to represent a threat.

3. Witchcrazes happened for social reasons

This is the view that witchcrazes are an expression of tensions and difficulties within society. Witchcraft does not exist, but society needs to find scapegoats, particularly in times of trouble, and witches are a convenient target.

One aspect of the witchcraze, undeniably, was an uneasiness with and hostility toward dependent older women. Witch charges may have been used to get rid of elderly women, past child-bearing age and too feeble to do productive work. As Barbara Walker has put it 'the old woman was an ideal scapegoat: too expendable to be missed, too weak to fight back, too poor to matter' (*Witchcraze* by A. Bairstow).

4. The geographical theory

Some historians have argued that living in the mountains, at altitude, affected people's belief system:

Historians have long debated the geographical origins of witchcraft. Josef Hansen, followed by Hugh Trevor-Roper, argued that witchcraft began in the mountains, where the thin air was conducive to hallucinations, severe natural phenomena such as storms and avalanches encouraged belief in demonic powers, and ancient sorceries lingered in benighted minds.

5. Human nature

Another historian, Russell, suggests that the witchcraze was a 'flaw in human nature' which is repeated throughout history:

Much has been said about the reasons for the origins, the spread, and the ultimate decline of the witchcraze. Fundamentally, the witchcraze was one particular form of a flaw in human nature, the desire of human beings to project evil on others, define them as outsiders, and then punish them horribly. The burnings at Bamberg and the hangings at Salem are functionally and structurally comparable to the ovens of Dachau, the massacre of My Lai, and the brutalities of the Gulag.

Do some research and find out what happened at Dachau, My Lai and the Gulag.

HELP

WRITING A FEATURE ARTICLE

1. Planning

No one is completely sure why the witchcraze happened. Working in groups of three, discuss each theory, making brief notes on the essential points which you feel are relevant to understanding the witchcraze.

2. Organisation

It is very important to have headlines and an opening paragraph which really capture the reader's attention. Spend time working on this together so that your first few lines make a real impact.

Once you have interested the reader, you can begin to develop your own theories about why the witchcraze occurred. Because you are writing a logical, persuasive piece, you will need to link the paragraphs together. Consider using some linking phrases such as:

'Another theory suggests ...'

'As a consequence of this ...'

'In contrast to Wilson, Murray suggests ...'

3. Composition

Remember, you are writing for adults who are reading a Sunday supplement. They will want to read an article which is informative and summarises most of the evidence but is also lively and interesting. Because you are dealing with a serious, adult topic, you should use a more impersonal style. It would be appropriate, for example, to write 'A possible theory is ...' instead of 'What I think is ...'

4. Sub-editing

All journalists have their work checked and re-written by a sub-editor before it appears in the newspaper. Ask a friend to be a critical reader of your work and respond to their suggestions.

As this is a newspaper article, it would be best to publish using a desktop computer format with columns, photograph boxes and different sized typefaces for headlines. If you do have software of this kind available as a resource, remember to spell-check and proofread to ensure accuracy and clarity.

sub-heading

Why did medieval Europe execute so many women?

Bewitched!

eye-catching heading

opening paragraphs should capture reader's attention and explain what article is about

When darkness comes and good people are asleep, the witches creep silently from their beds, rub themselves with ointment, and fly through the night to the deserted heath, where they sacrifice infants to their lord and master – the devil.

So thought the people of the middle ages, and "WITCH!" became the accusation that lead to the burning or hanging of thousands of innocent women. Why was this persecution allowed – and could it happen today?

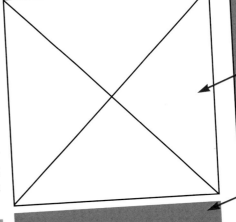

picture

caption

CASE STUDY OF A WITCH HUNT: THE HANGINGS AND HYSTERIA IN SALEM.

Now that you have looked at the main theories about why witchcrazes occurred, try reading this first-hand account of a real witch hunt which shocked America. The following events continue to fascinate people even today and Arthur Miller based one of the most famous plays of the twentieth century, *The Crucible,* on the Salem witch hunts.

THE SALEM WITCHES

Sarah Good was an old, argumentative woman who lived in Salem in 1692. She was one of the first to be accused of witchcraft.

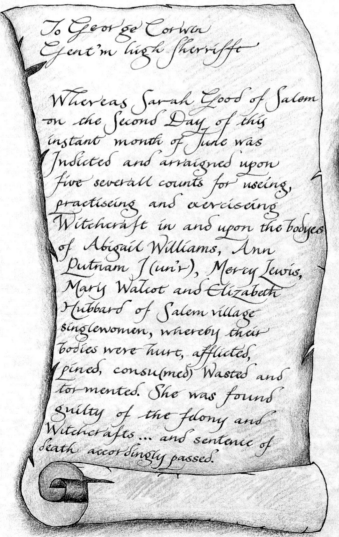

To George Corwin
Gent'm high Sherriffe

Whereas Sarah Good of Salem on the Second Day of this instant month of June was Indicted and arraigned upon five severall counts for useing, practiseing and exerciseing Witchcraft in and upon the bodyes of Abigail Williams, Ann Putnam J (un'r), Mercy Lewis, Mary Walcot and Elizabeth Hubbard of Salem village singlewomen, whereby their bodies were hurt, afflicted, pined, consu(med) Wasted and tormented. She was found guilty of the felony and Witchcrafts ... and sentence of death accordingly passed.

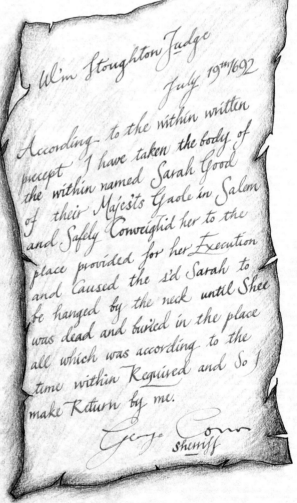

Wm Stoughton Judge

July 19th 1692

According to the within written precept I have taken the body of the within named Sarah Good of their Majesits Gaole in Salem and Safely Conweighid her to the place provided for her Execution and Caused the s'd Sarah to be hanged by the neck until Shee was dead and buried in the place all which was according to the time within Required and So I make Return by me.

George Corwin
sheriff

In Salem Village, Massachusetts, in the year 1692, four young girls, Betty Parris (9), Abigail Williams (11), Ann Putnam (12) and another girl who was a cousin of Betty, were playing together in the home of Reverend Samuel Parris, Betty's father. Their game was a childish dabbling in fortune-telling. Within the space of a year, twenty people had been executed and four others had died in prison as a result.

By the time the number of people hanged for witchcraft had reached twenty, the local government was becoming seriously concerned. Even wealthy people were being accused and no-one was sure how far the witch hunt might spread. Sir William Phips, the Governor-in-Chief of Massachusetts, set up a committee of enquiry to learn what had actually happened and to decide what to do about it.

'I am no more a witch than you are a wizard, and if you take away my life, God will give you blood to drink.'
Sarah Good's last words

• You and the other two or three members of your group, are advisers to Sir William Phips. It is your job to sift through the evidence on the following pages and, armed with your detailed knowledge of witchcraft, report back to Sir William on the events in Salem. You should consider all of the evidence, decide on exactly what has happened and include your recommendations in the report. Initially, your report will be a verbal one, but a written account will be required for the Court of Appeal in England.

EVENTS IN SALEM

The fortune-telling game took place in the house of the Reverend Samuel Parris of Salem Village, a few miles from Salem Town. The girls' behaviour following their little game became strange, and then bizarre. They began to take up odd postures, to speak in weird voices, to have fits and to roll about the floor. This was repeated several times until they became known locally as the 'afflicted' girls.

Rumours of their behaviour began to spread through the village and Mary Sibley, an older village matron, suggested to a black maid called Tituba that some witch cakes should be baked. These cakes, made from rye meal and urine from the afflicted girls, would then be fed to a dog. If the dog died, that would be taken as proof that the girls were possessed in some way. It is now thought that rye flour can cause hallucinations if it goes bad in hot weather. When Samuel Parris found out, the first whispers of witchcraft had begun to circulate.

The story is taken up by Paul Boyer and Stephen Nissenbaum their book *Salem Possessed*:

By this time, more than a month had elapsed since the girls' strange behaviour began, and still no legal action had been taken. By this time, too, the afflictions were beginning to spread beyond the minister's house; soon they would come to affect about seven or eight other girls as well, ranging in age from twelve to nineteen, and including three from the household of Thomas Putnam, Jr. For a time, even several young married women became afflicted. At last the troubled Village resorted to the law. On February 29, 1692, warrants went out for the arrest of three Village women whom the girls, under the pressure of intense adult questioning, had finally named as their tormentors: Sarah Good, Sarah Osborne, and Tituba herself.

The next day, Jonathan Corwin and John Hathorne, the nearest members of the upper house of the provincial legislature, made the five-mile trip out from Salem Town to conduct a public examination of the three women in the Village meetinghouse. Osborne and Good denied that they were witches, but Tituba confessed, volubly and in great detail, even volunteering a description of the devil as "a thing all over hairy, all the face hairy, and a long nose". After their examination, all three women were committed to Boston jail – At this point, anyone familiar with the pattern of earlier witchcraft outbreaks in New England – one or two accusations, arrests, and perhaps convictions – would surely have predicted that the matter was now at an end. But, for once, the pattern did not hold. Even with the three women in prison, the bizarre behaviour of the girls continued. Once again, the Village strove to deal with the crisis in its own way. Parris held several "private fasts" in his own household, and on March 11 he invited the neighboring ministers for a day of prayer. But in the very presence of these men of God, the children began to behave "strangely and ridiculously"; one even suffered a "convulsion fit, her limbs being twisted several ways, and very stiff."

… the fourth person to be arrested, Martha Cory of Salem Village, was examined by Hathorne and Corwin before a throng of several hundred in the Village meetinghouse. As she was led into the room, the afflicted girls, sitting together at the front, cried out in "extreme agony"; when she wrung her hands, they screamed that they were being pinched; when she bit her lips, they declared that they could feel teeth biting their own flesh. In the general hubbub, a Village woman named Bethshaa Pope flung first her muff and then her shoe at Martha, striking her on the head.

Martha Cory joined the three other women in jail, but still the outbreak showed no signs of abating, and now the arrests began to accelerate. On March 23 Dorcas Good, the four-year-old daughter of accused witch Sarah Good, was sent to Boston prison, where for nine months she remained in heavy irons. (Eighteen years later her father would declare: "She hath ever since been very chargeable, having little or

no reason to govern herself.") The day after Dorcas was jailed, at the packed examination of still another Village woman, Rebecca Nurse, the torments of the afflicted produced near pandemonium: Deodat Lawson, walking some distance from the meetinghouse, was amazed by the "hideous screech and noise" that poured from the open window. When it was all over, Goody Nurse, too, was committed to jail in Salem Town.

By this time it had become impossible any longer to treat the outbreak as a local Salem Village matter. The next examinations, on April 11, were held not in the Village but in Salem Town, and not before Hathorne and Corwin only, but before the deputy governor, six magistrates, and a "very great assembly" which included several ministers. Ten days later, Thomas Putnam, Jr., whose daughter and wife were both among the afflicted, dispatched a letter to the magistrate in Salem Town hinting at "high and dreadful" news – a "wheel within a wheel, at which our ears do tingle." The news was dreadful indeed: Abigail Williams had charged that George Burroughs, a former minister in the Village who had moved away to a frontier parish in Maine, was himself a wizard – indeed, that he was the mastermind behind the entire outbreak. In a matter of days, an officer was on his way to Maine with a warrant for Burroughs's arrest. A few days after that, the Massechusetts legislature, the General Court, ordered that a public fast be observed through the length and breadth of the colony.

Of the afflicted girls, two lived with the Rev. Parris and three lived with Thomas Putnam, Parris's most enthusiastic supporter.

The Putnams were a devout, independent and powerful family in Salem Village. Their religious views made them very suspicious of 'outsiders' from Salem Town whom they thought to be too commercial and individualist. As religious conservatives, they were poorer than most others but were very keen to build and keep control of a puritan church in the village. They had the Rev. Samuel Parris appointed as vicar, a man with similar views to their own. However, Parris's extreme views upset the other residents who refused to pay his salary and then tried, unsuccessfully, to remove him from office.

Most of the Putnams' supporters lived further away from Salem Town on the west side of the village, whereas the opponents of Parris and the Putnams lived nearer to the town on the east side.

Once the Rev. Parris and Thomas Putnam believed that their offspring (the afflicted girls) were in the grip of witchcraft, they exerted pressure on the girls to name their tormentors.

TESTIMONY OF ANN PUTNAM, JUNIOR

Three girls of Thomas Putnam's family testified against twenty-five people, and seven adult Putnams testified against thirty-nine. Nearly all of the accused were opposed to the Putnams in some way.

The deposition of Ann Putnam, Junior, who testifieth and saith that on the 25th of February, 1691/92, I saw the apparition of Sarah Good, which did torture me most grievously. But I did not know her name till the 27th of February, and then she told me her name was Sarah Good, and then she did prick me and pinch me most grievously, and also since, several times urging me vehemently to write in her book.

And also, on the first day of March, being the day of her examination, Sarah Good did most grievously torture me, and also several times since. And also, on the first day of March, 1692, I saw the apparition of Sarah Good go and afflict and torture the bodies of Elizabeth Parish [i.e., Parris], Abigail Williams and Elizabeth Hubbard. Also I have seen the apparition of Sara Good afflicting the body of Sarah Vibber [i.e., Bibber].

Ann mark Putnam

Ann Putnam owned this her testimony to be the truth on her oath, before the Jurors of Inquest this 28 of June, 1692.

And further says that she verily believes that Sarah Good doth bewitch and afflict her.

Still working as advisers to Sir William Phips, consider the cross-examination (on the following page) of Sarah Good on 1st March 1692. You may wish to work in pairs and reconstruct a 'live' presentation of the testimony so that you can make your own judgement about Sarah Good's evidence. When you have completed your analysis, look back at Sarah's last words on page 173. How would you judge this woman?

EXAMINATION OF SARAH GOOD AS RECORDED BY EZEKIEL CHEEVER

The examination of Sarah Good before the worshipful Assistants John Hathorne [and] Jonathan Curran.

Q. Sarah Good, what evil spirit have you familiarity with?

A. None.

Q. Have you made no contact with the devil?

Good answered no.

Q. Why do you hurt these children?

A. I do not hurt them. I scorn it.

Q. Who do you employ, then, to do it?

A. I employ nobody.

Q. What creature do you employ then?

A. No creature. But I am falsely accused.

Q. Why did you go away muttering from Mr. Parris's house?

A. I did not mutter, but I thanked him for what he gave my child.

Q. Have you made no contract with the devil?

A. No.

H[athorne] desired the children, all of them, to look upon her and see if this were the person that had hurt them, and so they all did look upon her and said this was one of the persons that did torment them. Presently they were all tormented.

Q. Sarah Good, do you not see now what you have done? Why do you not tell us the truth? Why do you thus torment these poor children?

A. I do not torment them.

Q. Who do you employ then?

A. I employ nobody. I scorn it.

Q. How came they thus tormented?

A. What do I know? You bring others here and now you charge me with it.

Q. Why, who was it?

A. I do not know but it was some you brought into the meeting house with you.

Q. We brought you into the meeting house.

A. But you brought in two more.

Q. Who was it, then, that tormented the children?

A. It was Osborne.

TAKING A STAND AGAINST THE TRIALS

Evidence from the trials reveals that, even during the intense hysteria generated by the accusations of witchcraft, some people attempted to give evidence to refute the hostile testimony of the girls.

- Consider, in small groups of four, what the atmosphere in Salem must have been like at this time. Draw up a list of the kinds of behaviour that you would expect to find.

- Working in two pairs, use the following petition in order to see whether you could persuade anybody to stop the trials. One pair supports Sarah Good and wants to persuade as many people as possible to put their 'mark', their signature on the petition. The other pair are waverers. They might like to sign but …

We, the undersigned, believe and confirm that Sarah Good is a God-fearing woman, who has never to our certain knowledge been involved with witchcraft or any such actions. We humbly beseech the court to refute the allegations and to set her free.
signed:

Nine years after the witch hunts in Salem, Ann Putnam, accuser of Sarah Good and others wrote the following: '*I desire to lie in the dust and earnestly beg forgiveness of all those unto whom I have given just cause of sorrow and offense, whose relations were taken away and accused.*'

> • Given that she has admitted her falsehood, what might Ann Putnam put in a letter of apology to the relatives of Sarah Good? Write a letter of condolence.

ENDING THE WITCH HUNT

The witch hunt was finally brought to an end by the Rev. Increase Mather. He achieved this by taking an enormous risk. He wrote and published a treatise which carefully denounced the hangings and the evidence of witchcraft in Salem.

He could easily have been accused of witchcraft himself if he had not argued his case carefully, calmly and logically. How would you have tackled the task that he set himself?

> • Put yourself in the same position as the Rev. Increase Mather and have a go at writing 'A Treatise Denying the Existence of Witchcraft in Salem'. Some help is provided below.

HELP

WRITING A TREATISE

A **treatise** is a very logical, systematic argument which attempts to prove a point of view in an unemotional and objective way.

Remember the four stages in producing any piece of writing that you were encouraged to go through when producing your feature article for a Sunday colour supplement.

1. **Content**
   You must remember that you are a member of the Salem society and that you could be accused of witchcraft yourself if you are thought to be sympathetic, so your treatise, your argument, needs to be very carefully

planned. Start by making a list of all the factors which have led to the accusations which can be explained rationally. For example:

- The accusers were young girls from 'decent' families.

- Sarah Good was foul-mouthed and people had reason to dislike her.

- Sarah Good was not a supporter of the Putnam family.

What other factors can you think of?

[continued over]

2. Organisation

Once you have your list of facts, prioritise them – place the best piece of evidence first and arrange the rest accordingly. Explain each piece of evidence in your own words using reasonable, unemotional terms. For example:

> Of course Abigail accused Proctor, she had every reason to do so …

3. Composition

When you begin your first draft, try to use repetition of the main ideas to keep emphasising your points. For example:

> So, when Abigail made the accusations, which were natural enough in her circumstances …

The length of this piece of work should be about two sides of A4 paper.

4. Sub-editing

Work with a partner to ensure that your treatise is ready for publication. To do this, you will each need a pencil and rubber and you will have to spend time reading and annotating your partner's work. Annotating means that you will mark every section where you think there might be a spelling or punctuation error; you will indicate where you feel that writing is unclear or where it lacks detail. When you have completed this exercise, swap back and do a final correction of your own work to produce your final draft.

COULD 'SALEM' HAPPEN NOW?

The whole point of studying the witchcrazes and the Salem witch trials in particular, is to understand the forces in society which create these horrors and to attempt to stop them from happening again.

The processes of stereotyping and scapegoating occur along these lines:

1. A person or a group of people (either within the society or on its margins) are identified by the majority as being different (e.g. an old woman who people believe has some healing potion).

2. This individual or group has distorted characteristics attributed to it (e.g. the idea of 'healing' becomes distorted so that people believe that there is some 'magic' quality to the healing).

3. The distorted characteristics begin to create fear and suspicion in the minds of the majority.

4. Problems or disasters occur and these problems are blamed on the 'different' person or group.

5. It becomes generally accepted that society's problems are the fault of this individual or group and that their persecution is legitimate.

- Working in groups, make a list of any individuals or groups, such as the Jews during Hitler's rise to power in Germany, who you feel have been persecuted in this way.

- See if you can find any parallels between what happened to them and the process outlined above.

Is bullying a modern version of witch hunting?

Read the following article. To what extent does Sally's story reflect the same process? If bullying is similar to witch hunting, what does that tell us about witchcrazes and human society in general?

The damage caused by bullying is now widely accepted, but, until very recently, schools often took the line that there was little they could do about it. Reader Helena Rogers describes what happened to her daughter just a few years ago:

'We moved from the north of England to the southeast when our twin daughters, Sally and Emma, were 11. After their tests, the girls ended up going to different schools. Emma was integrated into her small school quickly, but Sally's new school was vast – it had 1,500 pupils. Starting part way through the term, when the pupils already had their own groups of friends, made life difficult.

'After a few weeks Sally began having nightmares, but when I tried to find out what was wrong, she wouldn't open up at all. When I heard her crying in her room at night, I realised it was serious so I made an appointment to see her year tutor. She was very sympathetic, explained that it was difficult to keep tabs on all the pupils in a school of that size, but said she would see what she could do.

'But the nightmares and the crying continued, and in the end it was Emma who told me what was going on. It was mental cruelty most of the time, though the bullies did push and shove Sally as well. These girls would say to her, "Come and play with us" and she would think she had been accepted. Then they would say, "Go away. We don't want you."

'She would find a place to sit alone and have her lunch but they would come after her, snatch her lunch box and hide it, or throw her sandwiches into the bushes. Once they took her orange drink and poured it over her head so that she had to spend the rest of the day with this sticky mess all over her. They threatened that if she told anyone they would make it worse. That was why she had been too scared to say anything.

'It was a month since I had reported the situation and nothing had been done, so I went to the school again. This time I was able to give the teacher definite details about the bullying, and she suggested putting Sally in a different class. But it turned out to be a remedial class for troublemakers and children who couldn't cope with the work, and this only made things worse. Now the bullies taunted her about going to "the idiots' class". How can little girls – none of them were more than 12 – be such monsters, such torturers?'

The bully has to have some sort of power over the victim – a power not always recognisable to the teacher.

There is no such thing as a typical bully or victim. The 'traditional bully' has been seen as male and as, in some way, bigger than his peers; he bullies to have respect or power. The 'traditional victim' is often seen as a weak child, different in some way – racially, physically or socially. While this may be so, if teachers and parents only recognise these stereotypes, many victims can remain unsupported.

A quiet, self-contained child like Sally, for instance, can suffer in silence unless positively encouraged to speak out.

- Work in pairs as Sally and the editor of a teenage magazine's problem page. Write Sally's plea for help and an appropriate reply.

BUT WHAT IF SOCIETY'S FEARS ARE JUSTIFIED?

There are, however, some groups within society that are a threat. How do we decide which? In medieval days, simply accusing a woman of being a witch would bring a catalogue of horrors down upon her. Today, we may feel that we have a fairer sense of justice but, as in the bullying article, there are still deep-seated fears and prejudices.

Read the article opposite about a religious sect who were treated with indifference. No accusations were made against them, they were allowed to practise their beliefs without interference until they gassed people on Japan's underground system.

AUM – A JAPANESE CULT

This is the story of the ultimate cult: a wired, hi-tech, designer-drug, billion-dollar army of New Age zealots, under the leadership of a blind and bearded madman, armed with weapons of mass destruction. Like scenes of an apocalyptic future in a cyberpunk novel, it is also the stuff of nightmares.

Cultists wired electrodes to their heads while chanting ancient mantras and logging onto computer nets. Methamphetamine, LSD, and truth serum ran through their veins, the product of home-made laboratories equipped with the latest gear. Those same labs worked at refining enough chemical and biological weapons to kill millions. Other cultists attempted to build a nuclear bomb, while massive facilities were built to manufacture handguns and explosives. All this activity went toward preparing for – and then unleashing – Armageddon.

Aum's story moves from the dense cities of post-industrial Japan to mountain retreats where samurai once fought, and then overseas – to Manhattan and Silicon Valley, Bonn and the Australian outback, and then to Russia. It was there, in the volatile remains of the Soviet empire, that the cult's membership exploded and its leaders found ready suppliers of military hardware, training, and, quite possibly, a nuclear bomb.

Aum leaders systematically targeted top universities, recruiting brilliant but alienated young scientists from chemistry, physics, and engineering departments. They forged relations with Japan's ruthless crime syndicates, the *yakuza,* and with veterans of the Soviet secret police KGB and Russian and Japanese militaries. They enlisted medical doctors to dope patients and perform human experiments that belong in a horror movie.

For years this went on, with barely a question from police or the media on three continents. Before long, Aum had become one of the world's richest, most sophisticated, and most murderous religious sects.

In a world poised between the Cold War and the new millennium, the tale of Aum is a mirror of our worst fears. Heavily armed militias, terrorist cells, zealous cults and crime syndicates all find their voice in the remarkable ascent of this bizarre sect. For years, experts have warned us: the growing sophistication of these groups, combined with the spread of modern technology, will bring about a new era in terrorism and mass murder. The coming of Aum Supreme Truth shows just how close these nightmares have come to reality.

- Compare this group of 'outsiders' with those you have already discussed. How are they similar or different?

- You belong to a select committee of MPs who have been asked to recommend new laws to help to monitor new cults which have emerged in Britain. Write your report to the government making recommendations you feel necessary along with an explanation of why you feel these measures are necessary.

WITCHCRAFT IN THE 20TH CENTURY

As a result of interest aroused by the feature article that you wrote asking 'Why did Medieval Europe execute so many women?', you have been contacted by a broadcasting company who want you to devise a documentary for television which seeks to provide a balanced, informative account of witchcraft, its history, the theories surrounding its existence and its relevance to society today.

INDEPENDENT TELEVISION PROGRAMME MAKERS (ITPM)

is seeking interested parties able to make a convincing and gripping television documentary programme on

'WITCHCRAFT: its history and relevance to society today.'

A grant of £250,000 is available to the successful applicant.

Proposals for a 25-minute documentary should be submitted in writing to the Head of Programming.

Shortlisted candidates will be asked to make an oral presentation.

Your documentary can be planned in one of two ways:

- As an oral presentation to the Head of Programming (refer to the help box on 'How to make an oral presentation').

- As a storyboard (refer to the help box on 'How to develop a storyboard').

HOW TO MAKE AN ORAL PRESENTATION

1. Map out the main points you wish to make about witchcraft and agree what material you want to use from everything that is available in the unit.

↓

2. Working in pairs, time how long it takes to read the extracts that you have selected. By subtracting that amount of time from the 25 minutes that are available, you will be able to form some idea of how much time you have left for commentary, expressions of opinion, or further additional material.

↓

3. In order to win the bid, you will have to convince the Head of Programming that your ideas for the documentary are well thought out, logical, interesting and relevant. Run through your main points again and note where you could make persuasive comments, for example: 'One of the features of our documentary will be the graphic images which show the horror women had to endure'.

↓

4. Perhaps your biggest challenge will be to convince the ITPM of the relevance of your approach to a modern audience. Review all the work that you have done on stereotyping and scapegoating and use it to make sure that you have included some modern parallels.

↓

5. You may, if you have the resources, video your presentation and rather than present it in person. If not, present your plans for the documentary 'live' as an oral activity.

HOW TO DEVELOP A STORYBOARD

1. Working in small groups, divide a large piece of paper into about twelve squares. Each square will represent one section of the emerging storyboard.

↓

2. Discuss with the members of your group which are the twelve essential moments in the documentary.

↓

3. Each square will be devoted to an image of one of the twelve essential moments (perhaps a view of the torture of a witch or a single fact – 100,000 witches were burnt).

↓

4. Along the bottom of each square there should be a short caption (or comment) which neatly summarises the image in the square. This should be a brief comment because there will not be space for lengthy text.

↓

5. Additional commentary can come in the form of 'voice-overs'. These are the words which are spoken while the image is on screen. They can be lengthier, supplying more detailed information while an image is held on screen for the duration of the comment.

↓

6. When the storyboard is complete, you should be able to rehearse it using either a video camera (focusing on one square at a time) or by explaining it to the whole group as an oral exercise.

You might find that the following additional pieces of material will help you produce a more entertaining programme.

'SHE'S A WITCH!'

Crowds run excitedly through a medieval village shouting, 'We've got a witch! We've got a witch!' The young woman in question has obviously been dressed up as a stereotypical witch with a carrot stuck on her nose and a long pointed hat on her head. She is jostled along by the crowd of peasants towards a knight who is on a raised platform waiting for the crowd to arrive.

Peasant: We've found a witch. May we burn her?

Knight: How do you know she is a witch?

Peasants: She looks like one.

Knight: Bring her forward.

Woman: I am not a witch. I am not a witch.

Knight: But you are dressed as one.

Woman: They dressed me up like this … and this isn't my nose, it's a false one.

Knight: (*Removes fake nose and looks at peasants*) Well?

Peasant 1: Well … we did do the nose … and the hat. But she is a witch.

Peasants: Burn her, burn her.

Knight: Did you dress her up like this?

Peasant 1: No, no … yes … a bit … she has got a wart!

Knight: What makes you think she is a witch?

Peasant 2: Well, she turned me into a newt (*everyone looks at him*) … I got better.

Peasants: Burn her anyway!

Knight: There are ways of telling whether she is a witch.

Peasants: Tell us … what are they?

Knight: What do you do with witches?

Peasants: Burn them!

Knight: And what do you burn apart from witches?

Peasants: More witches … wood?

Knight: Good! Why do witches burn?

Peasant 3: Because they're … made of … wood?

Knight: Good! How do we tell if she is made of wood?

Peasant 1: Build a bridge out of her?

Knight: Can you not also build bridges out of stone? Does wood sink in water?

Peasants: No, it floats. Throw her into the pond.

Knight: What also floats in water?

Peasants: Bread, apples … very small rocks … gravy, churches.

Knight: A duck. So logically …

Peasants: If she weighs the same as a duck … she's made of wood … a witch.

From *Monty Python & the Holy Grail*

A NOTE ABOUT WITCHES

In fairytales, witches always wear silly black hats and black cloaks, and they ride on broomsticks.

But this is not a fairy-tale. This is about REAL WITCHES …

REAL WITCHES dress in ordinary clothes and look very much like ordinary women. They live in ordinary houses and they work in ORDINARY JOBS.

That is why they are so hard to catch.

A REAL WITCH hates children with a red-hot sizzling hatred that is more sizzling and red-hot than any hatred you could possibly imagine.

A REAL WITCH spends all her time plotting to get rid of the children in her particular territory. Her passion is to do away with them, one by one …

A witch never gets caught. Don't forget that she has magic in her fingers and devilry dancing in her blood. She can make stones jump about like frogs and she can make tongues of flame go flickering across the surface of the water …

A witch is always a woman.

I do not wish to speak badly about women. Most women are lovely. But the fact remains that all witches *are* women. There is no such thing as a male witch …

Which lady is the witch? That is a difficult question, but it is one that every child must try to answer …

Oh, if only there were a way of telling for sure whether a woman was a witch or not, then we could round them all up and put them in the meatgrinder …

From *The Witches* by Roald Dahl

Anjelica Huston in The Witches, *1990*

This is what one commentator had to say about Dahl's views on women and witches:

'The Witches, whose underpinning anti-female ideology could have almost come from a seventeenth century witch-hunting broadsheet, leaves a bad taste in the mouth, regardless of the narrative skill which the author displays. Here, Dahl's famous love-hate relationship with personal hygiene is centred around the female body as an object of loathing. It is a difficult book to like.'

WHAT NEXT?

As part of your course work, you may be asked to research and read books which focus on the themes or topics you are studying in class.

Bessie Dunlop, Witch of Dalry by John Hodgart and Martin Clark, is based on real events of the witch-craze in Scotland in the sixteenth century. The play is written partly in Scottish dialect, and it tells the story of a young woman whose skills in folk-medicine make her an important figure in her village as midwife and healer. However, Bessie's 'powers' become sought after for all sorts of reasons and, eventually, she becomes a threat to the church and the local gentry. The events in the play are based on the life of an ordinary, sixteenth-century woman, and explore the prejudice, victimisation and hysteria which accompanied the first witch hunts in Scottish history. The trial of Bessie Dunlop took place on 8th November, 1576, at the High Court of Justiciary in Edinburgh.

NARRATOR 4	**In a time of turmoil and change,**
NARRATOR 5	**A time of chaos,**
NARRATOR 6	**A time of fear,**
NARRATOR 1	**We look for convenient scapegoats**
NARRATOR 2	**People who are different**
NARRATOR 3	**People who are a threat,**
NARRATOR 4	**Enemies in our midst,**
NARRATOR 5	**Someone to blame,**
NARRATOR 6	**To vent our anguish on,**
NARRATOR 1	**Someone to persecute,**
NARRATOR 2	**To exterminate.**
NARRATOR 3	**The list of victims is endless,**
NARRATOR 4	**Their ashes scattered in the wind.**

Bessie Dunlop, Witch of Dalry, Act Three, Scene 11

- Read these lines aloud to a group of five other members. Then, with the other members of your group, take a part each and read the extract aloud again, giving full expression to the meaning of your part.

  Discuss why the writers might have chosen to have the lines read by different narrators, and the effects this gives compared to reading the lines as one speech.

If you have time, you might go on to complete one of the following assignments:

- Read *Bessie Dunlop, Witch of Dalry*. Bessie Dunlop experiences the hell of a witchcraft accusation. Write a diary of Bessie's ordeal during the accusations and the trial, showing her terrible dilemma.

- If you have read *The Crucible* by Arthur Miller, read *Bessie Dunlop, Witch of Dalry* and compare the plight of John Proctor with that of Bessie. How are their predicaments similar/different?

Preparing for your exam

ABOUT YOUR EXAMINATION

Answer the following questions as fully as you can without looking up the answers:

1 What are your set texts?

2 Which books are you studying for your timed examinations?

3 Which books are you studying for course work?

4 How many timed examinations are there and what is in each one?

5 Are all the questions worth the same number of marks?

6 How long is each paper?

7 What is the difference between the English examination and the Literature examination?

8 How many marks are there for Speaking and Listening?

9 How many marks are there for the course work folder?

10 How many marks are there for the timed examination?

11 In which month of which year will you sit the examinations?

12 In which month of which year does your course work have to be submitted?

- Now find out the correct answers to all of the questions on the previous page. Make a note of them and of any details about the exam papers which you think are important to remember.

How can you take this information into account in planning your revision?

▶ Give yourself time to re-read the examination texts well before the detailed revision period.

▶ Focus your energies on high-scoring elements of the examination.

▶ Pay attention to the quality of expression and to accuracy in your writing: even your understanding of literature is assessed through your ability to write about it.

WHAT IS THE EXAMINER LOOKING FOR?

In Speaking and Listening

Candidates must demonstrate their ability to:

- communicate clearly, structuring and organising their talk and adapting it to different situations

- use standard English

- listen to and understand varied speech

- participate in discussion, judging the nature and purposes of contributions and the roles of participants

An examiner comments:

For your GCSE assessment you may be required to take part in a variety of activities. You will join in a discussion, probably be asked to chair a discussion, or you may be asked to give a talk or to take part in 'role play'. All these activities require particular skills.

In discussion, you need to concentrate hard on the topic and listen carefully to what other people are saying. You then have to work out how you can further the discussion by asking questions or taking up someone else's point and giving it a new direction. Never let yourself become so obsessed with an idea of your own (however interesting) that you let it interfere with the points other people are making.

When you are chairing a discussion, you need to train yourself to restrain your own ideas. Your job as chair is to make sure everyone has a chance to speak, that nobody wanders miles off the point, and to give the discussion some shape. Listening skills are very important in this situation.

When you are giving a talk, the emphasis is on the way you relate to your audience and get their response. It is

important to appear pleased to be there and interested in what you are saying. No one wants to listen to people who bore even themselves. As in writing an essay, you need a clear beginning, middle and end, and you need to be aware of your audience. If they are sitting in front of you it will be easy to see how well they are taking in what you say. Try to look one or two of them in the eye and talk to them rather than into the air. It is better not to read a complete script of words but to make notes and use them to prompt you. Try to use the sorts of gestures and expressions you would normally use in talking to people, in order to make your speech more interesting.

Role play requires rather different skills because you are trying to get into the position of someone else and to concentrate on a particular way of talking or presenting a point of view. It needs careful thought about the way other people might speak and behave, and is a form of acting. It may be a way of giving you greater insight into many of the topics about which you have read or written during your English course.

In Writing

Candidates must demonstrate their ability to:

- communicate clearly, adapting their writing for a wide range of purposes and audiences

- use and adapt forms and styles for specific purposes and effects

- organise ideas into sentences, paragraphs and whole texts

- use accurate spelling and punctuation, and present work neatly and clearly

- use the grammatical structures of standard English and a wide vocabulary to express meanings with clarity and precision

An examiner comments:

It is important to plan your writing carefully, deciding which information will go in each paragraph. This will also ensure that you don't use up all your material in the first paragraph and then run out of things to say. You may use different styles of plan – some people use lists, others use diagrams.

One of the difficulties when you come to the actual writing is to keep to the point. As you write, all sorts of

ideas will come into your head and carry you away from your plan. You should be on your guard against this. If you put in a lot of detail which is only loosely attached to the title of your essay it will muffle the main points and be distracting for the reader, so keep the title in mind and ask yourself at the end of each paragraph whether what you are writing still relates to that title.

In Literature

Candidates must demonstrate their ability to:

- respond to texts critically, sensitively and in detail, selecting appropriate ways to convey their response, using textual evidence as appropriate

- explore how language, structure and forms contribute to the meanings of texts, considering different approaches to texts and alternative interpretations

- explore relationships and comparisons between texts, selecting and evaluating relevant material

- understand literary tradition and appreciate social and historical influences and cultural contexts

An examiner comments:

The question of range comes first. Of course, it is not easy to show you have responded to a lot of different novels, poems or plays in the exam but you may be able to show this in your written or oral course work. You are asked to 'respond' to what you read, which means bringing your own ideas to what you read and

forming an opinion of your own, but you must always base your ideas on the actual text as it is, not in the way you might have written it yourself. In developing the skills necessary for literary study you must always think about what authors are trying to do and the ways in which they achieve their effects.

And about poetry in particular:

Reading poetry and then writing about it requires a slightly different technique and is often more complicated. Some poems, of course, tell a story and can be read quickly and immediately, others are so full of meaning condensed into a few short lines that they have to be read more slowly. It often helps to read the poem through, then read it aloud to yourself before you concentrate on sorting out the meaning of particular phrases. When you have got a sense of the poem as a whole, go back to the bits you found difficult and try to work out a meaning. Let some individual words and phrases create an impression for you and don't worry if the impressions do not fit together with perfect precision. There may be several meanings and interpretations, so don't feel you are alone in being undecided between various alternative meanings.

When writing about poetry you are likely to be asked to write about two or three poems together and to compare and contrast them. It may be easiest simply to list them, but it might help you to make up a basic chart into which you could put similarities and differences.

Poetry questions are difficult to revise for. All questions are likely to be about one of the following: theme, a personality described in a poem, setting, or the writer's use of language. It's sensible to look at groups of poems together which either have characteristics in common or which contrast in those four areas. It will also be useful if you know a group of poems by the same writer. If you are using a prescribed anthology the poems will have been selected with comparisons in mind and it should be easy to pick out the points that you can discuss.

REVISION

Long term revision (early in the examination year):
Re-read the earlier set texts for examination to refresh your memory. As you go, check that your reminder notes are in order – you might not have the time to re-read again.

Medium term revision (from March):
Organise your course work ready for submission.
Construct a revision plan for each week from Easter onwards using a chart similar to this:

For example:

REVISION PLAN	WEEK 1 – 5th–11th April						
	Mon	Tues	Wed	Thurs	Fri	Sat	Sun
Before 9am			TUTORIAL				SLEEP
9–12	LESSONS	LESSONS	LESSONS	LESSONS	LESSONS		
12–2							LONG LUNCH
2–4	LESSONS	LESSONS	CANOEING	LESSONS		SHOPPING	
4–6							
After 6pm					OUT	OUT	

Think about all your subjects and work out how much revision time belongs to English. Divide this time into parts: time for each of the exam texts and for each of the main sections of each paper. Fill in your charts.

The revision period (May onwards):

Stick to your revision plan.

English isn't like a factual subject. There aren't reams of facts to remember. If you have refreshed your memory of the texts, spend time brainstorming, planning and organising essays so that the issues come to mind easily in the examination.

Ask the teacher for a list of key areas for revision. Write in full if there are aspects of writing which you find difficult, such as:

the opening paragraph

justifying a point

using a quote gracefully

explaining something tricky

using terminology

Practise just those parts until you find a comfortable style which suits you.

EXAM TECHNIQUE

- Make sure you know how much time you have for the exam beforehand.

- Invest a larger portion of your limited time in the high-scoring questions.

- Read passages once for gist, then again after reading the questions.

- Underline key words in the question.

- Mark and annotate the passages to pick out relevant details: this is more useful than marking off large chunks of it.

- To achieve a higher level of answer, and so to get a good grade, justify your views by giving examples or by quoting apt details. Examiners will mark higher if:

   'The answer is sustained by reference to the text' (Level 6)

   'Pupils use relevant and well chosen detail from the text' (Level 7).

- If you read slowly you will not have time to read passages twice.

   Either:

   Skim over the passage then look at the questions, then read it properly with the questions in mind.

   Or:

   Read the passage first for sense, then read the questions, then answer each question, stopping to scan the passage for relevant details as you go.

- Aim to make two or three clear, solid points in response to each question or point, rather than rambling or retelling.

- Plan longer answers in diagrammatic form – a star chart, 'For and Against' columns, or some other appropriate form (see page 192).

- When you see time running out, jot down any further points in note form, particularly for those sections assessed for reading rather than writing: the examiner will be free to give credit for abbreviated points.

JANE EYRE

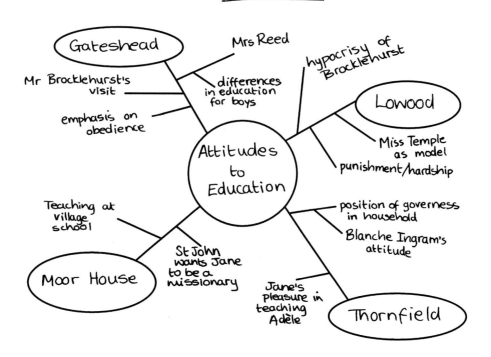

An examiner comments:

1. *Decide in advance exactly how much time you are going to spend on each question and keep a careful eye on the clock, planning for time at the end to read through what you have written. If you are asked to do four questions, it is no good doing three brilliantly and not leaving time for the fourth – you will lose one quarter of the marks if you only cover three quarters of what is required. Look carefully at the number of marks allocated to each question because that will tell you which questions are most important and need longer time.*

2. *At the beginning of the exam, before you start to write anything, read through the instructions to remind yourself of what you are being asked to do. Then find the sections you are going to answer and decide which questions to do. Read the questions very carefully and then jot down some brief notes for each answer. These could be in the form of a diagram which will be easy to refer to at a glance. While you are writing your first answer, your subconscious mind will be thinking about the others. Don't panic if you look round and see that everyone else is already covering sheets of paper. Time spent in planning is not wasted.*

3. *Remember that the examiner has got hundreds of papers to mark in quite a short period of time. If your answers are clearly labelled and set out on the page it will be more welcoming to the person reading it. Handwriting which is easy to read will also help the examiner to follow your ideas more easily, so try to keep it legible.*

4. *Answer the questions on which you feel most confident first and keep an eye on the clock so that you don't run out of time just when you are getting into your stride. Time spent at the end checking through what you have written and correcting spelling and punctuation is never wasted. If you really can't finish, you should write down the points you would have made in note form.*

5. *There are various phrases that often creep into exam essays which examiners are inclined to find depressing and which should be avoided. Try not to say that you enjoyed a play, short story or novel because it was 'easy to understand'. Although this may be true, it is not a critical comment. Better to assume that understanding is never a problem and try to make a firmer comment on the meaning or style of the text.*